AFRICA AND THE NOVEL

By the same author

The Survival of the Novel

Africa and the Novel

Neil McEwan

Humanities Press
Atlantic Highlands

© Copyright Neil McEwan 1983

First published in the United States of America in 1983 by Humanities Press Inc.
Atlantic Highlands, N.J. 07716

ISBN 0-391-02922-3
Library of Congress Catalog Card Number 83-12991

All rights reserved. No part of this publication may be reproduced or transmitted in any form or by any means, electronic or mechanical, including photocopy, recording, or any information storage and retrieval system, without permission in writing from the publisher.

Manufactured in Hong Kong

For My Parents

Contents

Preface   ix

1. Modern Africa   1
2. Colonial Africa: Achebe, Oyono, Camara Laye   20
3. Independence: Soyinka, Achebe, Armah   61
4. Stories, Themes and Impressions in Recent African Fiction   102
5. Outsiders? Nadine Gordimer and Laurens van der Post   128
6. Afterword   161

Notes   167
Select Bibliography   172
Index   177

Preface

This book is a study of how Africa has contributed to the novel during the last thirty years; it is not a complete survey of African fiction. Although I hope to assist the student or general reader who is relatively new to African literature in English, I mean to put a case of interest to everyone who reads new novels.

African writers express a view of the world from within a culture which has been more or less politely disregarded by our own, as though it were removed from the present day, ever since Conrad found it 'prehistoric' eighty years ago. Other terms have changed, but his kind of distancing remains. 'Barbaric' is now 'traditional'; 'civilised' is 'modern' or 'developed'. A recent complacency is to speak of 'hybrid' culture and of people who live 'in two worlds'. The art of a novelist who looks at what is real in his own knowledge of life finds it more complex, vital and unpredictable than that.

African novelists address readers at home in the setting of their present experience. Since they are still beset by outside assumptions about Africa's future, this is an urgent commitment. Addressing other readers in English, or French, the novels can be disconcerting to what Roland Barthes called the Doxa, the sum of our commonly received opinions — and to views publicised by Barthes. African styles of fiction are likely to discomfort readers who have been persuaded by the new prescriptive criticism. A frequent response is to say that Africa is at an earlier stage of the novel. But African novels are not underdeveloped. The most creative writers compete with those in older literary traditions in extending the possibilities and uses of fiction even in times and places which are gravely unpropitious. In this respect I hope their work can be seen in relation to Western literature in the 1960s and 1970s, and to European novels about Africa, without the imposition of our preconceptions on their culture, all over again.

I am indebted to many colleagues and friends in Fez for the loan of books, for advice, and for hospitality; especially to Michael Scott; to Abdulla and Griselda El Tayeb; to Tony and Jeannine

Newbury; and to Jean-Jacques and Christine Le Port. I am grateful to my parents, R. K. and J. L. McEwan, for many kinds of help with the book.

J. N. McE.

1 Modern Africa

Modern is a complex word which means different things to a geologist, an historian and an aircraft-designer. The senses of 'now existing' and 'of recent origin' have grown further apart in every century since the word appeared in English in 1500. Much that now exists is held to be obsolete, in life and literature. Competing voices claim their own modernity and *modern* becomes increasingly highly charged when it means what is now desirable and elastic in its sense of now existing. Podsnap's 'not English!' has been replaced by 'not modern!' Africans have suffered most from other people's misguided attempts to modernise them, and much of their literature has been inspired by a reappraisal of their own present place. But African fiction is worth the attention of everybody interested in the state of the novel. It poses various challenges, not least to developments in criticism which are losing touch with what novelists actually write.

My purpose is to offer an account of the best work of African novelists since 1950, and of some novels by outsiders inspired by experience of Africa, in the context of a discussion of the competing claims made on literature, and on all of us, by the idea of 'the modern'. When novels by Africans began to be published in London in the 1950s they were often discussed in terms of earlier periods of English literature. Amos Tutuola was said to be 'Elizabethan'; Cyprian Ekwensi was called an African Defoe – a comparison which became almost routine. It was even argued that an 'emergent bourgeoisie' in Africa was repeating the experience of England in the eighteenth century. There have been good critical accounts of the new African fiction in English, but studies of the contemporary novel have ignored them. Critics of African fiction have often seemed to justify that by assuming that new content has been put into old forms, African materials appearing in the traditional European form of the novel.[1] I hope to show that Achebe, Ngugi, Soyinka and others have been writing fiction which is fully contemporary.

According to one pervasive misconception Africans are not 'ready' for modern writing. Even Chinua Achebe has lent it currency in the course of disparaging certain trends in European literature. Ghana, he observed caustically on one occasion, 'is not a modern existentialist country'. No country is existentialist, and there are English novelists who share Achebe's poor opinion of 'existentialism', while an African writer can reasonably take Kafka or Camus into account. The view still to be found among London reviewers that African fiction is 'at the stage of Dickens' is akin to the notion once common in British Council circles that earlier English literature should be most interesting to African readers because they are at the same stage of development as Chaucer or Fielding or Dickens; no one was ever sure which. In fact certain features of the Dickens world may have a special immediacy for a Nigerian or Sudanese reader, and other features for readers in England. No society has entirely outgrown the conditions Dickens knew, nor has any retained or acquired them. A British, Irish, or American novelist has at his disposal a range of fictional possibilities extending from the earliest European prose narratives to the most ingenious techniques of post-modernism: the continuum includes Fielding and Dickens, Lawrence and Joyce, Nabokov and John Barth. To deny that one can still learn from Dickens's art or from his portrayal of life is shortsighted, since the complex, uneven passage of history has finished with neither.

An African novelist who writes in English has access to the same possibilities. It is not a matter of borrowing techniques (as for agricultural irrigation) but of working out in new circumstances possibilities suggested by older books. Modern criticism of Victorian fiction has shown the almost unlimited scope for types of narrative which were once supposed to have been superseded by new experiments – a misunderstanding which is still current in France. Solzhenitsyn, Roland Barthes claimed, 'is not a good writer *for us*' because 'someone writing, let's say like Maupassant or Zola, can't be judged the same way as one of our modern writers'.[2] Russia is very different from France, but equidistant in history from Maupassant. A Nigerian or Kenyan novelist is not writing in an older manner for an older society; he is writing as the contemporary of Roland Barthes and John Barth, in a type of society that has never existed before. Influences from his own culture in forms of narrative, in oral culture, in his own language will assist in his creation of an African reality, but 'influences' in good literature are only one kind of inspiration, and a novelist needs all he can find. No new novel with life in it can be like Defoe or like the tale of a bardic griot, although it may owe something hard to define to both.

Roland Barthes's condescension to Solzhenitsyn was characteristic of the attack on realism which began seriously in France in the early 1950s and has since spread to America, England, and Africa – as one sees in Marc Gontard's *La violence du texte* (1981), a study of Moroccan fiction in the fashionable French manner which has now added algebra to Barthes's ancient Greek in its attempt to mystify the young. Several recent books have helped to clarify the descriptive powers and responsibilities of the novelist and have shown that 'fictive' experiment is an old tradition compatible with realism.[3] Critics, overimpressed by Barthes, who say that British realism is not 'for us' subject themselves to a narrow view of what contemporary readers expect. African novels are refreshing in their claim to teach, to inform, to entertain, and – especially in recent years – to persuade, by reference to the real world. Critical acknowledgement of their competence to do so within the realm of modern literature is worth defending because there is a deeply established tendency to treat them as 'backward'.

Some African critics disregard the issue because their literature belongs to an entirely separate culture, whose independence it has been necessary to defend. Ngugi wa Thiong'o's *Homecoming* has an appendix 'On the Abolition of The English Department'. As a Professor of Literature he contributed to the replacement of Nairobi University's English Department by Departments of African Literature and Language. Ngugi has rightly insisted that African students must approach other cultures through their own, and through their own languages. Wole Soyinka has objected to outsiders' imposition of '*their* European world and *their* history, *their* social neuroses and *their* value systems'.[4] The 'universal' is a dangerous idea since it easily leads to cultural aggression. Chinua Achebe has explained the need for African autonomy in objecting to a claim that characters in one African novel might be Americans because the work is 'universal':

Does it occur to American critics to try out their game of changing names of characters and places in an American novel, say, a Philip Roth or an Updike, and slotting in African names just to see how it works? But of course it would not occur to them. It would never occur to them to doubt the universality of their own literature. In the nature of things the work of a Western writer is automatically informed by universality. It is only others who must strain to achieve it.[5]

It does occur to many of them to doubt the universality and realism of their literature, and writers with Achebe's objectives should concede nothing to these doubts. Overemphasis on separate realities yields to the substitution of 'structures' for the real. African and English writers and readers want to resist the creed that, in a phrase Achebe quotes, 'we are all Americans under the skin'. But such fiction as Achebe's historical books reminds us that humanism, as George Watson has recently reaffirmed in *The Story of the Novel* 'is a necessary ingredient in the claims of realism'.[6]

Discussing the question of verification, George Watson gives the case of an African schoolboy who knew a Lady Catherine de Burgh in his own village. Achebe might be irritated by that. But Lady Catherine was real to Jane Austen as the quintessence of a certain blend of the ladylike and the vulgar in Regency England, occupying an exact place in the sociolinguistic history of social arrogance – and as a proud, domineering, unfeeling woman with power over others. George Watson's African child recognised the woman in the lady, and rejoiced if he read *Pride and Prejudice* to the end where Elizabeth puts her in her place. The stubborn humanity of every culture is most obvious when we read works of the past. Marx's admiration for the ancient Greeks troubled him because he thought they belonged to a less developed stage of history than his own: 'the childhood of mankind'. Homer is still a best seller. Our capacity to enjoy literature seems to be the least explicable of all kinds of development. Literature breaks the rules by which we separate epochs and cultures. Even those who think that foreigners of their own time are retarded can feel at home with their stories. A Victorian reader who thought the Russians backward would have been impressed by their novels. African writers in the last thirty years have shown again that cultural barriers do not withstand good writing. Whatever a foreign reader's attitude to the Africa of Chinua Achebe's *Things Fall Apart*, it will not interfere with his absorption in the novel.

Defending what is *African* in African literature ought not to forbid its discussion as a contribution to writing in the modern world. A story can be a means of mitigating cultural prejudice. It might be illuminating to an African that a good man in Jane Austen can marry his brother's wife's sister,[7] or to a European that a good man in Elechi Amadi can take several wives at once. Varieties of custom and outlook can be learned in the course of reading the best novels. There are opponents of realism who deny that one book can be better than another except as a matter of personal taste; a useful refutation, if one is needed, exists in the fact that for all our cultural differences African and European critics have largely agreed about which are the best books — although foreigners have much to learn from Africans about how to read them. 'Literature', says Eldred Jones, 'is part of Africa's gift to the world'.[8] Novel readers are less numerous than novelists would like but they are now to be found everywhere; for the first time a writer in English can be in touch with a readership the great Victorians wrongly claimed to address: intelligent representatives of all mankind. The attack on realism, the denial that we can verify the truthfulness of our reading, is directed at all parts of this community. To ignore the claims of the 'universal' (an inadequate word for common experience) abets a cause which denies what African writers most vigorously claim, in the manner and purpose of their work: full participation in the modern world.

Wanting that above all for their novels and their societies, African intellectuals have engaged in prolonged debate about the relation of their fiction to European traditions. Whereas drama and poetry are African, the novel is said to be a European import. However well adapted to Africa, fiction is seen as a latecomer there; this is occasionally made a justification for polemical novels, as though all the art had been already accomplished far away. Western writers have also suffered an unnerving sense of a great institution behind them. Exaggerated respect for the history of the novel has been disabling in European and African literary theory.

In Nigeria it caused needless hostility when Amos Tutuola's *The Palm-Wine Drinkard* was published in 1952, although this is one of the finest minor works of its period. Its opening can hardly be quoted too often:

> I was a palm-wine drinkard since I was a boy of ten years of age. I had no other work more than to drink palm-wine in my life. In those days we did not know other money, except COWRIES, so

that everything was very cheap, and my father was the richest man in our town.

My father got eight children and I was the eldest among them, all of the rest were hard workers, but I myself was an expert palm-wine drinkard. I was drinking palm-wine from morning till night and from night till morning. By that time I could not drink ordinary water at all except palm-wine.

But when my father noticed that I could not do any work more than to drink, he engaged an expert palm-wine tapster for me; he had no other work more than to tap palm-wine every day.

The tapster dies and the bereft drinkard seeks him in 'The Deads' town'; he has many marvellous adventures. The sentences are shaped by the imperfectly educated Tutuola's remarkable sense of what will read well in modern English; the story's incidents are drawn partly from Yoruba folklore. Foreign reviewers, including Dylan Thomas, were delighted,[9] but at home it was felt that Tutuola was not dignified enough to be an African successor to Dickens and Lawrence (who would both have admired him). Other novelists were more orthodox.

Another reaction to the status of the Novel has been a refusal to 'compete' with a foreign genre, and critics have been attacked for pointing out Western influences in novels even when their authors admit to having profited from reading Hardy or Conrad or Joyce. Here is a different version of the European fear (or hope) that the prestigious novel is an exhausted genre. The Soviet critic Mikhail Bakhtin offers a valuable corrective: 'the higher a genre develops, and the more complex it becomes, the better and more fully it remembers its past'.[10] That is clear in the way fiction has been revitalised by the discovery of fresh starting-points in old novels, throughout the last half-century. Other critics have shown what the novel shares with other kinds of narrative and argued that its origins need not be located in Richardson and Defoe.[11] The differences between English and French accounts of fiction's development make the existence of a genre conditioned by one, European world view seem unlikely. There is another background to fiction, of which novelists are usually more aware than critics, in everyday story-telling, anecdote, gossip, argument by example, mimicry, confession, fantasy, dreams, elaborated jokes, and the impulse to reminisce about childhood or travels, or to grumble about one's husband or wife. The novel has always thrived on every kind of talk. An ear for people talking is perhaps a novelist's first qualification. Guillaume Oyônô-Mbia, the Cameroonian playwright and author of prose 'chronicles' of life in his village Mvoutessi began his first play *Three Suitors: One Husband* after listening to a palaver in the village. The stories in his *Chroniques de Mvoutessi* have the same source; Oyônô-Mbia's village is endlessly in palaver.[12] He is, as so many novelists have been, an extraordinary story-teller, mimic, wit and literary joker, in French and English. This aspect of the novel is neglected most of all in teaching and in guide books for students which stress themes and messages at the risk of representing a story as a tract. It may be that readers expect Lawrence's 'full play' of ideas and resent a writer's obvious designs on them because they recognise an affinity to conversation in which one anecdote is contradicted by another.[13] In talk nobody doubts his sense of the real, although we enjoy tall stories. Novelists must be more than good talkers, but at their most advanced they are true to their most modest origins, in our ways of discussing the world. Happily no one can decide whether talk has 'developed', or propose that the 'genre' is exhausted.

It is frustrating for the African novelist in English that the best talk around him is in another language. The language barrier frustrates the foreigner too, and excludes most outsiders from competing as African novelists. It helps to explain the worst of all misrepresentations of Africa, which continues to be a menace, and which African novelists of most intellectual persuasions have combated: the European charge of backwardness.

At the close of his *Chinua Achebe* David Carroll observes that Achebe 'is creating a new kind of fictional reality which makes the reader examine afresh both his own reality and his assumptions about the modern novel'.[14] Professor Carroll means the English reader, for whom this is certainly true. For the African reader Achebe's fictional reality *is* that of the modern novel and it conveys the Ibo life (in *Things Fall Apart* and *Arrow of God*) known in Conrad's and Cary's lifetimes as a reality of the modern African world. The foreigner is made to re-examine his own reality and his own novels, but above all he is made to absorb the fact that another kind of reality has coexisted with his.

Colonialism interrupted the course of many relatively homogenous societies at various stages of their own historical developments and found all of them hopelessly 'retarded'. The newcomers' cultural advancement had been less consistent. Modernisers working in conformity with European models introduced Calvinist theology, Victorian literature, and Marxist–Leninism; Napoleonic bureaucracy, Edwardian education, and the World Bank. European incongruities have become more startling in Africa where older institutions found new ground and less competition. The regime of South Africa draws authority from ideas which were at their strongest in the seventeenth century. So beset, African creative writers since Independence have asserted the modernity of their own worlds, not without opposition. Overlooking the presence of anachronisms throughout our own societies, we have found them everywhere in Africa. Few Europeans can visit Africa without feeling that they are looking into the past: life is 'nineteenth century', or 'medieval', or 'prehistoric'. Understandable as metaphors among non-historians these designations are inaccurate and unfriendly. An historian in Africa would certainly find points of comparison between modern societies and his period of study, and that would be possible in Europe too. Such comparisons need very careful definition and can be only speculative. When an Islamic city is called 'medieval', as V. S. Naipaul recently described Qum in Iran,[15] and as visitors almost invariably label traditional cities in North Africa, the effect is to claim the modern world for the West, and to disclaim the obligations of coexistence with peoples who live differently. Discussing Senghor's idea of Africa's mission to 'leaven' the world Achebe writes:

> In talking about the world here we really mean Europe and the West. But we have all got into the bad habit of regarding that slice of the globe as the whole thing. That an African writer can so easily slip into this error is a tribute to its hold upon the contemporary imagination. For those of Europe and the West such a habit if not entirely excusable is at least understandable. It can even be amusing in a harmless way — as when, for example, a game between Cincinatti and Minnesota is called the World Series. But it ceases to be funny when it consigns other continents and peoples into a kind of limbo; and it begins to border on the grotesque when these continents and peoples come to accept this view of the world and of themselves.[16]

The limbo into which Africa is cast is that of the past, not as Western historians understand it, but as it is commonly imagined.

Alberto Moravia's very readable travel book *Which Tribe do You Belong To?* records journeys in East and West Africa. Throughout the book Moravia presents himself as a modern man and locates Africans somewhere in 'the past'. In one sketch, 'The Abyss of the Centuries', he describes a young couple he saw in a shop in rural Kenya in 1963; the girl was 'adorned' with copper rings and the man with painted body-markings. They were, he says 'indecipherable' because 'between them and me there was a gap of ten or fifteen thousand years'. But he recalls the girl's 'glance of bashful, shy humanity; like a modest appeal to a remote, archaic brotherhood'. The chapter ends with an account of a Samburu hut where the author imagines himself, painted red, with a wife in copper rings: 'and I have gone back twenty thousand years; and this is my home'.[17] Elsewhere in the book Moravia finds other past periods reflected in contemporary Africa. A Gikuyu schoolmaster who speaks enthusiastically of European literature, but with little apparent understanding, reminds him of how Virgil and Latin culture were regarded in the Middle Ages;[18] a group of Englishmen observed in a hotel are 'perfect samples' of 'homo Victorianus'.[19] Among the Dogoni of Bandiagara in Mali Moravia is surprised by the normal appearance of boys who seem 'just like boys anywhere in the world', yet believe, he thinks, that 'the cosmos is merely crockery', and that the sun and moon are basins, of red and white copper. He finds 'points of resemblance with the myths of Greece and the Eastern Mediterranean', and he wonders why the Dogoni 'came to a standstill at the myths themselves, whereas elsewhere there was a progression from myth to science'.[20] History has followed another course in Rome.

The girl in copper rings has probably seen tourists before; whatever she thinks of the shop with its tins of food, umbrellas, and workmen's clothes, her thoughts belong to the present age. The schoolmaster's fellow-countryman Professor Ngugi wa Thiong'o has explained the irrelevance of much colonial English-teaching to the realities of modern Kenya; Ngugi might perhaps wish that the Englishmen would go back to the nineteenth century.[21] Moravia emphasises that he does not feel superior to the Dogoni. He was impressed by the courteous behaviour and conversation of the Dogoni boys who acted as his guides. He is aware that African hospitality to strangers and good manners in the young contrast just as disturbingly with Western social barbarity as Western astronomy with African myth. These differences nowadays embarrass the educated European who feels that Europe has no claim to be better than Africa but that traditional African world views are wrong, and traditional life 'limiting'. It is too easy an escape to find in the Dogoni or Samburu reflections of prehistory, twenty thousand years ago. We know little about life then, although we know that people were better fed, larger, and healthier, than most are today; and that they were undisturbed by Italian novelists. Moravia's assumption that he is epochs away from the girl in the rings, from whom he is in fact divided chiefly by language, is disappointing in a novelist. He could have wondered about how an African freethinker, contemplating the Pope, might mistakenly say: 'between him and me there is a gap of centuries', or how an urbane African might find 'living-history' in Calabria, or in Oxford 'which people call medieval, though it's not'. An African novelist visiting the United States and hearing of the movement to remove Darwin from school curricula might suffer the illusion of a past come back to life, so strong is the American insistence abroad that social and technological changes have made a wholly new world there, safely encapsulated.

In deriding the efforts of 'foreign triers' among Victorian and early-twentieth-century novelists for their inability to show the African world from inside and for distorting or ignoring their African characters, African critics have given various explanations: racialism, imperialism, Romanticism, laziness about language learning. Carl Gustav Jung, who identified modern Africans with Early Man, believed that Europeans are unbalanced by meeting in Africans the 'primitive' in themselves. However that may be, the first half-century of English fiction about Africa is a disappointment. Olive Schreiner's *The Story of An African Farm* and Conrad's *Heart of Darkness* are good novels flawed. We should understand why.

The presence of ignorance, stupidity, greed, and racialism, among Europeans in colonial Africa has been amply demonstrated. 'The conquest of the earth', Marlow observes at the outset of his tale in *Heart of Darkness* 'is not a pretty thing'. Whatever view would be taken today of Marlow's 'idea', had he explained it, there is no doubt that many Europeans had baser motives. But Africans were misrepresented by the most intelligent and imaginative outsiders, good novelists. At its best the European idea led to a view of Africans which diminished and blurred their humanity.

In the case of Olive Schreiner, a progressive-minded writer, a feminist and intellectual who had grown up in remote parts of South Africa as the daughter of a Calvinist missionary, 'new' men and women represented the real world which as a girl she hoped to join. *The Story of An African Farm* was written in South Africa and was published in England in 1883. The story concerns a group of white settlers, adults and children. The African servants and farm-workers remain in the background, less interesting to the author than the ostriches and chickens about the farm. Although this can be defended on the grounds that Olive Schreiner was not writing about race relations, it is implausible, in a novel concerned with the mental growth of adolescents living in so small a community, that the Africans should have contributed nothing to the Europeans' lives which was worth recording. We see just enough of two of the servants to wish to know more of them, but a fictional apartheid intervenes. Olive Schreiner was not a racialist: she is contemptuous of Tant Sannie who (in Part 1, Chapter 5) excludes the black servants from divine service because she 'held they were descended from apes and needed no salvation'. It is not race the author values but modernity: her characters can be placed on a scale of diminishing progressiveness. The precocious boy Waldo who invents a sheep-shearing machine at the age of fourteen, and the intelligent, rebellious girl Lyndall, are true Victorians who read Political Economy and are troubled by Doubts; they are most real to the author who treats them with solemn and lyrical respect. Lyndall's sister Em, a 'natural housewife', follows them on the scale, and further down are Tant Sannie, who thinks the Bible and Hymnary the only good books since the Devil is in all the rest, and her coarsely comic suitor Bonaparte Blenkins: they seemed to Olive Schreiner to belong to a colonial past which could not be presented to modern English readers except by figures of farce, reminiscent of Smollett and a time gone by. At the far end of the scale are the Africans who take no part in the story because they could not be seen in any connection with the distant English present day which was more vivid to Olive Schreiner than the world around her. The Africans are alien in race, language and culture: but that does not preclude what we are led to believe is a kind of friendship between Tant Sannie and her maid. They are excluded from the novelist's interest and sympathy because she could not see them as her contemporaries.

Joseph Conrad was well qualified to have done better in *Heart of Darkness*. In a ship's company race, culture, and class count for less than 'solidarity': 'backwardness' there means only lazy seamanship. Conrad had also known, in his early life in Poland, the injustices of life under an empire. He shows the sympathy we expect in a letter on the subject of Belgian colonialism, written in 1903 five years after *Heart of Darkness* was published. 'The black man shares with us the consciousness of the universe in which we live – no small burden. Barbarism per se is no crime . . . and the Belgians are worse than the seven plagues of Egypt.'[22] But although Marlow responds warmly to the African crew of his riverboat, he feels distanced from them by history. In the famous account of the journey up river Africans are heard in the forest:

> The prehistoric man was cursing us, praying to us, welcoming us – who could tell? We were cut off from the comprehension of our surroundings. . . . We could not understand because we were . . . travelling in the night of first ages, of those ages that are gone, leaving hardly a sign – and no memories.
> The earth seemed unearthly. We are accustomed to look upon the shackled form of a conquered monster, but there – there you could look at a thing monstrous and free. It was unearthly, and the men were – No, they were not inhuman. Well, you know, that was the worst of it – this suspicion of their not being inhuman. It would come slowly to one. They howled and leaped, and spun, and made horrid faces; but what thrilled you was just the thought of their humanity – like yours – the thought of your remote kinship with this wild and passionate uproar. Ugly. Yes, it was ugly enough; but if you were man enough you would admit to yourself that there was in you just the faintest trace of a response to the terrible frankness of that noise, a dim suspicion of there being a meaning in it which you – you so remote from the night of the first ages – could comprehend.[23]

It is usual to say of this passage that 'the primitive stereotype' denies humanity to the Africans.[24] In fact Conrad acknowledges a common humanity: 'no, they were not inhuman'. The man who can face the unfamiliar, Marlow asserts, 'must be as much of a man as those on the shore'. But he cannot accept that these are people of the 1890s, and he escapes the uncomfortable truth by assigning them to the furthest possible historical past. The Congolese are not the proto-man Marlow imagines, nor is he so securely removed from them in his civilisation. Had a late Victorian novelist been able to penetrate not just the continent of Africa but also the lives of its people he would have found much to disconcert his readers, and in more than their imperialist presuppositions. Ngugi wa Thiong'o properly claims that 'some African civilisations had not developed the conquest of nature to a very high degree; but they had developed to a high degree their control of social nature'.[25] English literature lost by the failure see it. The Victorians depended on twin stereotypes of savage African and civilised European because, amidst their own efforts at progress, savagery was so evident in the cities and the countryside of nineteenth-century England. Rowdy abandonment which *was* gravely uncivilised could easily be found in London in the 1890s. Marlow's journey leads him to Mr Kurtz, the civilised man who regresses into barbarism. But *Heart of Darkness* falsifies Conrad's knowledge that London in 1898 was itself one of the dark places of the earth, and that in the late nineteenth or early twentieth century there was no need to leave Europe to practise barbarities in the name of civilisation. *Heart of Darkness* is an indictment of imperialism, in revealing, inadvertently, how hard it was for even the most enlightened European to see Africans as men of his own time.

Some critics who attack the 'negative' view of the Congolese in Conrad's story and in later English novels — Joyce Cary's *Mister Johnson* is the most frequently castigated — object to the idea of an uncivilised human 'core' which is allegedly exposed in the African and dressed, however lightly, in the European. Ngugi wa Thiong'o, who has learned and gained from Conrad, comments in *Writers in Politics*:

> For Joseph Conrad, the African characters in *Heart of Darkness* are part of that primitive savagery that lay below the skin of every civilised being. For Joyce Cary, the positive creative African in *Mister Johnson* is a clowning idiot whose desire and final fulfilment is having to be shot dead by an Englishman whom we are led to believe loves him well. . . . So much for *Mister Johnson* and Master Joyce Cary.[26]

It would have been more obvious when the novel appeared in 1939 that *Mister Johnson* would provoke this kind of hostility, if it had been easier then for Cary to regard Africans as contemporary readers.

Ngugi condemns Conrad, Cary, and many other modern English writers, for a liberalism which he calls 'the sugary ideology of imperialism', an explanation which fits his book.[27] But it was the assumption that Empire, however dreadful its operations, represented the (single) course of progress which precluded liberal creative writers from taking more seriously African cultures apparently left behind by history. That limitation can be seen in many nineteenth-century analysts of British Rule. Karl Marx writing in 1853 believed that although the motives and results of Britain's activities in India were vile and criminal, they were historically necessary; his comments are often quoted: 'England has to fulfil a double mission in India: one destructive the other regenerating — the annihilation of the Asiatic society, and the laying of the material foundations of Western society in Asia'. There is no reason to suppose that he would have thought differently of what happened later in Africa. Marx wrote in the same passage that he was 'sickened' by the shattering of 'inoffensive' village communities but regretted more that they had always been deprived of 'all grandeur and historical energies'.[28] Without sharing Marx's belief in the inevitable progress of history towards socialist revolution, other writers on imperialism suffered the same loss of human sympathy with village communities in Africa which apparently 'confined the human mind within the smallest possible compass' as Marx wrote of India. Concern with the grandeur of historic energies so potent in their own recent history caused Europeans to overlook not so much (among writers of Marx's intelligence) the humanity of Indians or Africans, but the fact of their sharing our own times. Conrad and later novelists were more alive to individual predicaments, but were hampered by the ingrained habit of mind which designated modern Africa 'ancient' and found its cultures tiresomely incongruous.

African writers since the 1950s have been writing to proclaim their modernity, without meaning by that merely to claim a share of ours. In his Conclusion to *The Wretched of the Earth*, Frantz Fanon writes: 'we today can do everything so long as we do not imitate Europe, so long as we are not obsessed by the desire to catch up with Europe'. He reiterates the phrase 'to catch up' *rattraper*: although 'for many among us the European model is the most inspiring'.

> The pretext of catching up must not be used to push man around, to tear him away from himself or from his privacy, to break and kill him.

No, we do not want to catch up with anyone. What we want to do is to go forward all the time, night and day, in the company of Man, in the company of all men . . .

If we want to turn Africa into a new Europe, and South America into a new Europe, then let us leave the destiny of our countries to Europeans. They will know how to do it better than the most gifted among us.[29]

Fanon's alternative Africa, conceived on revolutionary socialist principles, is to be based on the present and past realities of the continent, not in complete independence of Europe, for he writes here of the need to 'have regard to the sometimes prodigious theses which Europe has put forward', but independent of the false hypothesis that Africa's present state can be equated with Europe's past. Whatever their opinion of Fanon's politics, all African novelists write with this certainty in mind. For Europeans it is easy to take the point but hard to take it in.

The novels discussed in the following pages are either very well known to readers of African literature, or very recent. They show great variety of style and technique and, as David Carroll observes of Achebe, they extend the range and vitality of fiction. Chinua Achebe's *Things Fall Apart* (1958) and *Arrow of God* (1964) brought a young man's point of view at the time of Independence to a fictional world sixty and forty years earlier in such a way that Africa's strangest half-century is seen as modern history. *Things Fall Apart* is no second-hand Africanisation of an old art form. Little is borrowed except the title and epigraph which are from Yeats's 'The Second Coming':

> Turning and turning in the widening gyre
> The falcon cannot hear the falconer;
> Things fall apart; the centre cannot hold;
> Mere anarchy is loosed upon the earth

After nineteen hundred years of Christendom and an era of paganism before that, Yeats thought a new cycle of history was about to begin. The second coming we have witnessed has been a coming together of Christendom with other civilisations, moving in their own gyres, which Yeats's rather exclusively European view of things overlooked; and mere anarchy has been resisted so far.

When Achebe modestly said that he would be satisfied to refute the colonial charge that African 'history was one dark night of savagery', ended by Europe, even if that reduced him to 'applied' art rather than pure, he was claiming 'commitment', as magic a word in Africa as in Europe, rather than explaining his full achievement.[30] Yeats observed that literature often requires the attribution of 'noble' qualities, in the public interest, which do less than justice to its real proceedings. Mindful perhaps of Conrad's uninhibited prehistoric man Achebe imbues his old Iboland with grave decorum, although this conception of dignity is large enough to admit the tensions of a real community and the indignity of real life. But he is not simply manufacturing *korma*. The village world is split by the arrival of missionaries but it remains energetic and adaptable. It is the British District Commissioner at the end of the book who seems to represent a defunct order, and in *Arrow of God* that impression is confirmed. An irony in both novels is that his Ibo characters are better equipped to cope with twentieth-century developments than his Englishmen who assume them to be lost somewhere back in history; the principal disadvantage for the twentieth-century Ibos is that of being overprotected. The elegiac element has been exaggerated by critics who feel that pre-colonial Africa was purely pastoral, 'like the old Age'.

Achebe's distinction has overshadowed — as in this book — the work of another Nigerian, Elechi Amadi; in *The Concubine*, *The Great Ponds* and *The Slave* stories of traditional village life are told as though by a villager, but written by an exceptionally intelligent scientist, teacher and administrator. The world of Amadi's novels has no contact with history as known to Europeans, but is subject to some of the same disturbances. *Wonjo*, 'the curse of the gods', which threatens to end the world and which fills villages with sad spirits of the departed, is identified in the last lines of *The Great Ponds* as the Influenza of 1918 which 'was to claim a grand total of some twenty million lives all over the world'. That is almost the first intervention by the 1969 narrator into the enclosed lives of the feuding villagers of 1918 and it neatly invites comparison of the novel's small war over the Pond of Wagaba with events in Europe at the same time. The world of 1914–18 was, we are reminded, larger than that of the First World War. Modern history was also taking place around the Great Ponds in a corner of Eastern Nigeria.

'The African novelist has turned his back on the Christian god', observes Ngugi with satisfaction.[31] In most of Black Africa Christianity is no older than first contact with Europe and has suffered from association with conquest and foreign rule – and with the more disagreeable aspects of education. Traditional social life was inseparable from the older religions which have lived on to coexist in belief and practice with Christianity, as happened in the Americas, and earlier in Europe. Mission policy appears to have varied; but in African novels in English and French the priest or pastor is usually a fool or a rogue or both, and is unable to grasp that African religion, at least as monotheistic as popular Catholicism and more practically serviceable than Christianity has ever been, had to be treated with respect. Some missionaries were intelligently sympathetic, as we see in the writing of Father Placide Tempels and others.[32] In *Houseboy* (*Une vie de Boy*) by the Cameroonian Ferdinand Oyono the boy abandons village life to put his trust in a priest and the life of *les blancs* as unreservedly as any missionary could ask; he has small thanks for it. Published soon after Independence, in 1956, *Houseboy* stresses the idiocy of priests, teachers and administrators; francophone countries were very given to retaliatory fiction castigating colonial types. Scenes of cruelty in some such novels confirm the view of those who take colonialism to have been one dark night of savagery ended by Independence: *The Poor Christ of Bomba* by Oyono's fellow Cameroonian Mongo Béti is such a story. The effect of unrelieved allegations of atrocity can be miscalculated though, as in the later stages of *Le Pauvre Christ de Bomba*, by provoking a degree of resistance even in readers who are sympathetic to the critique ('Our Father Patrick wasn't like *that*'). The strength of *Houseboy* is in exposing the attitudes of the French characters who see Africans as people who have recently emerged from prehistory. Camara Laye, a Guinean Muslim who died in 1980, will be remembered for *The Radiance of the King* (*Le regard du roi*) which is the best African novel in French. Published in 1954 it was, in effect, a startling reproach to Michel Butor and Alain Robbe-Grillet who were then at the height of their campaign to prove that modern fiction can owe next to nothing to tradition. The novel has attracted many interpretations, but it is a relatively simple reversal of the scheme in tales of tyrannical white priests. A European in Africa loses faith in his own culture and then finds God. The king may be pure poetry but the poetry is religious.

Commentaries on African fiction set in recent decades are given to speaking of characters who 'live in two worlds' (two *systèmes de verité* for French structuralists); this is a piece of stale figurative language which the ablest creative writers work their way past. The characters in Wole Soyinka's comic novel *The Interpreters* live in one 1960s world which they know thoroughly but find awkward to interpret. Characters in Achebe, in Ayi Kwei Armah, in Ngugi, experience conflicting claims between family and employer, religion and education, conscience and self-interest. The temptation for those who explain the books is to simplify with such large dichotomies as 'Africa and the West', or 'tradition and progress', which tend to be resolved into 'the past and the present'. In the Somali Nuruddin Farah's recent *Sweet and Sour Milk* the hero Loyaan wonders at one point whether he should live in the past or the future, in a world of the *Arabian Nights* or one of Orwellian politics, but he sees at once that the world about him is neither. Loyaan is resentful of Western and Eastern attempts to recreate Africa in their own modern image as though it were the raw material for other peoples' grand historical purposes. In Ngugi's *Petals of Blood* a supposedly 'nineteenth century' village is transformed in a decade into a town-of-the-future by Western forms of development which are disastrous for the people of this village of the 1970s. In picturing two forms of rapid development Farah and Ngugi are at their best in showing the lives of the people involved, whose present conditions have not been taken into account. Africans who are bilingual or multilingual, who have access to two or more foreign cultures, who watch several political systems in the outside world, are living with a greater range of choices than their ancestors, but it is their world still. To speak of two worlds is to imply 'theirs and ours', and underlying the implication is the myth of two epochs. These novels observe this epoch from their point of view.

Many are political; their authors are usually closer to a dangerous centre of power than their fellow-writers elsewhere. Since development in many countries has been misguided under the influence of capitalist and socialist outside interests, novelists often attack whichever developed political structure has been imposed on them; political doctrine differs as much as in Europe. Ngugi has become unreservedly critical of capitalism in the last fifteen years. Wole Soyinka has argued that 'ideologues' resemble Christian converts of earlier generations since 'both suffer from externally induced fantasies of redemptive transformation in the image of alien masters'. 'Like his religious counterpart, the new ideologue has never stopped to consider whether or not the eternal verities of his new doctrine are already contained in, or can be elicited from the world-view and social structures of his own people. The study of much contemporary literature reveals that they can.'[33] In *Sunset in Biafra*, his account of his experiences during the Nigerian Civil War, Elechi Amadi put the same idea: 'there is the belief that we need not, indeed dare not exercise initiative in these things government, technology and the arts until we have caught up with the advanced nations by copying every single achievement of theirs. Well, we will never catch up that way. We too must contribute.'[34] Like Soyinka, and Ngugi at his least doctrinaire, Amadi believes in a modern Africa which is no longer governed by foreign models. The pressures for Africa to become another Europe (West and East) are, of course, increasing with every decade. Amadi's best novel of pre-colonial Africa depicts villagers of the early twentieth century, who suffer as all peoples have done from war and disease but are able to resist both, with courage, imagination and intelligence which reflect unflatteringly on the European supreme commanders of 1918. The reviewer for the *Spectator* praised *The Great Ponds* for its subtlety, and compared its battles and parleys to those of Virgil and Homer.

African novels are inspired, whatever the authors' political views, by the wish to explore through the realism and freedom of contemporary fiction the integrity of modern Africa.

2 Colonial Africa: Achebe, Oyono, Camara Laye

One unforgettable image in Achebe's *Things Fall Apart* is of a bicycle tied to a sacred silk-cotton tree. Its owner was a white man, the first to intrude on the Ibo of the region; he has been killed because the Oracle warns that his kind will 'spread destruction' (Chapter 15). The bicycle is secured lest it 'run away' to tell what has happened. Animist interpretation, here, lags only a little behind technological invention, although a space-probe can communicate without moving. Bicycle mechanics are easily understood once initial surprise is overcome; they were new machines in the white world at the end of the nineteenth century as well as in Africa, and by inaugurating individual mechanised transport, they were a revolution which has affected almost everyone. Trust in such power as that of a sacred tree belongs to a different approach to things from that which results in bicycles, and neither has ever succeeded in ousting the other. Achebe is struck by the meeting of a culture mostly ruled by the sacred with a culture mostly devoted to the mechanical. The point of view is that of a mind to whom both are familiar, and historically placed. Trust in the tree is misplaced since the bicycle is observed by three other whites, accompanied by 'ordinary men', and their report to base results in murderous retaliation against the village. Incongruity which might have been pleasing turns out to be tragic. Conspicuous in this scene, in Chapter 15 of *Things Fall Apart*, the sense of disastrous consequences from the meeting of two cultures which might have managed better together is subtly present throughout.

An excellent critic and essayist willing to discuss his creative writing, Achebe has often been inclined, none the less, to make his novels sound less interesting than they really are. Achebe's commitment to dignifying his people's recent history, to combat bad colonial influences on morale, might have made this book an exercise in pastoral, or an essay in praise of former times. It is more. The richly developed social life of late-nineteenth-century Iboland is convincingly shown, in relation to a hero, Okonkwo, whose success as wrestler, farmer and elder is spoilt by a nature coarsened by fear of the 'feminine' qualities which he thinks disgraced his father. Okonkwo aims to embody every virtue of his clan but he fails to achieve the balance and caution valued by his culture. When the white men come these qualities in his people expose them to disruption while Okonkwo is adamantly hostile, and he dies in horrible circumstances, a remarkable victim of the imperial idea. The subtle artistry with which the story is told has been fully admired and various accounts have defended the novel's unity. Charles R. Larson sees unities in leitmotifs, in proverbs which 'draw threads together', and in the development of stories within stories; his explanation is among the most persuasive.[1] Others have tried to talk in terms of Greek tragedy. My purpose is to argue that the unity is in the point of view: that of a narrator of 1958 looking back sixty years and in so doing considering not only old Iboland but the whole modern period of eastern Nigeria. The book is original in technique; it is more than a revival of old types of story. Its outlook is challengingly modern because it is so loyal to traditional culture, whose 'dignity' Achebe has shown to the world. But he does not write as *laudator temporis acti*, even if he risks sounding it in his modest statement of his intentions. African novelists whose work is set in the past are sometimes said to have 'taken refuge in historical themes' — Achebe has done nothing of the kind. His original intention was to extend the tale of Okonkwo into a saga, to be complete with the story of Okonkwo's grandson in the 1950s; he was persuaded to issue the second part as *No Longer at Ease*. The last sixty years are always in view to the author of *Things Fall Apart*, and the title is misleading in so far as it suggests finality, rather than Yeats's fears for the whole modern world in trouble. The novel is misrepresented when it is explained as an elegy or an imaginative excavation of a lost world. It is of course a tribute to the dignity of the people and their ancestors, but also a critical appraisal of the drastic changes of Eastern Nigeria in recent history, of the subsequent transition from village community to nation state which has not yet been brought about at the end of the story, but which is contemplated on every page. The narrator is not a plaintive voice from the past but a sophisticated modern story-teller who has learned the story from people who remember. Ngugi wa Thiong'o has called Okonkwo's society 'emergent feudalism',[2] a classification which is disputed below; the connotations of that English phrase are so strong that to use it is to remove the world of Achebe's grandparents (and ours) from its real place in our time. *Things Fall Apart* sets it firmly where it belongs. Ngugi cannot say whether feudalism might have emerged among Okonkwo's villagers; what has emerged is Nigeria.

Some critics maintain that the narrator is a village elder. David Carroll comments that although

> the novel is narrated in the third person . . . There is no suggestion of an omniscient observer scrutinising and analysing the customs and habits of this Igbo community. The voice is that of a wise and sympathetic elder of the tribe who has witnessed time and time again the cycle of the seasons and the accompanying rituals in the villages.[3]

In fact the narrator discreetly merges two voices, one of which belongs to the village-world and the other to a more urbane Nigerian of 1958. The first is almost a 'communal' speaker, as though several villagers who had known Okonkwo were contributing their recollections to be edited and recast. The editorial voice, which becomes increasingly intrusive towards the end, can comment from beyond the villagers' standpoint; for him the people of Umuofia are 'they' rather than 'we'; and the Ibo are a larger people within Nigeria. In the village narrative, recent events are reported as if by eye-witnesses: muscles stand out on the wrestlers' bodies while Okonkwo slips through his opponent's grip (on the first page). Conversations are reported as though in gossip. A bad harvest is recalled with feeling. The ripeness of a bride's body is noted as a pleasing matter of fact. In the larger perspective, traditional life, colonial mentality and Christianity are observed with detachment. 'It was not the mad logic of the Trinity that captivated him', the narrator comments on the conversion to Christianity of Okonkwo's son Nwoye; 'he did not understand it. It was the poetry of the new religion, something felt in the marrow' (Chapter 16). To have written the story in the first person, with a story-teller of Nwoye's generation, would have altered the tone drastically; such a 'wise elder' who had lived under Okonkwo and the missionaries and remained so detached from both would be scarcely credible. The 1950s reader would have been conscious of a young recently educated mind behind the narrative.

For much of the book we have the impression of village reminiscence, anecdote, gossip, and formal 'tales of Okonkwo', mixed with folk-tales, songs and sayings. It is said of the young hostage who lives with Okonkwo that 'Ikemefuna's sad story is still told in Umuofia to this day' (Chapter 2), and the novel often seems to be giving an English version of the Ibo telling. Okonkwo distinguished firmly between masculine stories of war and heroism, and women's tales of the time long ago when the animals could talk. *Things Fall Apart* includes the equivalents of men's and women's stories, of conversation among elders and talk in the kitchen. Okonkwo's rise to power as a farmer and soldier is just such an improving sample of tradition as a father might recount to his sons; Okonkwo no doubt often used it for this purpose. Ikemefuna's life and death would teach the truth of the song sung after a woman's death: 'For whom is it well, for whom is it well? / There is no one for whom it is well' (Chapter 14). Although Uchendu repeats the verses to Okonkwo when he is exiled to his motherland, Umuofia would consider the lesson especially valuable for girls. Male discussions and debates are given as they might have been repeated for the benefit of a notable who had been away; women's talk is about babies and the rashness of husbands, told as it might have been passed on in gossip. In passages of this kind the interest is communal; all are affected by a death or by a good day's work by a willing farmer. Values are held in common and decisions are taken in public. Things are presented not as they appear to an individual consciousness through mood and character, in the European novel, but as everyone can see they plainly are. Little is secret in the villages. Okonkwo's barnful of yams and his wife-beating in the Week of Peace are common knowledge. No judgement on either means much if it is not shared by all. Here the point of view belongs to Iboland in the 1890s.

In the 1950s perspective there are implicit judgements of a different kind: 'these women never saw the inside of the ancestral masqueraders' hut. . . . If they imagined what was inside, they kept their imagination to themselves. No woman ever asked questions about the most powerful and the most secret cult in the clan' (Chapter 10). The last sentence would be superfluous among Umuofians. Following the hint about what the women may imagine, it delicately emphasises their exclusion. When the girl Akueke is to be married she appears briefly before her suitor and his relatives to be inspected, and 'when she had shaken hands, or rather held out her hand to be shaken, she returned to her mother's hut to help with the cooking' (Chapter 8). Her mother tells her to take off her waist-beads before she goes to the fire, and their careful removal is described. These details stress her desirability but also her submissiveness, and her exclusion — once those qualities have been established — from the marriage negotiations taking place in the men's house. The narrator is allowing for mixed opinions in his 1950s readers on the traditional status of women. In the paragraph which ends Chapter 7, Nwoye is shown to sense not indecorum but evil after his father has killed Ikemefuna, as he is said to have felt a chill of horror when he heard in the forest the crying of twins exposed to die; the narrator's sympathy with Nwoye there, and his implied aloofness from traditional practice are very clear. These private judgements are more effective for being tacit; they belong to a later period of Ibo debate.

The Umuofian and the Nigerian types of narrative, appropriate to the 1890s and the 1950s, produce different registers in Achebe's English. Where the point of view is strictly traditional, he gives an impression of Ibo. The diction includes about forty Ibo words translated in a glossary which is hardly needed since we learn them more pleasantly from their contexts. An *ogbanje* is 'a child who repeatedly dies and returns to its mother to be reborn'. *Uli* is a dye for patterning women's bodies. '*Ilo*' is 'the village green'. Some English words belong to Africa: 'yam', 'matchet', 'palm-wine', 'medicine-man'. Others are coinages: Evil Forest (both a place and a spirit), 'market week' for a unit of four days. Certain expressions translate Ibo literally: the masqueraders (*egwugwu*) who impersonate ancestral spirits address humans in the form 'body of . . .' followed by the name. Scores of other English words carry an African (or tropical) sense. In a world-language certain classes of vocabulary change meaning with climate, religion and other variables. 'Season', 'forest', 'rain', 'sunset', and 'grass' have unEnglish connotations in the tropics where, as Anthony Burgess once pointed out, April is no crueller than any other month. Achebe's Ibo world alters many other words. 'Python' to the Ibo is a sacred creature, addressed as 'Our Father'; or it is a rainbow. 'Royal' suggests 'yam king of crops' rather than a monarch; 'there is no king in Ibo'. The dead ancestors play an intimate part in daily life. Titles are worn on the ankle; wealth is measured in yams; a mask is a thing of power; a war may last ten days and involve the slaughter of twelve men; 'motherland' is the land of one's mother. A wife is one of several; a brother is a kinsman; a son a younger member of the clan. 'Evil' and 'crime' are offences against the *Earth* punishable by the goddess. 'Control' is more likely to mean magic or 'medicine' than technical aids. 'Village' has something of the force of the Greek *polis*. 'The world' soon fades into 'strangers' and implausible rumours beyond the nine villages. 'The dim past' is two generations away. The smaller physical scale and larger spiritual dimension of daily life in Umuofia brings about many other kindred semantic shifts, of which the author is plainly sometimes archly aware.

The 1958 viewpoint which accommodates these meanings has to allow for others. 'The world' has the global meaning for the Nigerian narrator, who uses 'government', 'religion' and 'education', with reference to new developments after the English arrive; these are alien to traditional Ibo, as are more down-to-earth terms such as 'handcuffs', 'court', and 'prison'. 'Iron-horse' translates bicycle since people take it to be alive. Communion is 'holy feast'; a new convert will take his drinking-horn. The court-messengers are 'Ashy-Buttocks' because of their khaki shorts, or *kotma* as English begins to supply Ibo with loan-words. But the perspective is increasingly distanced linguistically from the events; although nobody in the villages understands English and the missionaries depend on interpreters, Achebe intrudes vocabulary for which there would be no African equivalent throughout Part 2 and Part 3: 'pastor', 'parsonage', 'church', 'Sunday', 'service', 'heathen', 'Devil', 'prophets', 'temple', and 'missionaries'. These alien terms, which emphasise a division within the Ibo people, would of course have been familiar to an elder of Achebe's day, but they culminate in the last words of the novel which provide the District Commissioner with the title of the book he is planning: '*The Pacification of the Primitive Tribes of the Lower Niger*'. British English at its most assertive is given the last word by a narrator who is about to celebrate the end of British rule, and who is plainly seen at last as a Nigerian for whom the dangerous, unpredictable white man is no more than a typically shortsighted late-Victorian colonial officer whose book, or one like it, today gathers dust on the British Council shelves in Lagos. The novel's ending has been attacked and praised as a dramatic change of focus from Ibo to English eyes. In fact it is the proper conclusion of a narrative which has grown steadily more contemporary with its readers of 1958.

Even in Part 1 when we are immersed in the world of Umuofia and largely share its outlook, there is a narrative ambiguity, to be found in the novel's famous first sentence for example: 'Okonkwo was well known throughout the nine villages and even beyond'. We are at once enclosed in the village-world, whose boundaries are close in space and time; fifteen lines later we hear that Okonkwo's wrestling victory over the Cat 'was many years ago, twenty years or more'. The first and last sentences of the book contrast the tribal and the imperial world-pictures. 'Beyond' and what it implies to the twentieth-century reader is a quiet dramatic irony at the outset; 'many years' is also ambivalent. Talking later about varieties of custom in Iboland, Okonkwo observes that 'the world is large' (Chapter 8); the conversation then turns to 'the story of white men who, they say, are white like this piece of chalk . . . And these white men, they say, have no toes'. The narrator closes the chapter by noting that a 'polite name' for leprosy is 'the white skin'; at that point he plainly knows what the world holds beyond the characters' horizons, and is in effect an 'omniscient' on-looker.

English and Ibo registers coexist in the style. There are passages in which British idioms fit the Ibo world: 'the land of the living was not far removed from the domain of the ancestors. There was coming and going between them' (Chapter 13). 'Land of the living' and 'coming and going' are recharged with Ibo meaning, while their casual note in British English suits the Ibo context since the dead, enacted by masqueraders, are familiar figures in village life. But for most of the novel the Umuofians' dialogue and the surrounding narrative are so culturally Ibo that the modern British English from which almost all social, regional, and cultural nuances have been eliminated sounds coolly detached. Introducing Okonkwo in Chapter 1, the narrator observes that 'his fame rested on solid personal achievements', as a District Commissioner might note in a report, or as Achebe might have written for a news item for the Nigerian Broadcasting Service. In Ibo idiom Okonkwo is a 'ripe corn' whose value any farmer can see at once (Chapter 3); 'when a man says yes his *chi* says yes also. Okonkwo said yes very strongly; so his *chi* agreed' (Chapter 4). This pattern occurs throughout: judgements made in crisp English prose are supported by proverbs and stories from Ibo lore. 'And if the clan did not exact punishment for an offence against the goddess, her wrath was loosened on all the land and not just on the offender. As the elders said, if one finger brought oil it soiled the others' (Chapter 13). Images come from African life: Ikemefuna 'grew rapidly like a yam tendril in the rainy season' (Chapter 7); when a chill falls on Nwoye he is 'like a solitary walker at night who passes an evil spirit on the way' (Chapter 7); the clan is 'like a lizard; if it lost its tail it soon grew another (Chapter 20). In the Parts 2 and 3, the pseudo-Jacobean Biblical English of the missionaries creates a third voice although this seems to be subordinate to the 'editing' narrator who echoes it without any hint of affection or disaste. The Reverend Mr Brown observes: 'when I think that it is only eighteen months since the seed was first sown among you, I marvel at what the Lord hath wrought' (Chapter 18). Such conventional churchiness of speech, still to be heard throughout Africa, possessed an authority in 1900 which had receded by 1958. *Things Fall Apart* puts it in perspective.

Throughout the village stories we are aware of an artistic design which is not derived from the Western genre of the novel but is influenced by it. Many critics have emphasised the *African* character of the novel: the leisurely meandering of an oral storyteller, the brisk, reported transitions from one stage of Okonkwo's fortunes to another, the independence of Western techniques. Charles R. Larson points out how rarely characters are revealed through dialogue and how much of the technique is an outgrowth of oral narrative.[4] *Things Fall Apart* has a story rather than a plot, and it is a story frequently interrupted by set scenes which illustrate aspects of Umuofian life. 'There is no suggestion of an omniscient narrator', says David Carroll. No one denies that Achebe has written a novel, but the Novel is conceived as a genre to be filled in with more or less truckling to its 'European conventions'; Achebe is sometimes praised for Africanising the genre and sometimes reproached with 'looseness'. The unity of *Things Fall Apart* is easier to recognise when the narrator is seen as an editor of stories not themselves novelistic which are shaped by a novelist's eye for design.

The editor is omniscient, recording the most private feelings of Okonkwo, Nwoye, Ekwefi, and the thoughts of Ikemefuna moments before he dies. Chapter 11 begins with a folk-story told by Ekwefi to her daughter Ezinma. The birds are invited to a feast by the people of the sky. Tortoise persuades them to make him feathers, and he goes too. He tells the birds that new names are needed for such an occasion and takes the name 'All of You'. When the people of the sky announce that the feast is for 'all of you', Tortoise eats everything. The birds reclaim their feathers and arrange for him to fall to earth on the 'hard things' from his home, hoes, machetes, spears. His shell is smashed but repaired imperfectly by a great medicine-man. 'There is no song in the story', Ezinma objects. The story is skilfully told and the skill belongs to Ekwefi, to her mother, and her mother's mother. In the second part of the chapter, where Ezinma is taken by the priestess to the Oracle of Hills and Caves, events are presented through the terrified mind of Ekwefi who follows them through the spirit-haunted night, sustained by her love of Ezinma; the skill here is a novelist's, and so is that which combines the domestic intimacy of the children's tale with the awful exposure to night and the power of the goddess.

The Novel is one species of narrative fiction, and it shares conventions, as Robert Scholes and Robert Kellogg have shown at length in *The Nature of Narrative*, with other and older types of story. 'The best thing about a novel is the story', George Watson affirms in the first line of his Preface to *The Story of the Novel. Things Fall Apart* is written with a delight in story at its simplest and at its most subtle. The book's Biographical Note refers to Achebe's sister who, he says, 'told me many stories when I was young . . . I can say it was she who introduced me to the pleasure and art of storytelling'. Even in the set scenes where the curiosity created by a plot is entirely absent, we are led to read on by narrative art within the scene (the tale of Odukwe's judgement by Evil Forest, for example) and by the sense that Okonkwo and his village are living through a quiet time before the coming storm. Novels, however sophisticated their technique became in the late nineteenth and early twentieth centuries in the West, depend before anything else on the art of story-telling. 'Technique' and 'devices' are terms of almost magical force for some critics, as though the most 'advanced devices' could in themselves produce good books. Achebe has gained from reading earlier fiction, in learning what a novelist can leave out, among other things, but he owes more to his sister than to them, as the greatest novelists of advanced technique would have recognised.

Okonkwo believes that stories are fit only for foolish women and children unless they improve us, making us more manly. That view, not confined in the nineteenth century to Iboland, is still current, especially in Africa where teaching and novel-writing have usually been joint professions. Achebe challenges its cruder side with the weight he gives to womanly stories and their appeal for Nwoye, but his book is meant to educate. The recent past is dignified by the seriousness of the scrutiny its contemporary, 'omniscient' observer brings to bear.

Without writing, an African or a British nineteenth-century village depended on traditions going back no further than the old men's memories of what their fathers told. Ogbuefi Ezeudu, the oldest of Okonkwo's neighbours, reports his father's recollections, which belong to the dim past of eighteenth-century Umuofia. The unreliability of oral tradition is known to the Umuofians and although they accept myths, including the widespread belief in descent from an heroic founder who fought with 'a spirit of the wild for seven days and seven nights' (Chapter 1), they discount fairy-tales. 'We have heard stories about white men who made the powerful guns and the strong drinks and took slaves away across the seas, but no one thought the stories were true' (Chapter 15). 'There is no story that is not true', Uchendu replies in his surprise at the reality of white men. 'The world has no end.' The Portuguese had visited the coast of Benin three hundred years earlier and in the eighteenth century Ibos were sold in large numbers as slaves for the Americas. Christian missions were established on the Niger in the mid-nineteenth century, about the time of Okonkwo's birth. Guns and tobacco have reached Umuofia but no word of the Christian converts elsewhere in Iboland. Its people are as little aware of Nigeria and Africa as most country people in Europe at the same period were conscious of their geographical and historical setting, dividing mankind into 'ourselves' and 'strangers' in Eastern Nigeria, in Sicily, or in County Clare, and remaining sceptical or credulous in varying degrees on the subject of travellers' tales.

They are aware of change. Okonkwo's punishment when he violates the Week of Peace which precedes the planting of new yam-farms is a heavy fine.

This year they talked of nothing else but the *nso-ani* sacrilege which Okonkwo had committed. It was the first time for many years that a man had broken the sacred peace. Even the oldest men could only remember one or two other occasions somewhere in the dim past.

Ogbuefi Ezendu, who was the oldest man in the village, was telling two other men who came to visit him that the punishment for breaking the Peace of Ani had become very mild in their clan.

'It has not always been so,' he said. 'My father told me that he had been told that in the past a man who broke the peace was dragged on the ground through the village until he died. But after a while this custom was stopped because it spoilt the peace which it was meant to preserve.' (Chapter 4)

Although impulsive, Okonkwo is instinctively conservative; he disapproves of the modern weakening of the exclusive *ozo* rank in neighbouring communities. 'They have indeed soiled the name of ozo' he says (in Chapter 8) of Abame and Aninta where the title has become available for everyone. He agrees with the elder Nwakibie who holds the view that 'in these days' the youth have 'gone soft' (Chapter 3). Without falling into the trap of 'universalism', and recognising the wholly Umuofian character of Okonkwo, it is possible to think that such a man would have shared opinions with many Victorian farmers of military background.

Ngugi wa Thiong'o has referred to Okonkwo's society as 'emergent feudalism'; in some Marxist schemes of historical evolution 'higher barbarism' would be a more accurate classification for the nine villages, perhaps verging on the 'slave civilisation' which had appeared in other parts of West Africa. But comparison seems pointless either with Anglo-Saxon England's emergent feudalism, or with the rural communities from whose 'barbarism' Thucydides recognised that the urban Greeks had developed. Achebe might appear to be highlighting aspects of Ibo culture which would recall ancient Greece to a European reader: wrestling matches, and social status achieved by prowess at games; public debate; sacrifice of cocks; Oracular counsel; personal and household gods. Certain English terms needed in the novel automatically recall Graeco-Roman antiquity: 'priestess', 'goddess', 'oracle', 'hostage', 'shrine' and even 'abomination' in the sense of a religious offence requiring drastic purification. Only one purpose could be served by prompting such comparison however: that of recalling to the Western reader how civilised a people can be without high technology, and without Christianity. The Ibos of *Things Fall Apart* whose nineteenth-century level of civilisation was untouched by either, might have been envied by many Europeans of the 1890s.

European intellectuals of that decade were very conscious of the sociological distinction between 'community' and 'society', and of how their societies were developing from communities. Ian Watt has suggested that the ideas of Ferdinand Tönnies's *Gemeinschaft und Gesellschaft* ('community and society') of 1887 may have influenced Conrad's views on 'solidarity'.[5] A community, according to Tönnies, is 'obligatory' in membership, hierarchical and usually based on a simple rural economy. *Gesellschaft* or 'society' is made up of relatively 'free associations' which 'exist for the specific interests of individual members' rather than for a 'community'. Umuofia is in this sense a community, which is plunged into the different conditions of 'society' when Europeans intervene. Community life there is far better developed and more successful than the social conditions which colonialism brings, although it seems that members of a community are unlikely to resist the attractions of society when these are available.

Chinua Achebe's composition of *Things Fall Apart* was a social act — in Tönnies's sense; Ibo communities had no time or need for novelists, and could not have tolerated novelistic appraisal of their customs and values. Achebe's first purpose was to show that modern Africa did not begin at the time of British Protectorates, or at Independence, but that a 'dignified' and highly developed civilisation had existed two generations ago. But as an educated Nigerian of the 1950s he welcomed the different scope 'society' offered and was more optimistic about the immediate prospects than African writers are likely to be at present. Education under British influence recommended a balanced view of gains and losses, and Ibo culture taught that 'wherever something stands, something else will stand beside it'. Arthur Ravenscroft has rightly praised Achebe for his understanding of the complexity of historical processes.[6] *Things Fall Apart* sets traditional Ibo life in its late-nineteenth-century place, and weighs its values against those of Nigeria on the point of independence.

Okonkwo's grandson in *No Longer at Ease* is an unsettled and bewildered young civil servant in the Lagos of the 1950s. Although Okonkwo and Nwoye are troubled in their relationship and in themselves, the chief attraction of older village life lies in a freedom from various cares we think of as modern. Hard work on the farms and readiness for war are expected of every man, but leisure and recreation come naturally to most people, and the villages have learnt to avoid or at least to contain warfare. Life was cheaper in Europe. Okonkwo's father Unoka was, though a gifted musician, a failure in Umuofia because he was slack at his farming and at war. The village could not afford a specialist however great his talents. Untitled and in debt, Unoka appears to have been tolerated although not respected. He might have enjoyed his music at ease if he had worked hard to grow his yams. The priestess he consults has, not unreasonably, no patience with him.

African communal solidarity is sometimes said to have denied or repressed individuality. In Europe interest in the 'individual' is sometimes supposed to have formed in the Renaissance and to have grown, perhaps monstrously, in the 'bourgeois' centuries. Privacy – a condition of novel writing and reading – obviously has increased in this way and so has interest in all the senses of private life, but these are different qualities. *Things Fall Apart* corrects the view that Africans are centuries behind Europe in grasping individual character and worth. Okonkwo is a determined conformist, psychologically very simply conceived, but he is more memorable as an individual than many characters in modern fiction, including his grandson Obi in *No Longer at Ease*.

The Umuofians take a lively interest in character and allow for individual frailties in their laws, provided that the Earth and the gods are not offended. The ease of one villager's quarrel with his wife is sensibly judged by the senior masquerader 'Evil Forest'. When someone wonders why so trivial a case is brought before the *egwugwu*, he is answered: 'Don't you know what kind of man Uzowulu is? He will not listen to any other decision' (Chapter 10). Okonkwo is in many respects insufferable: a bully, a swaggerer, a hothead. But his neighbours make the best of him, and admire his achievements. A man's nature is governed by his *chi* but he can influence the governor. At every stage of life, and time of the year, he has duties to his family, to the village and to the gods, in ways that severely restrict his privacy and his freedom. He is bound to think what other people think on many matters but he may think more, as Okonkwo's friend Obierika does; and he may know the man his neighbours know more intimately and more clearly. While Achebe sees the limitations of community, he shows what can be achieved within them; Lagos today is more likely than old Umuofia to produce types and caricatures of men. William Golding's prehistoric Africans in the story 'Klonk Klonk' (in *The Scorpion God*) have little awareness of boundaries to the self and are happiest tumbled together like puppies. Achebe's modern Africans are not like that.

The mindless tribal member is, according to the stereotype, subject to superstitions which Europe has overcome, which belong to the Dark Ages or to 'the childhood of mankind'. Perhaps the most remarkable feature of the West in the 'Age of Analysis', of universal education, and the decline of Christianity, is the prevalence of superstition and of new religions of a kind the Ibos would have judged lunatic. Certainly rural communities in nineteenth-century Europe feared ghosts, respected wise-women, and acknowledged taboo. Achebe's presentation stresses the social usefulness of African beliefs. Any man who kills a fellow villager must go into exile; Okonkwo is obliged to spend seven years in his motherland after shooting someone by accident, to avoid the vengeance of the Earth. The Ibo's animistic sense of the numinous is linked to ethical and social standards in many other respects. 'Ancestor worship' and the ritual enactment of ancestral spirits affords authority to a system of justice. The strong sense of decorum governing all the social rites illustrated in the novel, from debt-collecting to burial, is supported by knowledge that the ancestors, the gods, and ultimately the one creator God are not to be mocked. Although the Oracle may sometimes require the death of innocents, the gods like those of Wole Soyinka are largely in the service of man. Belief in the presence and return to life of the ancestors ensures honour for the old, as for the dead. Elsewhere in Africa religious practice could be less humanistic, and bloodier. Achebe's Ibos, as Ezeudu's memory of his father's time implies, have developed a religion which should have deserved a modern Christian missionary's respect. The Christian understands history in terms of a single historical event, and must see the Ibo as a people nineteen hundred years behind the truth. Achebe's missionaries are quick to apply principles which Christianity had brought to the Roman world, claiming equality before God and the church for slaves, untouchables, worthless men, and women. While Achebe demonstrates with startling clarity how destructive of African community the first impact of Christianity was, he makes plain the appeal of this other religion in the conversion of Nwoye for whom an order of things which condemns twin babies, and Ikemefuna, and which condemns his father's arrogance, has been no more spiritually acceptable than it has been questionable, until now. The divergence between Christian principles and practice is a favourite theme of Ngugi and of many other African novelists. The Reverend James Smith is perhaps more of a tyrannical father than Okonkwo, although Okonkwo's slaves might disagree. But to an African Christian the preposterous Smith does represent the coming of history to Umuofia, and Achebe knows it. A novelist need not be expected to give a verdict on so momentous a change and to have done so would have divided his audience; Achebe's fiction always seeks to unite it. He sets one large ironic challenge to Christianity in Africa. As Nwoye learns of the crucified Christ his father hangs himself having lost in his son the honour he expects after death. Okonkwo dies in religious despair at what the missionaries have done to him.

The role of women in family and society was controversial in 1958 and remains so, especially in Africa. Achebe's portrayal of women and of femininity is loyal to the respect for both which he finds in the culture of Umuofia, although not in the practice of Okonkwo who fears so much in life — stories, tenderness, even fatherly emotion — because he labels it 'womanish'. He is never more absurd than when he regrets that his enterprising child Ezinma was not born a boy. He needs to reflect on the meaning of the goddess and of the motherland to which, appropriately, he is exiled. Laurens van der Post has said of Afrikaaner farmers that they treat women harshly because they reject 'the woman in themselves'.[7] It could certainly be said of Okonkwo. Achebe avoids polarising traditional and contemporary roles for women. His Umuofian women and girls are far from being wretched slaves, although he is realistic about their subjection. Rarely in literature can wives have been so battered, bullied, and insulted as Okonkwo's. While his fear of 'feminine' weakness makes him uncommonly severe, it is obvious that the villagers disapprove of his beating his wives too hard, and in the Week of Peace, rather than of his beating them at all. Achebe's female characters are vivid and lively individuals who know their place but do not always keep to it. Ekwefi's love for Okonkwo is convincing; it is felt especially at the end of Chapter 11 when the couple stand together before the shrine, where their daughter is with the priestess before the Oracle; both are brave here, and Ekwefi is the braver. Polygamous marriage has not enslaved her. 'Mother is supreme', say the Ibo. In this tough part of the world where nobody grows up without blows and hardships and where all need to know their places if the clan is to survive, women's lives complement those of their husbands; wiser men than Okonkwo respect them. When old Ogbuefi Ndulue dies, his first wife follows him the same day; it was always said that they 'had one mind' (Chapter 8).

M. M. Mahood has commented on the exuberance and nonconformism of the present-day Ibo contrasted to Achebe's graver characters, that 'they cannot have changed very much' in eighty years.[8] It may be that Achebe's stress on dignity and social cohesion exaggerates the submissiveness of women and the degree to which they were excluded from the counsels of men. Even in modern North African cities Islam has not been very successful with its own rule of *tacet femina*, and in country communities necessity gives wives and daughters greater social scope. The large body of Arabic proverbs on the subject implies that North African women have managed to be troublesome in many ways which illiberal measures were intended to obstruct. In Eastern Nigeria competitive spirit was perhaps less confined to Ibo men than appears to have been the case in the decorous set scenes of *Things Fall Apart*. There are hints of subversiveness. Okonkwo recalls the tale of how Mosquito proposed to Ear and, refusing, she ridiculed him: 'You are already a skeleton' (Chapter 9). 'Mosquito went away humiliated, and any time he passed her way he let her know that he was still alive.' Okonkwo fails to notice that the relation between the sexes in the 'old time' was more egalitarian than in modern Umuofia.

Achebe possessed one of the most up-to-date Nigerian minds of 1958 and in the best sense of understanding, in all its disunity, his own century. A natural instinct is to oppose separate cultures, as self-contained, single currents of human history, African and European, modern and traditional. That is how things appear to Okonkwo and to the District Commissioner. If it had been told from Okonkwo's point of view, or from that of a certain kind of Englishman, the novel would have shown a good old world destroyed by barbarians; told by a missionary or by a pacifying imperialist it would have presented Okonkwo's death as a misfortune incidental to the stamping out of paganism with all its prehistoric horrors, in favour of a new, civilised start. Achebe lets us see the extent to which both views are false. Neither Nigeria nor Britain in 1900 was a single, settled culture, although Umuofia approximates it as nearly as a Norfolk village in 1900 might have — and *is* made to seem in L. P. Hartley's *The Go-Between* of 1953. Although Achebe does not dwell on the point which Hartley makes, that the period between 1900 and 1950 is the 'longest' and most dreadful half-century in history, his sense of how things have changed is not very different from the Englishman's. Nigeria was like England in 1900 in being subject to violent, unpredictable upsets. Brown, Smith and the District Commissioner had more common grounds for belief with Umuofians than with many modern thinkers at home, as is suggested in the scene where Brown and an elder of the tribe hold an amicable discussion of monotheism in Chapter 21. By 1958 some Nigerians and Englishmen felt that they had lost a civilisation. If the last sentence of *Things Fall Apart* makes the DC look remoter from present realities than Okonkwo, he would of course, like James Smith, have seemed rather an anachronism to some in the England of his own time; and although the beliefs of all these men were still alive in 1958, they had lost for many Englishmen and Nigerians the appearance of being contemporary. Achebe's book reminds us of these complications.

'The most impressive achievement of *Things Fall Apart*', writes David Carroll, 'is the vivid picture it provides of Igbo society at the end of the nineteenth century'.[9] Its most impressive achievement is rather the manner in which the picture is created. The characters of *Things Fall Apart* illustrate the conduct of war, of religion, of the social roles of men and women in a relatively fixed and secure system. The Nigerian context in which they could be discussed was immeasurably different in 1958 and it included contributions, welcome or not, from outside. But such is the relation between the novel's narrator and its world that he and his characters are felt to be living in the same period of history, and so the past is dignified in the best way: by means of art and imagination it is still fully alive.

Achebe's third novel *Arrow of God* (1964), set in the 1920s, is a larger, denser work although not necessarily 'more ambitious' — the usual phrase to introduce it. The story of the priest of a village deity at odds with the British administrators and with his people is extremely complex and has been thoroughly analysed, by David Carroll, M. M. Mahood, and others. The present intention is merely to look at Achebe's treatment of two contrasted British views of Africa. The first, admired by young political officer Tony Clarke,

Colonial Africa: Achebe, Oyono, Camara Laye 37

is found in 'the first chapter of *The Pacification of the Primitive Tribes of the Lower Niger* by George Allen' (the chapter was headed THE CALL):

> For those seeking but a comfortable living and a quiet occupation Nigeria is closed . . . But for those in search of a strenuous life . . . who can grasp great situations, coax events, shape destinies and ride on the crest of the wave of time Nigeria is holding out her hands. For the men who in India have made the Briton the law-maker, the organiser, the engineer of the world, this new, old land has great rewards and honourable work. Our mothers do not draw us with nervous grip back to the fireside of boyhood, back into the home circle, back to the purposeless sports of middle life; it is our greatest pride that they do − albeit tearfully − send us fearless and erect, to lead the backward peoples into line. (Chapter 3)

The extract continues, recalling Crécy and Poitiers, Nelson and Clive, and ending, of course, with 'playing one's best in the game of life'. It is a mild burlesque. Angus Wilson, Evelyn Waugh, or Max Beerbohm, would have made more of the opportunity to ridicule the tone of popular imperialism. Achebe wants to keep his 'Call' just plausible in its wording, for it has its place in a discussion among his rather dim colonial staff as they try to hold their own against Ibo enterprise which is often more in tune with the latest *zeitgeist* in Africa than they are. The 'progressive' Tony Clarke finds Allen rather good but 'a little smug'. 'He doesn't allow, for instance that there might be anything of value in native institutions'. His superior, the old hand, Captain Winterbottom, has seen a man 'buried alive up to his neck with a piece of roast yam on his head to attract vultures', and he admires the French who are 'not ashamed to teach their cultures to backward races under their charge'. But soon afterwards Winterbottom receives a memorandum on the policy of indirect rule:

> To many colonial nations native administration means government by white men. You are all aware that H. M. G. considers this policy as mistaken. In place of the alternative of governing directly through Administrative Officers there is the other method of trying while we endeavour to purge the native system of its abuses to build a higher civilisation upon the soundly

rooted native stock that had its foundation in the hearts and minds of the people and therefore on which we can more easily build, moulding it and establishing it into lines consonant with modern ideas and higher standards, and yet all the time enlisting the real force of the spirit of the people, instead of killing all that out and trying to start afresh. We must not destroy the African mind, the whole foundation of his race. (Chapter 5)

Winterbottom is not impressed, and nor, for different reasons, is Achebe. Winterbottom recalls the roast yam on the victim's head [would it really attract vultures?]. Achebe shows in the course of the novel how misconceived is HMG's conception of 'the native system'.

The nineteenth-century assumption that 'backward' village societies were inevitably ruled by despots, caused the colonial authorities in Nigeria, following Lord Lugard's policy of indirect rule, to recruit native chiefs, even where — as in Iboland — these had not existed before. Winterbottom chooses for Umuaro its Chief Priest Ezeulu who has impressed him by testifying against his people's interests in a land dispute. But Ezeulu is at odds with Umuaro. His decision over the land was not affected by respect for the impartiality of British justice but by conflicts within changing Ibo society. Ezeulu, the arrow of his god Ulu who was created to unite the six villages of Umuaro, is opposed by the priest of an older god, Idemili, and by Nwaka, a powerful villager. When he refuses *Wintabota*'s offer of Paramount Chiefship, Ezeulu is jailed; he takes advantage of the interruption to monthly ritual to delay the planting season in a bid to uphold the power of Ulu. But Ulu is overthrown, since the Ibo destroy gods who are no longer useful, and Ezeulu goes mad. The Christian Church benefits: harvest festival takes the place of the ceremony of the New Yam. Meanwhile the British have decided to reverse the policy of ruling Iboland through Paramount Chiefs.

There are many further complications to the tensions within Umuaro, among the British administrators, among the missionaries, and among the various Ibo factions. *Arrow of God* is an ironic study of political and religious authority, and of the discrepancy between systems to which men commit themselves and the unforeseeable turns of real events. Its omniscient narrator, who adopts various points of view and controls of range of English and Ibo—English registers, is more obviously novelistic in the

Western sense than the narrator of *Things Fall Apart*. If it is less than fully successful in comparing Ibo and British conceptions of power and truth, it extends the earlier book's vision of their coexistence within a phase of recent history whose course of development lay outside anyone's control. It is most effective, perhaps, and most lively, in the scenes which show how actively the African characters took part themselves in changes they were confident belonged to their world.

The white man is now accepted as a painful but unavoidable fact of life. Moses Unachukwu sums up the situation in a passage which neatly complements Winterbottom's views on 'backward peoples': 'I have travelled in Olu and I have travelled in Igbo, and I can tell you that there is no escape from the white man. He has come. When suffering knocks at your door and you say there is no seat left for him, he tells you not to worry because he has brought his own stool. The white man is like that' (Chapter 8). Nweke Ukpaka replies that 'the white man is like a hot soup and we must take him slowly-slowly from the edges of the bowl'. Guile is needed, he says, in dealing with a man who thinks you are a fool. In Umuaro the English are thought amusingly foolish, yet their power is acknowledged. The best way to take them, slowly, is to learn what they know and take advantage of the new states of affairs their presence creates, in the Church, in 'gorment' service, or in trade. Even Ezeulu sends a son to the missionaries, which leads to sacrilege when the boy tries (since God told Adam to crush the serpent) to suffocate a sacred python in his school-box. Ezeulu's motive was one that all seem to have respected, and which enabled them to live with their times: 'The world is like a Mask dancing. If you want to see it well you do not stand in one place' (Chapter 4). *Arrow of God* constantly surprises and pleases with the shrewdness of its Ibo characters. Wisdom cannot keep self-deception and failure from their lives, either in Ulu's last days or in the 1960s when they had full charge of their own affairs. Eastern Nigeria was threatened at the time Achebe was writing and since the Civil War he has declared that he can no longer write novels. *Arrow of God* has, among many purposes, the message that responsibility did not come to the people with Independence; however tiresome British assumptions of having backward peoples in their charge, Umuaro and its neighbours have lived their own twentieth-century history, and responsibility was always within their scope.

Achebe's rival among West African writers in the late 1950s was the Cameroonian Ferdinand Oyono. His best novel is *Une vie de boy*, translated as *Houseboy* in the African Writers Series. It is an elegant work of irony in the form of a houseboy's diary. Most of the main characters are French and the author's purpose is satirically corrective. As in another Cameroonian satire, Mongo Béti's *Le pauvre Christ de Bomba*, published in the same year, 1956, the narrator's naïvety is the author's strength. The tone of an enquiring, developing but immature mind is so skilfully caught that we believe in the two exercise books found, the prologue tells us, in the possession of a dead youth, a refugee in Spanish Guinea:

> Je m'appèle Toundi Ondoua. Je suis le fils de Toundi et de Zama. Depuis que le Père m'a baptisé, il m'a donné le nom de Joseph. Je suis Maka par ma mère et Ndjem par mon père. Ma race fut celle des mangeurs d'hommes. Depuis l'arrivée des Blancs nous avons compris que tous les autres hommes ne sont pas des animaux.

> [My name is Toundi Ondoua. I am the son of Toundi and of Zama. When the Father baptised me he gave me the name of Joseph. I am Maka by my mother and Ndjem by my father. My ancestors were cannibals. Since the white men came we have learnt other men must not be looked upon as animals.]

The irony that *les Blancs* look upon Africans as animals is pervasive, and Oyono begins to affirm it a few pages later; it is in mind throughout. Toundi tells us that he loves his 'benefactor' Father Gilbert: *c'est un homme gai qui, lorsque j'etais petit, me considérait comme un petit animal familier*'. He has no consciousness that the priest might have thought him anything more. After Father Gilbert's death, Toundi's adolescence is passed as *boy* to the *commandant*. As he gradually loses his respect for the French, the tone and style of the narrative became more adult; but the satire is nowhere stronger than in the early sections. Toundi's first account of himself suits the context of a school exercise-book — it comes not in 'Chapter I' but in the '*premier cahier*' — and seems to be a repetition of a lesson learned from Father Gilbert — perhaps a *dictée*. 'Everything I am I owe to Father Gilbert', says the small Toundi; Oyono's French is more exact: *'je dois ce que je suis devenu au Père Gilbert'*. In the lines 'my name is Toundi . . .' we see him becoming the '*chef-d'œuvre*' of the priest who has adopted him, and who shows him off to visitors as his 'masterpiece', happy to repeat as facts what we have to see as an interpretation of the white man's coming. As a cultural creation, Toundi and Joseph, child of one race and pupil of another, the boy characterises the colonial period he lives in and slowly learns to judge at the house of the *commandant*.

The novel's most painful irony is that, leaving home to go to the Father, Toundi has supposed that he would be joining their community. To do so he relinquished his own, joining the Father on the eve of his initiation 'when I should have met the famous serpent who watches over all the men of my race' ('*qui veille sur tous ceux de notre race*'). Gilbert clothes him and teaches him to read and write. '*Rien ne vaut cette richesse*' ['nothing can be more precious'], says Toundi, a little doubtfully since he adds that he has to wear old clothing. (No nation has more dandies than Cameroon.) By a related irony the riches of literacy give him all that he bequeathes, his record of rejection and mistreatment by *les Blancs*. Torture and death in exile punish his presuming, in the novel's later stages, to judge the whites as a moral equal. But Toundi is excluded from the start, although he is not only wholly dependent on Gilbert, but also, as French says, *formed* by him. He is not the Father's son but his *boy*. The role of *boy* is central in many African novels because of the extent to which it is socially as well as linguistically ambiguous.

The servant's place has been rich in literary possibilities from Pamela and Joseph Andrews to Jeeves and Felix Krull. Oyono's story makes another exploration of the balance of power. When the *commandant* and his wife come to know that Toundi knows that Madame is unfaithful to her husband, his presence becomes unendurable to them. Desire to keep things from the servants, and what a servant may make of knowledge can create tension in a novel set within a single culture, as in several of Iris Murdoch's books. Where the servant is a child of the house the tension can be more tightly screwed, a situation well treated in the Egyptian Fathy Ghanem's novel *The Man Who Lost his Shadow*.[10] Where two races and cultures are involved, the ironic force can be as highly charged as in *Houseboy*, although in this case colonial authority allows the master an escape from embarrassment and he sends Toundi to jail on the first pretext that offers. But the irony is not less cutting because the situation is quickly resolved. The educated Toundi observes the *commandant* with a French as well as an African understanding of shame and the *commandant* has a French atheist's abhorrence of (silent) censure from the priest's boy. The servant who judges his master is punished himself.

A further irony derives from a scene which is the key to Oyono's attack upon the French approach to their protectorate. Toundi serves at a reception in the Residence where M. Salvain the schoolmaster makes a remark which breaks a deeply respected European taboo.

> Drôle de pays! dit la femme du pasteur americain avec un fort accent.
> Ce n'est pas New York City! dit bêtement sa grosse amie.
>   Les autres Blancs ne semblaient pas comprendre. Elles rirent toutes les deux comme si elles étaient toutes seules.
> Il n'y a pas de moralité dans ce pays, gémit la femme du docteur, faussement désespérée.
> Pas plus qu'à Paris! riposta l'instituteur.
> Cette phrase avait été lancée comme un courant électrique dans les chairs de chaque Blanc de la salle. Ils tressaillirent à tour de rôle. Les Oreilles du docteur devinrent rouge sang. Seule, Madame était restée impassible.

> ['What a country!' said the wife of the American pastor with a strong accent.
> 'It's certainly not New York City', said her plump companion, fatuously.
> The other whites pretended not to understand. The two of them laughed together as if they were alone.
> 'There are no morals in this country', groaned the doctor's wife, trying to sound as if she were in despair.
> 'Nor in Paris for that matter', came back the schoolmaster.
> The remark ran through the bodies of the Europeans in the room like an electric current. They shuddered, one by one. The doctor's ears grew blood-red. Only Madame remained unmoved.]

M. Salvain may be more combative than usual because his plain wife has been irked by Madame's beauty and elegance. He is dealt with promptly by a fellow guest, whose job involves 'disinfecting' the town.

Le désinfecteur de Dangan allait-il lui sauter à la gorge? La situation était tendue.
——Eh coullon! Vous n'êtes qu'un demagogue! lâcha-t-il.
——Vous êtes un traître, vous êtes un traître, monsieur Salvain!

[Was the disinfector going to fly at his throat? The moment was tense.
'You nasty little rabble rouser', he snapped.
'You're a traitor, M. Salvain,' he said, 'a traitor'.]
(First Exercise Book: 'After the Funeral')

The excessive reaction is convincing and funny. Oyono is better than Achebe at catching the false tones in European conversation; perhaps French colonials are easier to portray than the English because they play their social roles more broadly. Oyono's plain points include a jibe at the French assumption, amusing to other peoples, that France *is* civilisation. Nobody hears the reference to New York, whose morals have not been put explicitly in question. '*Pauvre France!*' sigh the guests. The yellow peril has not yet been overcome, and the black peril is threatening already. What will become of civilisation? Another point is that Madame remains unmoved; she has brought her Parisian *mœurs* to Dangan, and the doctor's wife's remark is, ironically, appropriate to her. Another concerns the tribal instincts of the whites. No people is free from chauvinism, or from the urge towards solidarity, seen in the disinfector's '*traître!*', when confronted with danger to its own interests in another. Oyono is a better satirist because his comedy and indignation do not stifle his feeling for the sadness of the colonials' predicament. The French will not allow Monsieur Salvain to make a comparison between the morals of Dangan and Paris. They tell him that he will teach the Danganais to think themselves as good as their protectors – 'as if they hadn't got a high enough opinion of themselves already' – and so threaten the French empire. But admitting the possibility of comparison is insufferable to them: flesh quakes and ears redden. It is well that no one knows that Toundi is following every word with a diarist's curiosity, or that the fascination he finds in *les Blancs* has already made him able to note comparisons. The lesson he has been taught has made that appear unthinkable: '*ma race fut celle des mangeurs d'hommes*'. He has *les Blancs* to thank that he is not a cannibal. In fact he has learnt from reading Father Gilbert's diary, 'a grain-store of memories', a novelist's interest in detail, and from learning a new culture he has developed a novelist's alertness to behaviour although he lacks Oyono's sense of irony and humour. None of the guests is watching him as keenly as he watches them. For all his puzzlement, his is the best available point of view in this scene, which is itself an irony.

Throughout the novel, refusal to compare confines the French characters in a world far less rich, less interesting, less amusing, less human than the real world about them, reflected in Toundi's diary. Oyono makes their failure a source of comedy, partly apparent to Toundi. In one particularly good scene Madame interviews a would-be chambermaid, Kalisia, a girl who has been even more promiscuous than Madame. '*Les Blancs sont fous de son derrière*', and she has lived with white and black men on the coast. Toundi is amused by the meeting of two fine women, Kalisia refusing to appear submissive, Madame in a suppressed rage at the girl's dumb insolence.

> As tu déjà été femme de chambre, demanda-t-elle à Kalisia.
> Ououououiii . . . repondit Kalisia avec un sourire.
> Ou ça?
> Là-bas . . . vers la mer – répondit Kalisia en tendant le bras vers l'ouest, du côté de la mer.
>
> Je n'en pouvais plus. Je me mordis les lèvres. Kalisia avait une conception particulière de son métier. J'intervins et expliquai à Madame qu'il fallait lui poser la question autrement. Quelque chose dans le sens de 'As-tu été boy de chambre?'
>
> ['Have you been a chambermaid before?' she asked Kalisia.
> 'Yeeeeeesss', said Kalisia with a smile.
> 'Where?'
> 'Over there – by the sea', said Kalisia pointing with her arm westward towards the sea.
> I could hardly hold myself. I bit my lips. Kalisia had a rather special idea of what her job was. I broke in and explained to Madame that she would have to put the question in a different way – something like, 'Have you ever been a lady's houseboy?']
>
> (Second Exercise Book)

Madame recovers her composure when Kalisia admits that she has never been a servant but wishes now to change her calling.

Colonial Africa: Achebe, Oyono, Camara Laye   45

Madame is not amused, but comforted by what seems a 'half-excuse'.

By excluding the Cameroonians from their real view of the world these French characters miss much of the life about them. Madame learns from Toundi that his father's occupation was setting porcupine traps, and this amuses her. *'Tiens! c'est drôle ça!'* It is hard to believe that a Frenchwoman who had tried *porc-épic à la camerounaise* would scoff at Toundi's father's calling; she cannot have tried. Toundi too can trap porcupines but she shows no interest in how it is done. If the French of Dangan seem at times unusually stupid, they are unusually brutal. Sent to prison on the faintest of suspicions of complicity in theft, Toundi is repeatedly whipped and otherwise tortured in the course of 'questioning'. But the scenes of violence are more than fictional allegations because the brutality is shown to develop from indifference, and that from lack of imagination and narrow cultural assumptions. It is not that the *commandant* or the others think Africans less than human, although 'other people must not be looked upon as animals' is an undermining irony, and although Toundi at the end has, metaphorically, been eaten alive. Father Gilbert baptises Toundi, and his curate appears to have a lustful interest in the bodies of all his parishioners. Racialism arises here from the notion of the *race des mangeurs d'hommes*. The Africans seem too remote to take seriously, although to the reader they are vividly present and as interesting, especially in conversation, as the Europeans. It galls Madame that Toundi hopes to become more than a houseboy, and when she calls him 'Monsieur Toundi', a sarcasm he cannot grasp, the sources of her bitterness have been made clear to the reader from every stage of his account of *les Blancs*. She is happier thinking of him as a trapper of porcupines because, irrationally, that seems to her remote as a fairy-tale.

Because the novel is an exposure of imaginative failing, the satire is both irresistible and pertinent twenty years after the colonial period, while novels which are only 'denunciations of colonialism' through examples of misconduct tend to provoke resistance even against the reader's will. Reading *Houseboy* as such a novel can lead to misinterpretation through a wish to find satire everywhere. Father Gilbert is said to be popular among small boys because he gives them sugar lumps and because he is a curiosity, dressed like a woman. Eustace Palmer comments that 'there is satire here . . . at the white man's effeteness and the spiritual bankruptcy of the Roman Catholic Church whose priest attracts boys to Christianity by throwing them lumps of sugar'.[11] Oyono's reference to *une robe de femme*, incidentally, seems aimed at French rather than African anti-clericalism, since robes are not thought effeminate anywhere in Africa and since for African villagers a cassock signifies powers which are thought manly. But no reader would think the priest 'effete' for wearing the cloth, especially not today. Even if we disapprove of the sugar lumps — and Father Gilbert shares his dinner with Toundi when the boy first calls on him — one priest's error does not in itself reflect on spirituality in the Roman Church. Those who dislike the Church may be pleased, and the faithful pained by this interpretation, but the passage remains a realistic picture of a commonplace priest and a normal boy. Toundi is further intrigued by the man's hair which looks like a maize-cob beard; no satire seems intended there.

Professor Palmer rightly dwells on the French police and prison chiefs who conduct beatings with an ancient Roman savagery, and on the 'fellow-feeling, solidarity and humanity of the African characters'[12] — the conversations among Toundi's cronies are particularly good. But the arts of a novelist are not needed to establish that prolonged beating with a hippopotamus-whip is degrading to victim and perpetrator. These scenes have a place in the book partly because they support the point that those who claim to be civilised uphold their rule by means which their own culture judges uncivilised, but more crucially as means of convicting the imaginative failure of even the more refined characters which blinds them to an Africa where, Oyono shows, they need not have been unwelcome. Toundi is full of admiration, for Gilbert and for Madame. Madame's momentary amusement, followed by boredom, when he tells her about the porcupine traps; Father Gilbert's corrective kick when Toundi mimics him; the schoolmaster's belief that education must start by assuming that Africans know nothing — these are the proper targets for satire. Certainly Oyono is determined to compose his cast of the most disreputable possible samples of every kind of European; and he compensates for the portion of humanity in Father Gilbert in the portrait of his dislikeable curate. But the scenes of horror are made meaningful by passages which convey the wasteful, witless colonising of Toundi. Nobody doubts that colonial life was harsh. Toundi is whipped by his father in the first pages and by the police in the last: one such account in fiction is very like another. Toundi sitting down to write about himself for the first time (*'rien ne vaut cette richesse'*) and putting down *'ma race fut celle des mangeurs d'hommes'* touches upon what can be called a tragedy. Equally useless would be to set a French boy to write 'my people is one of police-torturers'. The atrocities are undeniable, and in themselves beyond a novelist's interest. It is reluctance to look at the world that requires a novelist's attention; Oyono's best satire attends to his characters' shortsightedness. His book is not just a record of 'barbarity', but a portrayal of how the word itself has caused them to arise.

Le regard du roi (*The Radiance of the King*) by Camara Laye is a novel which places a modern European in an old Africa and strips him of his modernity for his spiritual good. The book has been widely praised and discussed: it is a unique blend of whimsy, wit, farce, story-telling and mystical prose poetry. There has been some discussion as to whether Laye is a French or an African writer. The quality of his African sensibility was shown in *L'enfant noir* (*The African Child*), the story of his childhood in rural Guinea, published in 1953. In 1954 when *Le regard du roi* was published in Paris he had been living in France for ten years, well aware of the various achievements of the modern European novel. His translator James Kirkup has written that he combines 'the instinctive poetry of the native African with the observation . . . of a lively Western mind'. Laye has pleased African and European readers and critics. There is a hint of the divisiveness of *négritude* in James Kirkup's remark; Laye certainly said that Africans have 'a natural religious and poetic sense', but he recognised that European civilisation must not be 'confused with its technical, rational side', but be found in the finest creations of art and literature – 'in voices which call from the depths'.[13] *Le regard du roi* has a quotation from Kafka as its epigraph, omitted in James Kirkup's translation. Attempts have been made to prove Kafka's 'influence' on the novel; 'an African Kafka' can be praise from some European critics, disparagement from some Africans. When Laye referred to Kafka in his introduction to *Le Maître de la Parole* (1978) Camara Laye linked his name with those of Bernanos, James, Lautréamont, and Leonardo, in all of whom he says the primacy of 'soul' is recognised.[14] Influence, in fact, means little in the case of this novel. It can suggest innumerable European writers, as one sees in the published criticism; *Le Maître de la parole* (*The Guardian of the Word*), a fictional version of oral traditions among the Malinké singers, the *griots*, has demonstrated, as Kirkup says in introducing his translation, that the novel owed as much to African reality as to European imagination.

It was a gift to contemporary criticism. Even the meaning of the title is debatable. (It might have been more exactly translated 'The Look', 'The Eye', 'The Gaze', 'The Regard' or 'The Watchfulness' − 'of the King'.) Apart from the question of influences, there are many 'polarities': African and European, sleep and waking, dream and vision, rights and favours (law and luck), flesh and spirit; all these are present, although none rules the author's imagination. Symbolist, allegorical, mythic, archetypal, psychological, and comparative-cultural studies seem called for; indeed there are passages, as in many works of modernism, in which one suspects that the author has deliberately provoked and mystified critical attention. The novel is very literary, but the impression in reading is of a freshness and naïvety, which the English translation recaptures. It can be called a 'deceptive naïvety', but it is difficult for critics to approach the particular quality of *The Radiance of the King* because critical method tends to be so much heavier in touch than Camara Laye, and because the novel tends to mock intellectual solemnity; even the king has a smile about his lips. It mocks analysis. The white man Clarence is reproved for excessive enquiry: '*tu questionnes et tu requestionnes; tu es comme un enfant: tu passes ta vie à questionner!*' (Part 3, Chapter 1); he spends his life childishly asking questions. Laye's is partly a self-mockery; he was a scholar. Most accounts concentrate on the familiar 'meeting' and 'conflict' of cultures. Laye sets a rational European among wiser Africans, but schematic contrasts of Western and African fail to focus the novel. Clarence has been rejected by his own people; he does try to live in Africa; the king accepts him at the end.

What is crucial is that Camara Laye was more concerned with his characters' souls than most novelists have been. Critics are reluctant to admit it. Clarence is not redeemed culturally or socially but spiritually. He enters a world where nothing is of twentieth-century origin; separation of white development and black tradition is absolute here. Laye was not discrediting progress. He said that technical achievements are only complementary to civilisation. He defined civilisation as a way of life, and a passage for the soul: 'and after all the soul comes before the body . . . even though the body too, as long as it lives, is not to be disdained'. Wole Soyinka's strong defence of the novel under the heading 'Ideology and the Social Vision' contrasts 'Clarence's Western form of rationality' and the community system which 'offers fulfilment for the individual within society and bends man and his environment into a complementary existence'. Laye, says Soyinka, asserts 'its fullness of separation from the occidental world, and from the traditional one dimensional conception of African reality, a largely anthropological creation'.[15] This is better than looking for Kafka's influence or hunting polarities. But in arguing the 'fullness of separation' between Clarence's reality and Africa's he disregards the point at which Clarence's experience coincides with the Africans': their love of the king. Soyinka's is a brief account which enlists the novel in the cause of a larger argument, but he is less than just to his author's intentions when he dismisses the final chapter: 'despite the mystical effusion at the end, the aesthetics of the novel are secular'. That involves dismissing the title, and the story in which Clarence progresses towards his meeting with the king. Laye's is a more transcendent god than Soyinka likes; Laye was a different sort of writer. Although Charles Larson thinks the ending the most beautiful passage in African literature, he refers to religion as though it were another African 'material'. He writes of 'an indication that the Western world may gain something positive from the African continent'.[16] In Clarence's meeting with the king, Laye, says Professor Larson, is 'fusing Clarence into total oneness with Africa'.[17] In fact the novel's final sentence places Clarence in the presence of God; his African experience, which he has never liked, is finished. Professor Larson should have said so. *The Radiance of the King* is a religious novel. Laye's love of Africa and greater love of God are apparent throughout.

It has been remarked that Clarence is a white man as seen by Africans. The African characters find him a simpleton, a child, a joke, a nuisance, a curiosity — and a commodity, for he is sold and in a way exploited. He is ridiculed, but pitied and gently dealt with. Modern-minded Europeans are especially liable to such belittlement and Clarence's role can be seen as that of a 'modern' European in Africa. Earlier Europeans in Africa, at least in fiction, were either victims of savagery or bearers of enlightenment; recent intruders have been expected to keep quiet and be grateful for whatever comforts are offered. Clarence complains about Africa but he does not seriously expect to alter things. He expects to be valued, and when we first meet him he is looking for a job with the king.

> Je suis venu pour parler au roi, dit il . . .
> Inouï! dit le noir, C'est proprement inouï. Croyez-vous donc que le roi reçoive n'importe qui, jeune homme? . . . Je ne suis pas n'importe qui, dit Clarence. Je suis un blanc.
>
> ['I came here in order to speak to the king', he said . . .
> 'But it's unheard-of!' said the black man. 'It's absolutely unheard-of. Young man, do you think the king receives just anybody?'
> 'I am not just anybody,' replied Clarence. 'I am a white man.']
>
> (Part 1, Chapter 1)

This is Clarence's meeting with the beggar who is later to sell him. His pride is gradually humbled in an Africa which thinks him less than just anybody, and the process, humorously and tenderly managed by the Africans he meets, is one course of the novel's development. The other traces a spiritual progress through the same events which culminates in the final pages.

There are various jests at the expense of Clarence as a European who cannot interpret Africa. The first is that he thinks himself employable because he is a European. The beggar offers to 'see what he can do' for him, but Clarence's offer to work at anything is apparently rejected at court. When he says he would have worked even as a drummer, he is told that drummers come from noble stock and learn an art of which he knows nothing. He is slow to adjust to a different system of social roles. 'Only a beggar', he condescends to his companion, who sees himself as a skilled and experienced professional. There is of course a contemporary social reality to that, as well as to Clarence's thoughts of himself a *coopérant* without portfolio; in North Africa there are fine social distinctions among beggars. Clarence's other companions are a pair of boys, Nagoa and Noaga, in the early stages of apprenticeship as dancing-pages; they too are inclined to condescend. Since Clarence is destitute after gambling at his grand hotel, his luggage impounded by the management, he might have seen himself as a beggar; but instead he plays *le grand blanc* and invites all three to dinner at an inn where he forfeits his jacket as payment.

Wole Soyinka exaggerates, none the less, the inaccessibility of Laye's Africa to 'Western forms of reason'. The beggar reasons speciously, when the bill arrives for example: 'Where's your hospitality? . . . was not the white man your guest?' (Part 1, Chapter 2) The innkeeper is, fairly, indignant; he is properly hospitable but his is hospitality one pays for; the white man knew the terms. The beggar spits on the landlord's lowness and on that of the food and wine, which have been for him and the boys an exceptional feast, but that is understood – a friendly, customary procedure before Clarence has to part with his coat. The innkeeper's claim on his trousers is normal, affable haggling. Kipling or Graham Greene would have been at home; although Clarence represents certain humdrum contemporary Western assumptions, rather than Western forms of reason, he is willing to learn. The beggar tells the boys they must eat last. Clarence says he would have thought they could share the meal freely, but he will accede to custom – '*vous savez mieux les usages.*' It seems likely that the beggar is inventing *usages* from fear of the pages' appetite.

Inexperienced, Clarence is easily deceived. The court scene after his arrest on the charge of having taken back the coat, is as neatly illogical as Lewis Carroll; the beggar decides that the judge, '*monsieur le premier president*', is in league with the landlord. They escape, helped by a dancing-girl whose father appears to be the judge, although she denies it firmly: her father is 'an honourable man'. Here is an alien system, although close enough to the French to permit Camara Laye incidental satire, but reason is partly restored when the coat is found, divided, under the smocks of Noaga and Nagoa. Clarence is certainly lost in unfamiliar ways but a brighter European would have grasped the laws of predictability which elude him. More disturbing to him is the loss of 'rights'; he can only expect 'favours', the beggar tells him, and points out logically that Clarence has recently been relying not on rights but on luck at the gambling-table. Perhaps, Clarence reflects in stray thoughts which are not pursued, having money to pay for dinner is chance or 'favour'. The beggar lives on favour not by rights, like the social system to which he belongs. The various implications of this distinction, familiar too in Asia, are not beyond the compass of Western, Asian, or African forms of reason. But they puzzle Clarence.

It is common critical practice to simplify the novel's subtle treatment of cultural convention by forcing it into a scheme by which rational Europe misunderstands syncretic, harmonious Africa. Laye certainly has in mind a reversal of roles: under colonialism the African most often suffered culture shock in unfamiliar judicial and bureaucratic systems; now it is the European who is constantly disturbed by the beggar's first reaction to him: '*c'est inouï*' – unheard-of! But Clarence is bewildered by the shock to his conventional assumptions, not by the irrational. Laye has made him a vaguely middle-class, suburban, liberal Frenchman, and has designed his Africa, plausible although its contrivance was unhampered by any precise setting, to contradict his assumptions as fully as possible. The author's own sharp reasoning fills the comic scenes with ironic views of how it is that different customs seem reasonable to different peoples.

Clarence is well cared for by the beggar and the boys. There is a firm contrast between their friendly acceptance of him and the hostility of the Europeans who see him expelled from the hotel. 'Did it ever enter your head to abandon the white man?' Nagoa asks Noaga. 'I should never have dreamed of doing such a thing,' he replies (Part 1, Chapter 1). The boys protect Clarence from the mob, and when the beggar offers to take him south in the hope of meeting the king, they help him through the forest. It is ironic that Clarence should claim his rights when he is surviving by their favour. But in so far as he feels grateful, he is, partly, misguided. The boys regard him as a 'find', amusing and perhaps useful. The beggar sells him to the naba of Aziana, the boys' village, in exchange for a donkey and a woman – although Clarence remains unaware of it for a while. '"What has the beggar bartered?" asked Clarence. "Did he have something to sell?" "Haven't we all got something to sell?" said Nagoa eyeing Clarence rather narrowly.' (Part 1, Chapter 5) In future he will be obliged to live on favours. The beggar is ingenious in arguing for his own system. Clarence thinks he should have asked the court for a full pardon, in the matter of the coat. That would have been his 'right' says the beggar:

> car ce que vous appelez votre 'grâce', c'est votre 'droit'.
> A plus forte raison, alors! dit Clarence.
> Mais non, pas à plus forte raison, dit le mendiant. Ne pouvez-vous comprendre qu'un droit ne se quémande pas? J'aurais

pu quémander une faveur, je veux dire: une chose qui n'est pas due; je ne pouvais pas quémander un droit, qui vous a dévolu d'office. D'ailleurs je n'ai pas appris à quémander les droits: cela ne s'enseigne nulle part. Comprenez-vous, à présent?
——Vous me cassez la tête, dit Clarence.

['. . . because what you call your "pardon" is your "right".'
'All the more reason, then?' said Clarence.
'No, not at all', retorted the beggar. 'Can't you get it into your thick head that one cannot beg the favour of receiving something that is one's right?'
'I could have asked for any favour, I mean something that is *not* due to you. I could not possibly have asked for something that is your "right", something which devolves upon you officially. Anyhow, I never learned how to beg for "rights" — that sort of thing can't be taught. Now do you understand?'
'My head's reeling', said Clarence.] (Part 1, Chapter 3)

He is of course an *ingénu*. Laye is amused at the cultural varieties of common sense, and perhaps affected by the modern French philosophical emphasis on social conditioning; the beggar's world and Clarence's are differently 'structured', to some extent. The author's reason plays upon both systems. Word-play is involved in the more specious logic, but the beggar's attitude, that a favour is better than a right, is widespread, and a target of satire in African writers who see it as a corruption in modern societies. It is not endorsed here. Laye's white man is a fool, and his beggar is a rogue.

Where critics do not take for granted African superiority, they are more complacent than the novelist about cultural relativism. Camara Laye has not tried to endue his Africa with 'dignity' as Chinua Achebe, for example, conceives it. Beggary, vagrancy, theft, trickery, gluttony and lust abound in his Africa, and often dismay the decent Clarence. One serious affront to his modern liberal humanist conscience comes at the naba's court when the master of ceremonies is publicly whipped, an incident which occupies a large portion of the novel's second part. The master of ceremonies is a disagreeable functionary whose animosity prompts him to risk revealing to Clarence the service he has been unconsciously providing for the naba — the second affront to his white man's decency. The *maître* is tried and sentenced and his punishment is treated as a 'show' (*'spectacle'*); there are not many forms of entertainment in Aziana. Nagoa, Noaga and Samba Baloum, eunuch of the naba's harem, enjoy the proceedings as much as the crowd. 'Is it not his job to organise public spectacles?' asks Samba Baloum. Clarence protests: 'Noaga, I should never have thought it of you . . . I tell you that this man is suffering, and that you ought to have pity on him. And you laugh.' (Part 2, Chapter 2). When he refuses to join the others in spitting on the inflamed bottom, they reproach him with lack of compassion, for the spit is cooling; and when he persuades the naba to stop the beating, not only the crowd but also the master of ceremonies is disappointed. He will suffer public resentment now, and enjoy no sense of having satisfied justice. 'Clarence has yet to realise that justice in one culture is not necessarily the same in another', comments Charles Larson. It seems from *The African Child* that Camara Laye saw the justice of such traditional punishments but disapproved of them as forms of entertainment. In this section of *The Radiance of the King* the comic baffling of Clarence does not exclude signs of the author's disapproval. The naba is moved more by personal irritation and the wish to put on a popular show than by justice. Noaga is vengeful; reproached by Clarence, he answers 'bitterly' that the master of ceremonies has not spared him, on a previous occasion. The crowd relishes 'justice'. 'But believe me,' Samba Baloum tells Clarence, when the naba has agreed to be merciful, 'the people of Aziana won't like it. You've offended their sense of justice'. 'They're certainly far from being pleased', says Nagoa as the master of ceremonies is helped away. 'They are just men', (*des hommes justes*) says the eunuch. 'That is why they are looking so ugly', says Noaga. Laye is not simply contrasting two concepts of justice; although the festive atmosphere of the whole scene is out of harmony with Clarence's reaction, he looks least ridiculous at the moment when he makes his protest.

Dignity depends on convention in many respects. Self-esteem in the master of ceremonies is offended by the interruption of his chastisement. Nobody is ashamed of drunkenness or of spectacular gluttony. Clarence has already forfeited much of his dignity at the start; he is the first white man to be thrown out of the grand hotel. Asked if he agreed that *The Radiance of the King* is the greatest African novel, Chinua Achebe said he hoped Africa's masterpiece would not have for its hero 'a disreputable European'.

The white man's remaining dignity is steadily eroded. He has been provided with a girl for his hut; but she is nightly replaced, in the dark, by members of the harem who visit in turn. The harem fills with light-brown children, whom some critics suppose to symbolise the 'leavening' of Africa. Nagoa and Noaga try to convince Clarence that the children are born light and darken as they grow up. Whatever the purpose of the naba's whim, the effect is shaming when their father learns the truth. Finally the master of ceremonies lets him know that he is a slave, and moreover '*un coq*', unfit to be presented to the king. On the last pages he has no self-esteem left. Dignity is often referred to as a pride which has its social uses, as has pitifulness. White men, the beggar reflects, do not inspire pity; the boys would if they were less plump; he can live on pity, for a while, in each place on his travels. But the boys decide that the beggar has made a bad exchange for Clarence. 'He won't be able to carry out his professional duties with a donkey that arouses pity and a woman who arouses desire. He'll be giving away with one hand what he takes with the other' (Part 1, Chapter 5). The proud and pitiful are alike absurd in this view of social man. True worth is beyond social criteria. Clarence does not adapt to this African village, and for all its attractive warmth and vigour it does not in itself satisfy the African characters completely. They too are waiting for the king.

In calling this novel poetic, critics may have in mind the 'medieval' appearance of Laye's Africa; and 'archetype' is as good a word as 'symbol' for discussing the poetry of Laye's imagination. Although the meaning of 'poetry' when applied to fiction is hard to define, anybody can recognise its appropriateness for Dickens or for Camara Laye – two writers whom it would otherwise be futile to compare. Laye is a poet in the sense of Sir Philip Sidney's formula: he never lies because he ever feigns. We do not read the *Radiance of the King* for information about Africa as we read Achebe or Oyono, but the more we know of Africa the more his work recalls it, and recalls too, if not 'the universal', elements in African culture which arise in many literatures. Adele King has set out in *The Writings of Camara Laye* some of the background in African cultures (and her notes provide for further reading).[18] The poetic effect depends on sensing a background, available in part to any reader because present in European, Arabic and African traditions, which gives depth to characters and symbols. Wily beggar, mischievous pages, sensual eunuch, aged wise-woman, dedicated smith, and king laden with gold, belong to centuries of story-telling in the two continents from which the characters come. The waves beating on the reefs which surround Africa in Clarence's mind, the red earth and red walls against the forest green, the sultry odour of the South, belong to an Africa of the mind, soothing to the author who had lived ten years in France. The narrative and certain incidents can recall Kafka, and the style that of Flaubert whom Laye used as model for his literary French. It could equally suggest Arabic tales in which trickery is seen as a principle of life in this world, or the parable-like stories in French by Ahmed Sefroui.[19] The atmosphere especially might recall Sefroui in whose writing the real world of the Moroccan city of Fez blends with magic, and Paradise can be seen in pure white robes or in the perfection of a well-shaped pot on the wheel. Laye is an artist in whom sources are entirely absorbed and the question whether this novel is French literature or African seems pointless; it is Camara Laye's.

He will not fit into any particular tradition, or any movement. *The Radiance of the King* cannot usefully be claimed for *négritude* or for existentialism. The wish to make the book fit which has encouraged critical polarities — reason versus instinct, Cartesianism versus the African world-view — has been strengthened, perhaps, by a fear lest it turn out to be 'old-fashioned'. It is a remarkably modern achievement to have won critical praise in Paris and respect from the Malinké *griots* of Guinea. As the son of a Malinké jeweller and goldsmith and a student of literature and mechanics in Paris, Laye was able to take a wide view of the modern world. In his next novel *Dramouss* he was to engage in political satire which compelled his exile from Guinea. In *The Radiance of the King* his imagined African world is removed from 'the mechanical' and all its implications, and he deliberately adopted a very old-fashioned dichotomy.

Few novels have so strong a sense of an ending. The last pages cannot be dismissed for the sake of reading a secular interpretation against the text because the story is of Clarence's progress towards the final scene. The structure is episodic. Succeeding incidents, adding to Clarence's humiliation and bewilderment, are linked by his growing understanding of the king. When and how they are to meet is the chief source of narrative interest and as we follow his misfortunes we realise that the king can be glimpsed but not encountered in his life.

'For if a man's body has needs, so does his soul, and after all the soul comes before the body . . . even though the body, too, as long as it lives, is not to be disdained.' In his introduction to *The Guardian of the Word* Laye continues this thought with reflections on the restricting spiritual influence of modern cities 'oppressed . . . by so much progress of no concern to the soul'. Most novels are concerned with the social and moral consequences of material progress, and in African fiction 'soul' usually means aesthetic, moral and political integrity. It is rare for a character's eternal destiny to be at issue, as it may be in Greene, Golding, Iris Murdoch, or even Kingsley Amis.[20] In African religions older than Islam or Christianity, the soul returns to the ancestors and may be born again. But the background to Laye's treatment of Clarence's spiritual quest is Islamic, and, perhaps, Christian too. It asserts that although the body has its needs, the soul which outlasts the body is what matters.

The tone of *The Radiance of the King* is easier to place if its religious purpose is fully acknowledged. One reviewer wrote of a use of words 'after the manner of an inspired child' with 'a keen and adult brain behind them'. The beating of the master of ceremonies is a good example. It is full of physical details savoured by the eunuch and the pages, but managed so that we respect Clarence's revulsion but do not share it. The victim is removed from normal sympathy not by caricature but by an innocence of tone which is almost reminiscent of Samuel Beckett but less studied in its indifference. Accounts which make the novel a re-education of European Clarence in African values and this scene a 'mistake' on his part in condemning a foreign system of justice, have to disregard the reality of his compassion, which is not ridiculous. What is absurd is the body itself: 'it's no use getting worked up about a pair of buttocks', says Samba Baloum, and that is consistent with the novel's tendency to treat the body as a jest or a frailty, in contrast to the soul.

The body is 'not to be disdained'. Physical satisfactions are cheerfully enjoyed by all the characters. But there is a grotesque aspect to them all. The feast at the inn in Part 1 fills the beggar and the boys to bursting; Clarence finds the food's texture offensive and wonders if it causes teeth to fall out. Clarence's flesh is treated like an animal's. It is squeezed by various other characters, and inspected. Fatness and thinness are viewed with impersonal interest; either can be useful. Like skin-colour it is more a joke than a problem. Clarence grows fatter in Aziana; his whiteness fades in the sun. We are kept in mind of how physique varies. Samba Baloum is monstrously fat; he minces on tiny steps. As a eunuch he is hard to categorise. Although much larger than they are he is akin to the boys, but his hips sway like a woman's. Although the body is not to be disdained, embodiment gradually comes to seem preposterous.

Changes of clothing raise questions, as so often in literature, but in this novel bodies may be equally misleading. Clarence's girl Akissi changes every night. The pale brown children are part of an extended joke at the expense of the body. The way in which features imply status is unpredictable, from the initial downgrading of whiteness onwards; the white man (who is *'l'homme blanc'* in the French text rather than *le blanc*, to stress his peculiarity in Aziana) wonders whether filing his teeth in the village style would make him look more or less like the others. He cannot attend the trial because he is unbearded. The naba's beard is a mark of status, but compared to the beardless king he is said to be like 'a goat'. Clarence can never quite decide whether nudity is shameful or natural. Another sort of unreliability arises from physical weakness. The forest and all the odours of Africa have a soporific effect on Clarence; a sleepy dreaminess is often induced in him. Sleep and related states, including hallucination, are liabilities of the body. In a dream Clarence is frightened by 'fish-women'; somewhere between sirens and manatees, they are animal, or supernatural distortions of the female form. Afterwards Clarence visits Dioko a wise-woman withered as a sibyl: 'one would have sworn she had no buttocks left' (Part 3, Chapter 1). While she performs an erotic dance with her serpents he has a vision of the king. In Laye's world the body's weakness can open the eyes of the soul.

Sunk in sensuality as the naba's 'cock', Clarence becomes oppressed by the sight and smell of bodies. 'Buttocks and breasts – that's all one saw, and perhaps that's what one breathed too' (Part 2, Chapter 1). For him the South has its odour, 'provocative and cruel, lascivious and unmentionable'. He is troubled by a smell which will not leave him and which he fears will be offensive to the king. Intent on his soul Clarence wearies of the flesh.

Irritated by critics, Camara Laye asserted that in Africa it is possible to meet God.[21] The king is physically present among his people and surrounded by court, palace, vassals, and all that troops with majesty. But his frail adolescent body is weighted with gold, symbol of his subjects' love we are told, to keep him in this world; he has to be supported by pages when he moves. Although young, he is also very old. He is radiant and his look is divine. Clarence insists on approaching him naked. Critics who emphasise the European/African polarity argue that his whiteness is now 'acceptable' through grace, although the novel does not say so. (Thinking about his whiteness Clarence has decided that 'it's the soul that matters and in that respect I am exactly the same as they are' [Part 2, Chapter 2]). Clarence goes naked in order to be clothed. The king parts his robe to reveal the faint beating of his heart which calls and 'inflames' his believer.

> C'était cet amour qui dévorait. – Ne savais-tu pas que je t'attendais? dit le roi. Et Clarence posa doucement les levres sur le léger, sur l'immense battement. Alors le roi referma lentement les bras, et son grand manteau enveloppa Clarence pour toujours.
>
> [It was this love that enveloped him.
> 'Did you not know that I was waiting for you?' asked the king.
>   And Clarence placed his lips upon the faint and yet tremendous beating of that heart. Then the king slowly closed his arms around him, and his great mantle swept about him, and enveloped him for ever.]

James Kirkup's version keeps close to the cadences of the French, but he should have retained the final naming which is tender, after all the mockery, as Clarence is received to the unearthly body in the robe of eternity. There has been considerable discussion about whether Clarence dies. That enveloping of his body is clearly the end ('*pour toujours*') of its absurd, unreliable condition. Adele King is a critic who fairly acknowledges that Clarence is united with God, rather than 'fused into total oneness with Africa', but she regards the book's comedy as an addition to its serious quest.[22] In mocking our physical state the comedy contributes directly to the religious ending in which Clarence is not a disreputable European, but a soul set free.

Comic satire on 'modern' misconceptions of Africa has the same effect. Clarence is ready to meet the king only when he has lost all pride in his kind of civilisation. He finally rejects sensuality, in which Africa has steeped him, and all belief in his own modern

European worth as an individual. He realises that his '*bonne volonté*', his 'goodwill', which is all he has to offer, is unacceptable to the king (a theological point disputed in Christianity and Islam). The surrender of his preconceptions is made possible by Africa, but Clarence does not turn to African forms of reason, although he might have done so with profit, by learning for example from the beggar's remark that there is no such thing as a fool's errand. Fearing that the naba will keep him from the king, he thinks with horror of remaining in Aziana. The king is God in Africa rather than an African god (Islamic, African and Christian analogues are assembled in detail in Adele King's *The Writings of Camara Laye*). The African characters frequently tell Clarence that none of them is worthy of the king. The blacksmith Diallo, who has been waiting for 'year after year', means to present the finest axe he can make, but that, he knows, will not be good enough. The king does not look at the gifts which are piled before him. But God is undeniable for the Africans, however long awaited and undeserved.

The Radiance of the King is easily attacked by those who judge less by a novel's fulfilment of apparent intentions than by influence or *tendance*. Some critics are disabled by their belief that 'any religion', in the words of a character in Ngugi, 'is a weapon against the workers';[23] the feudal naba *is* a vassal of the king. Mongo Beti decided that the novel is close to bourgeois European philosophy. Senghor, on different principles, was troubled by the apparent 'rejection' of the physical life which is highly valued in *négritude*.[24] Laye has borne the brunt of most current ideologies. If the novel is admired by some ungodly readers because its story and atmosphere remind us of the appeal of the numinous, of longing for God, there are countless readers in modern Africa who experience such longing themselves and may find comfort and encouragement in Camara Laye where so much African fiction neglects or disparages their aspirations. John V. Taylor's *The Primal Vision*, an intelligent book on Christianity in Africa, is evidence that missionaries more astute than those pictured by Ferdinand Oyono would be sympathetic to a story of colonial Africa in which a European comes not to teach but to discover the numinous.[25] This is a novel with a meaning and if the meaning is unfashionable in literary circles *The Radiance of the King* is none the worse for that.

3 Independence: Soyinka, Achebe, Armah

Wole Soyinka's *The Interpreters* (1965) is among the liveliest of recent novels in English. It is a bright satire full of good sense and good humour which are African and contemporary: the highest spirits of its author's early work. Soyinka had lived in England and there are critics who imply that something English, beyond an exceptional gift for the language, has rubbed off on him. Britishness in an African is less a theme for Soyinka than a joke. Behind the jokes of his novel is a theme that he has developed angrily elsewhere: that whatever progress may mean for Africa it is not a lesson to be learned from outside, however much of 'modernity' Africans may share with others.

The novel's characters live in the complex Nigeria of the early 1960s; they have dealings with people from equally unpredictable societies in the outside world — German, British, American, French; and they find it all hard to interpret. In form and content it is a novel of the middle 1960s, which were good years for comic fiction. Comparison with Amis's *One Fat Englishman* (1963), with Michael Frayn's *The Tin Men* (1965) or with Anthony Burgess's *Inside Mr Enderby* (1963) would show *The Interpreters*, like many of the world's best books, to be a novel of its moment as well as of its place. It shares with them a willingness to experiment with technique, combined with a respect for the power of narrative and especially for the dramatic scene (Soyinka was of course already an accomplished dramatist). Its main characters have recently returned from Europe and America; they are the sort of young men to have read such novels; they have, like the people of Amis, Frayn and Burgess, an intelligent, irreverent exuberance which can turn to anger or to melancholy. Because it is of its period, reminding us in some ways of English and American novels, it has unfortunately not only been welcomed but also claimed by the West, as though to be contemporary were to be Western. Charles Larson's remarks in

The Emergence of African Fiction imply the claim. 'The Western reader is already familiar with the kind of experimentation found in *The Interpreters*', he concludes his discussion.[1] There is a strong tendency with this novel to find those aspects of life which are of recent (and often foreign) origin 'modern', as though what is of older, African origin were irrelevant when not a tiresome inconvenience soon to be outgrown.

Professor Eldred Jones in *The Writing of Wole Soyinka* repeatedly contrasts the new African and the old: 'the primary society with which the novel is concerned is contemporary Nigeria in which, although the ancient traditional life still makes its appearances, the predominant impression is of a society in the grips of a turbulent modernity'.[2] Commenting on an incident in which the elderly Chief Winsala is unable to pay an hotel bill and reflects on his predicament 'in the words of traditional wisdom', he writes that 'this curious intrusion of the old Africa into the new is interesting'.[3] Here again is the metaphor of two worlds and the sense that modern life is alien to 'ancient' Africa which quaintly intrudes at times on dynamic modernity. Behind Professor Jones's sensitive, careful account lurks the myth of historical Africa as a 'limbo' (Achebe's word) to be filled with modernity. Impressed with how modern a novel this certainly is, he finds older habits of mind intrusive, fading anachronisms.

The Interpreters shows more clearly and extensively than any novel set in present-day Africa that what is characteristic of turbulent modernity is the constant interaction of old and new. Chief Winsala is both a villager rather drunkenly respectful of traditional wisdom, and an unscrupulous member of a newspaper board; he is, however deplorable, as fully a 'new man' and a product of his times as any of his juniors. The aristocratic Egbo, heir to a kingdom among the creeks and a public servant in the Foreign Office, is unable to choose between two options in life which cannot easily be combined. When tempted by the prospect of a king's harem, he refuses to be called anachronistic:

'Oh I've dreamt of me and a household like that dozens of times. And the future prospects for the country's traditions. By example to convert the world.'
'You are the first genuine throw-back of this generation.'
'On the contrary. Polygamy is an entirely modern concept. Oh I don't deny the practice is old, but whoever thought it was polygamy then?' (Chapter 1)

The concept is new to West Africa at least. Egbo's jest catches the truth that whatever kind of warlord of the creeks he might become, and his people are hoping for an 'enlightened ruler', he would be acting in new conditions; it is a fear of unforeseeable obligations rather than a wish to be a modern man of the Foreign Office that keeps him from accepting his inheritance. That would present a more challenging, contemporary role than his present post among the 'dull grey file cabinet faces' at the office where old routines protect him.

The interpreters are professional young men who have returned from places of higher education 'scattered over the face of the Western world', but none of them is a hybrid torn between two worlds. Sekoni is no less a devout Muslim because he is a skilled engineer and sculptor. Sagoe is as enterprising (and as drunken) as any Western journalist, but he finds the British and the Americans tiresome, and he declares at one point that 'I happen to be born into a comparatively healthy society.' (Chapter 13). Bandele the lecturer who has been patient with every fashionable affectation in Africans and foreigners, delivers a curse upon his superiors, at the end, in a traditional formula: 'I hope you all live to bury your daughters.'

The ultimate interpreter is the narrative voice of Soyinka: while he knows the wider world and delights in the best of the modern, he thinks African values would seem progressive anywhere. Anachronistic elements in those who are false to them are quite likely to be British. He tells us, for example, that Professor Oguazor who talks, like a conventional English academic, about 'moral turpitude' has an unacknowledged daughter 'had by a housemaid' hidden in a private school in Islington, where a child out of wedlock might have been concealed by a nineteenth-century gentleman. Soyinka is less concerned with scoring an English moral point at the expense of Oguazor's hypocrisy than with showing the man's betrayal of the West African principle that no child is illegitimate. Where Nigerians who think themselves 'evolved' are false to tradition they are more likely, as in this case, to be preserving an antique standard of Western manners than to be victims of modernity. Oguazor's manners and hospitality are unAfrican; and, without pressing a claim that the English have grown warmer in either respect, an English reader might argue that his particular chilly social style would seem rather out of date in Britain.

When Sagoe goes to his interview for a newspaper job he finds on the appointment board the judge—politician Sir Derin, sitting with Chief Winsala. The Chief's attempts to contribute are met with severity from Sir Derin, and he repeatedly withdraws to the 'friendship' of a cupboard where drinks are kept. When one pronouncement of Sir Derin's seems to have an Oracular effect, 'Chief Winsala grew quite creative in the new atmosphere, feeling at home in the re-establishment of the wisdom of elders.' (Chapter 5). The scene is comic at everyone's expense, and the Chief is the best of the figures of fun, but the wisdom of the elders, whom he perhaps remembers, is a reproach to this kind of contemporary nonsense, and Sir Derin is imitating just such establishment buffoons as English satirists of the 1960s were portraying as sad survivals from an earlier time. (The treatment of language in this scene is considered below.) Later in the novel the snobbish Dr Faseyi confides his ambitions, as one man of the world to another, to the painter Kola whom he assures that art, like medicine, may lead to a lucrative sinecure. Although Kola knows that he is not *truly* an artist, as Sekoni was when he sculpted his 'Wrestler', he has enough of Soyinka's respect for the African artist's role in society to turn a deaf ear. In all these encounters with the affected and the corrupt, they are made to sound like second-hand foreigners, and the standard by which they are judged is drawn from Nigerian customs. The power-station Sekoni builds in the bush is a clear symbol of what modernity has to offer; it is welcomed by the Village Head. The plant 'would bathe Ijioha maidens in neon glow — the Village Head had chuckled over that.' (Chapter 1). Sekoni is offered three wives, including the Head's daughter. It is neither the 'new' man nor the 'old' who obstructs useful progress there, but bureaucrats whose standards are imported and old. Soyinka is mocking a foolishness which often bedevils modern life in Africa, while his conception of African culture admits what is promising in the modern. A power-station or a newspaper board is not unAfrican in itself: how to use it is the African's decision and for guidance he ought not to have to go abroad. The 'apostates' who do so are usually backward old rogues and charlatans.

The Interpreters seems post-modernist to Charles Larson, who even refers to Robbe-Grillet, because it is plotless and figural in narrative, with uneven stretches and jumps in time.[4] Students who are unaccustomed to the wilder flights of structural fancy in

France and America are sometimes put out by the abrupt and casual connections between scenes. Soyinka has taken advantage of the fashionable freedom to present scenes in odd sequence: literary reviewers approve of it, especially in an African writer since it is felt that shows signs of progress. His book is no better for lacking a story – and, in so far as it creates difficulties for inexperienced African or English readers, worse. We move from one interpreter to another, from present-day experiences to memories of childhood and youth, through a series of loosely connected scenes, mostly very clear in themselves, which could be read out of context. The novel probably is reread for favourite passages. The hero of Farah's *A Naked Needle* rereads the sections in which Sekoni appears. The narrative power of the longer episodes will make some mature readers regret Soyinka's waywardness. Some may feel that the novel is too short (the most complimentary of reactions) since the author creates more characters who attract our curiosity than he can treat in depth. Noah, Lasunwon, Dehinwa and Bandele are people it would be good to know better. But Soyinka has included a variety of experience which could hardly have been accommodated within a fully organised story which tried to treat the lives of its characters from childhood on.

The book can be read as a modernist work made of patterns of leitmotifs and themes, as Charles Larson suggests.[5] But although recurring images are conspicuous on first reading these seem almost incidental products of Soyinka's creative energy – thoughts for later poems or poetic dramas. Here and there are the Four Elements (especially Water) but to dwell on them would be to miss the busy life of this novel. The most conscientious critics have soon abandoned that course of enquiry. Eustace Palmer is 'uneasy about the language and structure of the novel' and thinks that the most 'poetic' passages are only exercises in words. Looking at the first unexpected change of scene, on the second page, he notes that water provides a connection, but only tenuously.[6] Eldred Jones, uncharacteristically, broods over the same transition: 'Egbo sits staring at a 'talkative puddle' and his mind goes back to a significant journey by water. The thematic link here is water.'[7] He sounds more solemn than the novel's light, playful manner justifies.

There is unity in the warmth and sharpness of its comic vision. There are moments which sadden or anger; but they do not diminish the fun. The best comedy tends to demonstrate its limitations, and unalloyed comedy tends to cloy. Sekoni's story lies outside the reach of humour; Oguazor's blustering about morality is a joke which ceases to be funny when turned against the student who carries Egbo's child; Noah the thief turned apostle is a tragicomic figure, but the circumstances of his death are not amusing. In 1965, before the *coups d'état*, the war, and his own imprisonment, Soyinka could find most outrageous social scandals amusing. If the comedy can be classified by reference to European literatures, it may best be called *menippean*. The Soviet critic Mikhail Bakhtin, who has come to be better known outside Russia in the course of the last ten years, has offered an original, if broad interpretation of what he calls a 'carnival' attitude to the world. One of Bakhtin's attractions to the student of African writing is the range of literature from different backgrounds which he is able to take into account. In *Problems of Dostoevsky's Poetics* he treats the menippean as a category of narrative from Aristophanes, Lucian and Apuleius (perhaps the first African novelist) to Dostoevsky by way of Rabelais and Swift.[8] Bakhtin's menippean world is complex and unstable, comic, satirical, fantastic, poetical and committed to pursuit of the truth. The hero can travel anywhere in this world or beyond. Fantasy and symbolism are combined with low-life naturalism. Odd vantage points offer changes of scale. Heaven and hell are close and may be visited. Madness, dreams and daydreams, abnormal states of mind and all kinds of erratic inclinations are explored. Scandalous and eccentric behaviour disrupts 'the seemly course of human affairs' and provides a new view of 'the integrity of the world'. Society is very unpredictable; roles can quickly change. Current affairs are treated with a satirical, journalistic interest. Genres are mixed. Stories, speeches, dramatic sketches, poetry and parody are absorbed into the menippean. In *The Survival of the Novel* I have discussed Bakhtin's menippean attitude to literature with reference to the modern British novel, arguing that its 'relevance to fiction today is in the assertion it makes of a revitalising power'. Connected with principles of carnival, Bakhtin's menippea 'is a medium of renewal, quick to absorb and rework other genres but always true to its basic, unsettling, unseemly drive'.[9]

As a dramatist, and as a scholar and critic Soyinka is sympathetic both to the spirit of carnival and to the culture of ancient Greece in which the menippean view of the world can first be found, in recorded literature. Perhaps he may be prepared to tolerate the view that his novel is an African manifestation of this old and revitalising spirit which belongs to no particular people. Novelists elsewhere share with the African writer a sense of having come late to the formidable institution of the Novel and of a need to renew fiction in radically changed conditions, without losing the appeal of story, drama, poetry and satire, which are all older than any literature and common to all peoples. The menippean mode offers not merely renewal but, as 'an attitude' to life which belongs to no particular people, common ground in the modern world. It results in comedy which exposes the incongruity of things, with a relish for absurdity, but always pursues the truth, disconcerting in a world of frauds. It rejoices in jokes but does not see life as a joke. To say that Soyinka's novel fits Mikhail Bakhtin's characteristics of the menippean is not to claim *The Interpreters* for a European genre, but to free it from misleading classification as an experimental novel in the fashion of the 1960s whose European readers are already familiar with its techniques. Soyinka is not a decade or so late in the race for novelty. He has written African menippea in the form of a novel as he has written African tragedy in his plays.

The gods have a role in both. Although Kola's Pantheon is not perhaps great art it commemorates the gods. Chapter 16 begins with the flooding of the land and an evocation of the gods, Obatala lover of purity with Ogun lover of gore, the maker and lover of cripples and the master of the forge and of art. As one of many Biblical allusions it may suggest that the world has grown corrupt; but Soyinka's Noah, as we see at the end of Chapter 15, has no spiritual strength. In the conversation which follows, Kola, Egbo and his girl Simi are discussing the sacrifice of a ram – meant for reconciliation. Noah is later 'sacrificed' (as Bandele says), but pointlessly and grotesquely in flight from the homosexual Joe Golder. The novel constantly shifts from the divine scale to the human. Sir Derin, the shameless judge with an English title, returns in a dream from the afterlife as a figure of farce, clad for the grave in a brassière, on which he wears the medal of his knighthood. The prophet Lazarus believes that he has turned albino in the course of his resurrection: a joke at the expense of hymns in which one is to be washed white from sin. Sir Derin and Lazarus are characters in whom fantasy merges with a sure social realism. In his adventures with them Sagoe moves from high life to low life, from boardrooms and grand hotel to the criminal underworld.

Sagoe's states of mind change from drunkenness to a scatological mysticism of his own invention, but it is Joe Golder who is subject to the most erratic inclinations. Sagoe and Golder disturb the seemly course of what Oguazor likes to call decent society where things are blatantly not what they seem. Amidst the multitude of incongruities, categories are blurred. Is Golder a man? Is he a Black? Is Lazarus a madman or a miracle? The whole question of what is modern and what is traditional in this African world tends to dissolve in the overwhelming impression of how fortunes and standards are constantly turned upside down. Meanwhile, the interpreters persist, however incompetently, in seeking the truth.

The novel draws on many other genres. The author is clearly a dramatist and a poet: he is also a satirist, a parodist, a journalist, a teller of tall stories, a student of Yoruba myth and French philosophy, and a young man with a wild and ungenteel sense of humour. His characters are made to serve so many kinds of writing that they are (all but one), although vivid and interesting, insubstantial. Some like Noah are merely figures. Bandele is mostly an authoritative shade. 'Simi of the slow eyelids' is an object of lust. Sir Derin is a satirical butt. Chief Winsala, met trying to find in his voluminous robes the receptionist who is escaping between his feet ('where is the bitch? . . . she was here just now, I had her') belongs to stage comedy. So does Dr Faseyi, another representative target for satire who at times risks developing an individual character with which we might sympathise, the Shakespearean in Soyinka tending to overcome the Jonsonian. Lazarus is a gloriously extended joke with a serious side. Sekoni is idealised; representing artist and saint, he is a doomed figure; he stammers with truths too great for words, and Soyinka is wise to let him die in a car crash before the reader disbelieves in him. Sagoe is the most entertaining of the interpreters but he suffers as a character from the variety of modes in which he has to appear. He is sometimes a Lord of Misrule, sometimes a brilliant frantic child, sometimes a voice for the author's parodies and sometimes for his more earnest thoughts on life. In its own way this is true to life, but not to the type of coherently organised fictional character which is to be found in Achebe. Monica Faseyi and Dehinwa might have grown into substantial characters in a different sort of novel.

Egbo is the exception. He is a central figure. He connects the piracy of the creeks with the Foreign Office, the gods with Christianity. More than any character he invites psychological analysis.

He suffered exceptionally brutal and bewildering treatment in childhood and grew up to fear, later to seduce, women. He represents robust sensuality and manliness in one code, selfish exploitation of women in another. Full of suppressed violence, and yearning for silence and escape, his blend of strength and vulnerability is more intriguing than his perhaps related obsession with water and drowning. He looks artificially staged at times, brandishing a sacrificial knife or clenching his fist in disgust at Golder's queerness. But he is always interesting. Golder sings that he 'feels like a motherless child'; Egbo appears to feel so too at times, but he copes better. The story of his affair with the student girl is broken off before he has learned her name. Although Egbo occupies a large share of the narrative, his treatment is incomplete; but there is more to him than to the other characters. He does more than play roles in the satire. To have presented all the interpreters in the same depth would have required twice the length, and another type of novel.

If Mikhail Bakhtin is right about the emergence (after tragedy and epic) of menippean literature in antiquity as a new response to the unpredictability of society in Mediterranean cities, then the renewal of such writing in contemporary Britain, America, and Africa may offer a parallel. Conditions in all our societies have become ever less predictable in the last half-century. Lucian was amused by new philosophies and by Christianity. Scores of new religions, creeds, prophets and messiahs sweep the world today, as in late antiquity. Soyinka is amused by the rumour of a new Christ who has come this time not for suffering but for pleasure. Social mobility and insecurity were as striking for Lucian as they are today. For educated Africans as for the interpreters, the prospects and risks of life are especially dramatic. In 1965 men like Sagoe, Egbo and Bandele were soon to be at war, or in prison. Hedonism and doubt, exhilaration and danger shape their attitude to the world. Such analogies must not be pressed far; parallels might equally well be found between life today and the France of Rabelais or the Russia of Dostoevsky. It is better, Alain Robbe-Grillet has argued talking to African students, to live with several *systèmes de vérité* than with one.[10] It is certainly exciting. Robbe-Grillet would be dismissive of any quest for Truth. Soyinka, who deals with many *systèmes*, is not at all like Robbe-Grillet, whose work he has attacked; but he shares with older writers of menippea a truth-telling instinct, and he shares with many European novelists a concern to preserve an honest (for him African) moral sense.

The District Interpreters of colonial times were alert to the comic nature of language. Achebe and others have depicted their role as go-betweens so as to bring out both the absurdity and fun of what words can be made to do, and to show how human language is in possibilities and limitations. The elusiveness of meaning, a pervasive theme in modern literature, is most evident to African writers working in what is and is not a foreign language. Whatever the relations between language and truth — which can be made to seem demoralisingly obscure — we believe we know falsehood when we hear or read it, and Soyinka is skilled in spotting every shade and tone of verbal camouflage.

Sagoe and his friends are highly articulate, and their mastery of English puts them at an advantage over most of the other Nigerian characters, many of whom are trying to sound like native speakers. They talk rather better than the English-speaking foreigners, speaking their own brands of Nigerian English, but drawing like the narrator on Yoruba if they care to: 'black *oyinbos*' avoids the awkwardness of 'black white-men'; *ologomungomu* is feebler when rendered as 'a spectral figure' (Soyinka provides a brief glossary). Word games in the dialogue as in the narrative can be facetious or satirical. Sagoe is the most inventive: his 'drink lobes' are jarred or torn whenever his fastidious, often unsober sensibility is offended; whiskies 'burn out' his negritude; in a cold spell he longs for 'some negritude . . . anything to keep me warm' (Chapter 7). Contemplating government villainies he coins (or recalls) 'Ministerial in-lawfulness' (Chapter 5). In the same scene he finds that the newspaper offices have three lavatories: 'one masculine, one feminine and one [clean] for the Neuter Board'. Egbo can be crisply dismissive: 'I do not like apostasy. He has the smooth brass face of an apostate', he says of Noah, in Chapter 12. Kola gave him that word in one of the opening scenes: 'apostate . . . an absolute neutrality'. The interpreters discover various kinds of apostasy, of neutrality or betrayal, in the language of those about them.

Justly considering English as one of their own languages they take a poor view of its misuse by those — British or American — who lay first claim to it. The German–American journalist Peter speaks idly:

Yeah. Wall, not really. I'm German but I use 'merican passport. . . . So soree couldn't come down wi' ze others to Lagos, burra had a date wiz a Minister. I'm a journalist, you know, reckon

Bandili told you. . . . Fabulous guy your Minister, real feller of a guy. Invited me to spend a weekend at his country residence.
(Chapter 10)

'Quite unbearable as a social animal', observed Bandele to Sagoe. The carelessness of speech reflects Peter's inattentiveness of mind, his unaffected indifference. A few pages later Sagoe and Bandele have escaped from Peter, only to fall among the British, gossiping at an academic party. A shrill voice greets them − 'it was a strange dialect of some British tribe' − and it talks petty campus slander, among giggles. One of the drawbacks of learning a world language is that one must endure so many varieties of its common usage. Linguists have urged us towards a detached enjoyment or tolerance of all; novelists teach us the attitudes which lie behind slack speech. Soyinka is very effective in ridiculing the hypocrisy of much British small-talk, and of our effusive, smothering polite phrases. 'I am *so* sorry'; 'Thank you *so* much'; when not meaningless these are often ironic, and even when innocently meant they tend to sound unfriendly and not only to Africans. 'They are much more so wicked even when they are saying Yes please and No thank you,' Chief Winsala fairly observes in Chapter 6. The tonal aggression possible in good British English is an apostasy, Sagoe thinks, when adopted by Africans. His hosts at the university cocktail party, Professor and Mrs Oguazor, are good at it.

'To hell with patriotism!', Sagoe shouts when he spies apples in a fruit bowl; nothing beats the European apple. These are plastic, and he feels that his hostess's words of welcome are of the same stuff. '"Did you manage to find something to eat, by the way?". . . The plastic apple was nice thank you. . . . But Sagoe only simmered, silenced.' Her husband takes trouble with his vowels: 'Cem en der, we mustn't keep the ladies wetting'. Before leaving, Sagoe throws the plastic apple into the garden. At the end of the novel, when the Professor condemns Sagoe's student girlfriend, his elocution-school drawl undermines his authority, or so it seems to Bandele who is allowed the final judgement. 'Merals mean nothing to these modern girls.' 'The whole century is senk in meral terpitude.' '*May they live to bury their daughters!*' Kingsley Amis has a sharp ear for falseness behind pronunciations, and among English novelists he is the best at phonetic mis-spellings. In Soyinka the satire, though as deftly done, is angrier and the interpretation is more blunt. What is absurd in England is here unacceptably artificial. The Oguazors are putting a colonial distance between themselves and their guests. They are apostates, and the fruit of their plastic tree of knowledge deserves to go out of the window.

Meral terpitude extends much further into the ruling class of the country than Professor Oguazor appears to know. Applying to a newspaper company Sagoe appears before members of the Board whom he will be expected to bribe before his appointment can be confirmed, and there for once he resorts to silence. Asked why he wants the job he says tiresomely that he doesn't know. The Board proceed to an ill-tempered debate among themselves which is reminiscent of the Mad Hatter's tea party.

> 'These small fries they all think they are popularly in demand, just because they have a degree . . .'
> And Sir Derin interrupted him, gravely. 'A degree does not make a graduate.'
> It had the pacifying effect of an Oracle . . . Chief Winsala grew quite creative in the new atmosphere . . . 'The Chairman has said it,' he contributed, 'just as a tree does not make a forest.' The Managing Director nodded in approval.
> (Chapter 5)

Sir Derin tries to put the chief right, but little progress can be made since the knight is not quite abreast of his own idea. These men are attempting self-importance in a register of the language which they control imperfectly, and which is scarcely worth imitating anyway. Sagoe's silence, and his flight from the interview, are typical: he is an awkward character. He is fleeing, however, from yet another strange British tribal dialect, absurd in English appointment-committee members, and here gone hopelessly wrong. Sagoe is more at ease with the pidgin of the messenger Mathias, in spite of small cultural confusions. '"You see, you and I are kindred spirits." "Spirit? Oga a no sabbe dat one o."' He is at ease in the caustic, wordy, literate English he talks with his friends. They and Mathias belong equally to the Nigeria of his time.

The interpreters are attentive to the language of social signs. Their own social style is based on a distaste for pretension. Sagoe is dumbfounded when Mrs Oguazor tells him his informality is American. They are surrounded by formalities which they feel should properly belong nowhere today, and by symbols of status which are valued everywhere. *My Mercedes is Bigger than Yours* is a novel by Nkem Nkwankwo which catches in its title one spirit of our time, more effectively captured and mocked in Soyinka's novel.

'I happen to be born into a comparatively healthy society', Sagoe tells Joe Golder. The interpreters, 'scattered over the face of the Western World' in the course of their education, have returned sceptical about the health of Western cultures. Golder, the novel's one American character, is a wretched, socially inept homosexual and his inner disturbances, it seems to Sagoe, are typical of life in the United States. Oxford and Paris have aggravated his troubled nature. He and Sagoe can at least agree about the awfulness of 'the best Oxford accent' — and the insincere politeness that seems to afflict the British. The artists of the Latin quarter and the beatniks of San Francisco are symptomatic of a Western *malaise* which Joe Golder has brought with him. Sometimes the characters' judgements on America and Europe are superficial; as soon as he sees Sekoni's sculpture of the Wrestler, Golder wants to buy it, 'and impatiently, with a tinge of envy in his voice, Kola snapped, "Oh damn your American acquisitiveness" (Chapter 6). Golder's truer motive, we learn on the next page, is a 'feminine greed' for the starkly masculine figure. Acquisitiveness is no more particularly American than lying is, as Golder alleges, African. Sagoe claims to have learned to be cautious in judging others. However risky snap interpretations of alien ways of life, the worst features of the Western world are unmistakable when they appear in Africans; in Soyinka's preposterously Anglicised Nigerian circles some foreign diseases, at least, are easy to diagnose.

Perhaps the least characteristic episode is the story of Sekoni's power-station which is retold by most commentators of the novel, presumably because it belongs to a favourite type of cautionary tale, common in African novels of social and political satire, in which a good man falls among thieves in high places. The risk in these satirical *exempla* is that a predictable disposition of villainous officials around an idealised, well-meaning innocent may seem arranged by literary convention, so provoking doubts: are officials always corrupt? Is the able young man always thwarted? Is the foreign 'expert', who agrees to condemn Sekoni's work in exchange for a fraudulent claims payment of £8,000, an exceptional rogue or do they mostly behave in the same way? Soyinka comes closest to this danger when he makes the most of a chance to ridicule the term 'expert' which is so often applied by international organisations to novices and amateurs; '"Is it unsafe for operation?" and he winked a truly expert expat. expert's wink' (Chapter 1). The fatuous title is nicely undermined but the picture of twisted foreign consultants winking at twisted African chairmen, with varying degrees of expertise, could create resistance to the satire in some readers. The circumstantial detail, in this case, does convince us that adviser and chairman have learned certain Western skills which enrich them and obstruct development. The chairman's company, held in the name of a baby niece, receives compensation. 'I always say it, the Write-Offs pay better than fulfilled contracts': those first four words are just right.

The scene of the embassy reception in Chapter 3 shows a more complex interaction of British and African social standards. Ayo Faseyi, of the Teaching Hospital, has brought his English wife Monica to be presented to the Head of State. Although Monica is educated, has 'moved in society' and is no 'bush-girl from some London slum', she has come without gloves. Ayo feels disgraced; he is distressed again when she refuses champagne and is found drinking palm-wine obtained from a steward. 'Even those in native dress are wearing gloves!', he moans to his wife. Would she go gloveless to a garden party where the Queen was to be present? Eustace Palmer comments on the quarrel that 'this passage exposes Faseyi's uncritical absorption of non-African values, his willingness to descend to whatever depths are necessary in order to ensure social success and his complete unawareness that gloves, the Queen and garden parties are completely irrelevant and out of context in an African setting.'[11] Alas they are not, today.

Professor Palmer is obviously right about the novel's general view of the upper-class group to which Faseyi belongs. The concept of 'moving in society', linked with 'decent society', is European and, here, British; at times both Oseyi and Oguazor appear to be recreating in Lagos and Ibadan a new version of English polite society at its most vulgar and amoral. They pursue alien and old-fashioned symbols of success and a style of middle-class life which has long undergone searching criticism. It is an effective joke that the English wife drinks palm-wine, in gloveless 'seminudity', while her African husband fusses like an Edwardian *parvenu*. Coming so soon after the story of Sekoni, the word 'disgrace' is inappropriate: there are more disgraceful matters for the leaders of Nigerian society to think about than white gloves and champagne; not that Soyinka fails to acknowledge that these are of interest too.

Soyinka's presentation of this diplomatic scene is far more than a self-righteous African assault on apostasy. The best satire allows a sympathy and understanding for its victims – Greene's favourite 'There but for the grace of God go I' – which diffuses the righteousness a satirist needs. That generosity is not always present in *The Interpreters* for the author's scorn and humour are sincerely engaged, but Soyinka's intelligent sense of his characters tends to spare them from being simply targets. Ayo Faseyi is narrow-minded and over-anxious. Why doesn't he borrow gloves? Embassies keep emergency spares. Kola despises him – 'The man likes to worry' – and teases him into worrying more. But the man is not a simpleton. 'He is supposed to be the best X-ray analyst available on the continent' as Bandele tells Kola after reproving him for ragging Ayo. A nervous perfectionism which looks foolish at a cocktail party could be useful in the lab. Faseyi likes things to be done correctly; and if his preoccupation with British social habits is out of place, his values are not necessarily unAfrican. Gloves are nothing here but a mark of respect, and Ayo feels that his wife is slighting the dignity of the country into which she has married. Such details of decorum have a place in modern African society which is often disregarded by foreigners with a breezily modish contempt for courtesy in dress. His panic is moreover very human. Who likes to be laughed at? Modern embassy receptions, with their bizarre congregation of guests mostly unsure what their best behaviour ought to be are mined with embarrassments along invisible frontiers. Neither Bandele nor the British ambassador could advise anything more than caution in this milieu. We are likely to sympathise a little with the humourless Faseyi who takes it all too seriously, unaware that he like everyone else is out of his element.

The menippean attitude to the world, like Soyinka's, is amused by ideologies; it makes comedy of their contradictions, and of how real life subverts their formulations. When Ngugi objects to Soyinka's 'liberal humanism' which cannot 'explain' society with the efficiency of Marxism (*Homecoming*, p. 65), he misses the point of this kind of writing, which is to play with ideas, testing them out. Soyinka has been no friend to the '-isms' of intellectual debate in the West. 'Negritude,' he writes in *Myth, Literature and the African World*, 'adopted the Manichean tradition of European thought and inflicted it on a culture which is most radically anti-Manichean'.[12] Sagoe's private philosophy of Voidancy (or mystical defecation) provides a scatological comedy which is used to taunt the anglicised Africans of 'decent society', and to make fun of 'European ideological confrontations'. 'Of -isms I dirge this day, from homeopathic Marxism to existentialism', Sagoe intones to Mathias at the start of one Voidante lecture, in Chapter 6. Later in the same chapter he discusses Voidancy in Europe, praising the tangible silence of an English suburban lavatory and dismissing false French claims to sophistication since he was there compelled to retreat to the woods with a book and a shovel. He has argued the nature of orthodox Voidancy with a pair of French students in a bistro.

> They were, I remember, converted to what, for me, was mere resourcefulness. In the humid soil and wet undergrowth they claimed, in sly concealed manipulation of creepers and shrubs lay the true Voidatory. Back-to-the-bush stuff, I shouted, Voidatory requires the art and science of man. . . . For three days we were surfeited with Voidante dialectics. You are a bourgeois Voidante, they yelled – you know how the French love polemics – and I replied, and you are Voidante pseudo-negritudinists! You deviationist fools.

Behind Sagoe's irreverence is Soyinka's serious belief that negritude was a Romantic distortion, characteristic of European rather than of African world-views. The perhaps over-elaborate joke of 'Voidancy' allows him to parody certain styles of philosophical discourse which are alien to Africa and which, as an observer of Europe, he finds unimpressive. Sagoe finally undertakes to burn his Book of Voidante Enlightenment when he marries Dehinwa. The Book is, as he admits at times, egoistic and escapist. More reputable philosophies of the 1960s, the novel implies, serve the same purposes.

Menippean writing can be religious but it is never pious. 'I shall begin by commemorating the gods for their self-sacrifice on the altar of literature, and in so doing press them into further service on behalf of human society, and its quest for the explication of being.'[13] So began Soyinka's first Cambridge lecture, with a touch of pomposity, proper there, which is absent from his novel. Soyinka prefers gods to '-isms', for they are the 'projections' of his own culture. Christian and Yoruba religion provide 'reference-points' (Soyinka's own term) in *The Interpreters*, but whereas many African novels presuppose that conflict is bound to arise between different world-views, Soyinka seems here to be at ease with both.

Christianity is often a source of superficial metaphor: the thief Noah, for example, is compared to Barabbas and to Christ. There is nothing enriching to the novel in Biblical allusion as such, although some critics think so; they are reminders, preparing for the comic play with Christianity. The albino Lazarus, recently risen from the dead to found a cult among disciples selected from sinners like Noah might easily have been treated as yet another joke. Sagoe sees him as a fund of newspaper articles; such prophets are a feature of modern West African life. But Lazarus is also taken seriously because he preaches his faith as a contemporary, African truth. Here he is preaching: 'He wrestled with Death and knocked him down. . . . But Death never learns his lesson, he went and brought boxing gloves. When Christ gave him an uppercut like Dick Tiger all his teeth were scattered from Kaduna to Aiyetoro.' (Chapter 12). Death runs to his farm for a machete and attacks from behind but this Christ, quite at home in Africa, is ready for him. The new Lazarus is a living revelation of His victory. Bandele takes the prophet seriously and his approval is at the heart of the novel's interpretation of religious belief. In the educated eyes of Soyinka's people, Christianity is suspect and probably discredited, but still, such is the novel's spirit of tolerant curiosity and impatience with anybody's *Doxa*, able to impress. Lazarus has already shown his calibre in rescuing the street boy Noah from a hue-and-cry.

Placed between the very rich whom they despise, and the very poor who perhaps despise them (although that is not shown), the interpreters observe the extremes of social life from a privileged position. In Chapter 5 Sagoe watches a poor thief on the run and feels an instinctive sympathy; 'Run poor negro, run', from a bad poem almost forgotten, runs through his head. The lean youth who is dragged naked through the crowd and beaten by gleeful ruffians is pitiful enough. 'Lagos staged such pursuits daily, the unfortunate snatcher and a bored crowd. It was a moral demonstration and the prospect of indiscriminate beating was an incentive'. Soyinka's laconic prose reflects Sagoe's distaste for the vicious instincts of a street crowd and for the morality of 'the bigger thieves' who control Sagoe's newspaper, and decent society. He cheers when 'Barabbas' gives the mob a chase but he does not intervene. Lazarus does. 'In fact the boy may be innocent', he remarks; and should he be a sinner, Noah will be all the more ripe for redemption.

The Christian content of Lazarus's service is comical but not, except to the most austerely pious reader, altogether irreverent. The sermon spreads a sunny shared laughter at the puny efforts of Death in a world which is made brighter by Lazarus's gift for words. He is a figure of fun in the very best sense, and he seems to pose no great threat to the gods of the land.

These deities belong to the rivers, the forests, and the creeks where Egbo especially is sensitive to their presence. The narrative celebrates them from time to time in passages of rather ostentatiously poetic prose with which some critics have found fault. They embody the beliefs of the past which live on among the creek-people to whom Egbo might return if he wished, and so oppose Egbo's irritated desire for the past to leave him alone. They stand too for a future free from the posturing affectations of 'decent society' at its Nigerian worst. *They* have certainly never belonged to decent society, and would not be welcome there except in the safe framework of the canvas on which Kola portrays his pantheon.

Soyinka writes most lucidly and appealingly of Yoruba gods, in *Myth, Literature and the African World*, when he discusses their weaknesses, which 'bring them firmly within the human attribute of fallibility'. Obatala, who shaped our bodily forms, was too fond of palm-wine. Whereas Christianity tries to reconcile the malformed, the crippled and the blind, with the omnipotent love of God, 'the Yoruba assert straightforwardly that the god was tipsy and his hand slipped.'[14] Fallibility involves the need for adjustments by gods and men. The worshipper of Obatala is expected to abstain from wine, but he may later become 'beatifically drunk' in honour of Ogun — himself a drinker.[15] Contemplating Kola's picture of Ogun in his image, Egbo is annoyed that the most irresponsible, bloodthirsty aspect of the god has been emphasised at the expense of Ogun the artisan and creator. The angry, unsparing side of Egbo's nature is of course out of proportion as Kola has shown him. He is in part responsible for the death of Noah whom he left with Joe Golder. He has forgotten even to ask the name of the girl he seduced and who is now, an unmarried mother, scandalising the university authorities. But we feel at the close that Egbo is not to be judged by a Puritan morality.

Most of the interpreters fall well within 'the human attribute of fallibility'; they are given to lust, drunkenness, sloth, anger, jealousy, selfishness, folly and doubt. Eustace Palmer reflects rather sadly on their shortcomings. They do however, like the gods, possess the powers of 'adjustment', of co-operation, of sensing proportion. Bandele is somewhat regal when he pronounces his 'Word' on his seniors (on the last page): 'Bandele, old and immutable as the royal mothers of Benin Throne, old and cruel as the *ogboni* elders in conclave.' Sekoni, with the stammer the wise and strong are marked by in many folklores, a Muslem who married a Christian wife and went as a pilgrim to Jerusalem, preached tolerance within the 'Universal Dome' which covers all good paths – Sekoni alone was saintly. The other interpreters are ready, although not always quick, to assess one another, and friends and apostates. As they do so they appear more human than Bandele or Sekoni, and so perhaps more godlike.

'A Man of the People' would make a good title for a political novel anywhere in the modern world. Achebe's book poses a number of questions which arise throughout African and world literature today. What is political authority and especially what is that of a man of the people? What is the role of an educated élite – and that of an idealist in a corrupt society? How is personality related to political outlook? How do personal relations affect political allegiances? What is meant by commitment in personal relations in conditions which are changing so quickly that custom is unsure? What are people entitled to expect from their political 'men'?

It was not Achebe's intention to use a West African setting to reflect upon world-wide issues. He looked at African reality, not at remote analogues in other cultures. His story of rivalry between the politician Chief Nanga and the intellectual narrator Odili Samalu illustrates the uneasy relationship which has existed between two castes in the ruling class in most African countries. But while the roles of Nanga and Odili can be seen as 'products of colonialism', they experience fears and aspirations which belong to the later twentieth century. The novel shows us two distinctly contemporary figures living in an (unnamed) African country which is caught in the complexities of the contemporary world.

Introducing himself Odili will sound familiar to readers almost anywhere. Odili wants independence:

> A common saying in the country after Independence was that it didn't matter *what* you knew but who you knew. And, believe me, it was no idle talk. For a person like me who simply couldn't stoop to lick any Big Man's boots it created a big problem. In fact one reason why I took this teaching job in the bush, private school instead of a smart civil service job with car, free housing, etc., was to give myself a certain amount of autonomy . . . much as I wanted to go to Europe I wasn't going to sell my soul for it. (Chapter 2)

That is not a gentlemanly hauteur, although other characters laugh at him for playing the gentleman. Nor is it a traditional integrity. Okonkwo's pride does not prevent his looking to a bigger man for help at the outset of his career. It is a modern principle of sincerity acquired by Odili in the course of his education in the 1950s. The banal self-righteousness of 'I wasn't going to sell my soul for it' detracts from Odili's dignity; 'for a person like me who simply couldn't stoop' has just the right tone of current adolescent pomposity; 'to give myself a certain amount of autonomy' marks him off from his village background and makes him sound like any young man of the 1960s. Odili has undergone a 'Western' education, but when he spots the clue to Nanga's success, the Chief too seems a familiar hero of our time:

> Chief Nanga was a born politician; he could get away with almost anything he said or did. And as long as men are swayed by their hearts and stomachs and not their heads the Chief Nangas of this world will continue to get away with anything. He had that rare gift of making people feel — even while he was saying harsh things to them — that there was not a drop of ill will in his entire frame. (Chapter 7)

Readers in England and America will then no doubt agree with Odili's reflections on 'the Nangas of this world'. Political conditions in many types of present-day society make such charisma especially effective.

'The great Honourable Minister Chief Doctor (in advance) M. A. Nanga', MP, is more precisely a hero of our time in that he holds great power in the name of the people. He has been elected by the villagers of his own locality who see in him their champion. In the 1940s he was an elementary teacher with limited education; as a man of the People's Organisation Party (POP) he has become a 'warrior' who helped to drive out the British: when Odili attends one of Nanga's campaign meetings at the end of the novel he knows what the villagers will think if he intervenes: 'Was [Odili] not here when white men were eating; what did he do about it?' (Chapter 13). The position of Chief Nanga and his colleagues is that of men 'smart and lucky and hardly ever the best', Odili tells himself elsewhere, who have 'seized the one shelter our former rulers left', and have 'barricaded themselves in' (Chapter 3). The one shelter is government administration; beyond that lurks 'British Amalgamated'; Nanga has taken full advantage of both. He pockets 10 per cent of the money for government contracts; he presses for a road to be tarred so that he may run a fleet of buses on it, the money advanced, or perhaps given (since he takes 'never-never' at its word) by British Amalgamated who also fund his elections; he is eating. Following recent custom he is acquiring a new 'parlour-wife', young and presentable at receptions in town, to add to his 'bush-wife' at home. His house in the capital is a mansion with seven bedrooms and seven gleaming bathrooms. A lady lawyer visits him there at £25 a night. He drives a Cadillac. Nanga believes that one may eat the food which is put in one's hand; and he is ruthless in preserving the supply. He bribes his constituents and cuts off Party posts and amenities from any recalcitrant village. His henchmen are thugs who in the last resort will institute a reign of terror. Nor is he qualified for his post as Minister of Culture; his reading is limited to Rider Haggard and *Speeches: How to Make Them*.

He is far more than a crook and a boor, for all that, and he is popular although everyone knows his seamy side. He has boundless energy and humour. His charm is hard to resist. At times, as the tempter of Odili, he resembles the Vice in a Morality Play; but like Falstaff he fills others with his own laughter and relish for life, which are not always vicious. His English is restricted but pungent. Among the people he is at home at various levels of pidgin English: 'Minister de sweet for eye but too much katakata de for inside. Believe me yours sincerely.' (Chapter 1). As we see here he can joke even at his own hypocrisy. The pidgin is warmly reassuring and unites him with the villagers. After the cold Winterbottoms of

British rule, here is a man of the people. If his gifts are bribes, his largesse is welcomed at home in a convivial spirit. Like everyone there he prefers bitterleaf and egusi to 'chicken-puri, whatever that was'. The spirit of carnival is strong in him, and those he represents can take a vicarious satisfaction in his feasting, perhaps.

To Odili, at first, he is 'bush', and a national disgrace. Later Odili comes to feel that the Chief is exploiting his own culture to endear himself to the villagers without submitting to the true principles of village life. A trader is denounced in the village for having 'taken away enough for the owner to notice' (Chapter 9) – the owner being the village which will tolerate pilfering but stamp out anything worse. The man of the people has taken enough to be noticed but justice cannot reach him, barricaded as he is into institutions, including British Amalgamated, which are so far removed from the villages. But Achebe has not presented the indignant, helpless country people one might find in a cruder novel. Nanga's audiences cannot quite begrudge him his success so long as they receive their 'share of the national cake'. Their son may do the best he can for himself so long as he does something for them. Nor are the people free from corruption. An ex-policeman involved in a local fraud defends the POP on the grounds that 'we know they are eating but we are eating too' (Chapter 12). When Nanga performs at his inaugural campaign meeting towards the end of the book, he casts a more potent spell than that of a demagogue. However suspect his motives such a man can be hard to resist; he can appeal to the best in his audience, the festive and communal, and the worst, their wish to share the spoils. His personality itself is a force. 'We admire firmness', Odili observes, when imposing his own will in the last chapter.

Power has its own fascination in the persons of the Nangas of the world, and Odili is not entirely proof against it until his pride is wounded. Our vulnerability to that appeal seems to be common to all cultures. Achebe's version of a 'power-man' is a less sinister type of modern politician than can be found in other recent novels. Anthony Powell's Widmerpool who broods coldly on the satisfactions which might be had from governing black men, but joins a Labour Cabinet instead, is more frightening than Nanga.[16] He is of course created on a far larger scale in *A Dance to the Music of Time*, but the key difference is that he lacks all sensual enjoyment, all sense of humour, all interest in people; such qualities Powell maintains are lacking in those who truly love power. Although

Nanga is monstrously greedy, there are, if not worse, deadlier men of the people in the world and in African fiction, as will be seen in the next chapter. Achebe's is an intriguing portrait of the man who befriends us for his own good because the novelist loves what is human in his victim. He can make us believe that we might vote for the man.

Nanga's familiar defence, that politics is 'a dirty game' does not originate in Africa. The Minister urges Odili to go and 'learn more book' — to withdraw to the relative purity of a university. Academics and schoolmasters are certainly not free from the attractions of power in their smaller domains, which may help to explain the critical interest they frequently take in the exercise of political authority. Odili Samalu is introduced as a young 'intellectual' who observes the failure of parliamentary democracy with detached disapproval. He has watched Nanga supporting the Prime Minister in shouting down a 'gang' of Ministers who have been disgraced after a cabinet quarrel over economic policy. The principal victim is a man of high academic qualifications and the POP Daily Chronicle attacks Odili's own kind. 'Never again', says the Prime Minister in Parliament, 'must we entrust our destiny and the destiny of Africa to the hybrid class of Western educated and snobbish intellectuals who will not hesitate to sell their mothers for a mess of pottage.' Achebe is a good mimic of such formulaic rant. Behind the words is a sore point for Odili, who never again visits the Public Gallery. While he can see that the hounding of apparently responsible men, some of whom have been physically attacked, is unworthy of older West African traditions and reminiscent rather of European developments, the language in which he condemns it is no more in the style of the people than that of the Prime Minister. Odili is in a sense 'above his people': he calls village solidarity 'primitive unity' and thinks the villagers ignorant fools. Achebe's authorial point of view is almost teasingly objective, not sparing Odili his note of smugness, or his British airs. His colleagues at school accept the head's arrangements for Nanga's visit, declining to be 'roused' by Odili into even formal opposition. 'The teachers in that school were all dead from the neck up', he tells us in Chapter 1, using a tartly British idiom and that particular, petulant tone with which the highly educated increasingly damage their credentials as critics of the people and of their imperfectly chosen men. Nanga is an energetically practical villain from the start; his rival enters the book as a theorist and a prig: the villainy and the priggishness take typically up-to-date forms.

University graduates must expect to be abused as a class from time to time, and should fear it. But they enjoy a prestige, wealth and authority in the twentieth century which philosophers, clerks, and bookmen rarely knew in the European past: a role more akin to the status of the *griot* and the seer. It is no longer true that learning and poverty shall ever kiss, especially not in Africa. In English literature, in Shakespeare, Lamb, Dickens and Waugh, the schoolmaster is most often a comic, pathetic or monstrous figure; in African literature he can be a hero – not merely because the writers are usually teachers too. As education has become more technical and a broadly open route to expensive comforts, schools have attracted more attention from politicians and from novelists. Although Odili considers that he has sacrificed the perquisites of official life, he belongs as a graduate and an able man to a privileged caste, for all the Prime Minister's carping – in his own country and, should he go abroad, in the world. He looks forward to visiting Europe where he hopes that white taxi-drivers will carry his bags and call him 'sir'.

Education was in fact the second 'shelter' left by European rule; and the authority and public responsibility of graduate teachers is further developed there than in England or America. When Nanga learns that Odili has been to the University he exclaims: 'I use to tell the other boys in my class that Odili will one day be a great man and they will be answering him, sir, sir'. He is flattering and teasing Odili, but it is quite feasible for him to do so in such terms. In this respect the young man has a higher title than the Minister who is eager to acquire his promised American honorary doctorate and boasts of it already. There is a touch of respect in his playful form of address, 'the great Odili'. When they meet at the school they are already potential rivals, and when towards the end Odili refuses to be bribed into standing down in the election he sees fear in Chief Nanga's eyes. The Prime Minister attacked graduates because they threatened him with their 'expertise', as Odili might threaten Nanga's. Achebe's African situation is a more urgent, direct version of a conflict which exists everywhere, now, between the 'expert' (whether or not expert) and the 'democratically elected' politician (whether or not democratically elected). As for Odili, he cannot remain detached for long from the issue of Chief Nanga. His problem will be how to act without becoming involved in the 'dirty game'.

Once he is involved, his idealism is tested twice by the pressures of public life. As a guest at Chief Nanga's house he is dazzled by the material trappings of the wealth which office brings. Were he to be a Minister he would wish to be so for ever. It is 'man's basic nature', he tells himself: one cannot pass from poverty to ministerial opportunities and fail to be corrupted; and in his country everyone has recently been poor. Opulence quietens for a time his objections to the Minister of Culture's lack of scruple and lack of culture, even when it turns out that Nanga has never heard of the country's most famous novel. When he does break with his host, denouncing him as a fraud, it is a quarrel over a girl which provokes him. His convictions have been latent, and might have been submerged. Whatever the truth about man's basic nature — and the fruits of office have always challenged a poor man's honour — the opportunities for the able and unscrupulous to acquire the mass-produced appearances of luxury have never been so evident as in recent decades, not only in Africa. If not in Nanga's house then somewhere soon Odili would be startled by the gleaming bathrooms which, for all the justice of the idea about the white man's 'shelter', colonial officers never knew. Western advertising presents a taunting mirage for such people as Armah's poor and virtuous man in *The Beautyful Ones Are Not Yet Born*. It does so throughout the world. Odili in the guest suite at Nanga's might be an emblem depicting the poor man of principle today.

When Odili fights Nanga's constituency, for his friend Cool Max's Common People's Convention (CPC), he is troubled not only by Ministerial interference but also by the Party's money which apparently comes from Eastern Europe, and by the CPC's amorality. Nanga offers him a scholarship and £250; he refuses. Cool Max has taken his bribe of £1000 and means to fight on in the CPC cause using the other side's money. Although Odili sees this to be dishonourable, against all village principle, he soon finds himself 'eating the hills like yams' in a free Party car (a 'bourgeois' symbol, he used to think) and he ends by paying his bride-price out of Party funds. When Cool Max tells Odili's villagers that POP and PAP are two vultures whom the hunter shoots, a section of the audience reckons CPC to be the third and youngest vulture: there are signs that it may be. Odili hires armed bodyguards and provides money with which to bribe key figures. He has not been long in politics before adjusting somewhat to the 'dirty game'. Achebe allows him to be firm however in rejecting Cool Max's justification of the means by the end. Acceptance of POP money on false pretences, he believes, destroys the moral position which alone can bring terror to Nanga's eyes, and 'which in the end was our society's only hope of salvation' (Chapter 12). If that now sounds old-fashioned, the world's Nangas of POP and CPC may take comfort.

For some readers that will sound a quaint idealism, a principle taken from Barthes's *Doxa*, intended to reassure bourgeois liberals like Odili. Achebe shows his characters' political views in relation to their social and psychological background. Odili is the son of a District Interpreter who prospered in his position as a colonial 'minor god'. The elder Mr Samalu enriched himself with gifts of food and drink from those who had business with the DO. Fifteen-year-old Odili, visiting a schoolfriend, was sent home on the first evening when the family discovered whose son they had received. The boy came to resent his father's need for ever more wives and children — signs of wealth and status — and he was further isolated by a village prejudice: because his mother had died in childhood he was said to be a 'bad child that crunched his mother's skull' (Chapter 3). He was not, he tells us, lonely or unhappy in childhood. But he grew up a purist, a successful scholarship boy, aloof from worldliness. A combination of circumstances, within the culture and beyond it, have alienated Odili. His vulnerability is touching because it is so understandable. When he finds a moral position recognised by rural practice and by the university he is, in an unpleasantly modern sense, 'above his people', but supported by a maturity which is hard to explain away.

Achebe presents politics in the individual politicians: 'society in man' in the current phrase. Odili's relationship with Chief Nanga is the heart of the story, and this is made subtler than an allegorical struggle would have been. Odili first knew Nanga, his teacher in standard 3, as a 'most impressive scoutmaster', handsome, popular, and imposing in his uniform. That role is nicely chosen. It fits Nanga's self-importance, ambition, and taste for power; and it represents an alien, even imperial formulation of values which the Chief will not live up to himself; a scout is to be pure 'in thought, word, and deed'. It suggests also Nanga's tutelage of Odili who remains for him 'the great Odili', the favourite pupil whose success in life will perhaps exceed his master's and bring him credit. The irony, when Odili is 'at Chief Nanga's feet' to learn the ways of practical politics, is complicated by the older man's genuine affection and pride in his former pupil. An element of the fear in the Minister's eyes comes, it is implied, from a fleeting sense of older loyalties in their relationship. Nanga is hurt by the young man's contempt and seems pathetic as well as ruthless when his men attack Odili at their final meeting.

At the heart of their first scene together the politician embracing a possible recruit merges with the teacher embracing his former pupil like a father finding 'a long-lost son'. It is one of those images in fiction – Oliver bowl in hand, Jude by the walls of Christminster, Archdeacon Grantly at his father's death bed – which stick in the mind even if novels which contain them fade in memory, because they catch a permanent truth in a particular social context. Required by his headmaster to stand in line with the children who are to meet the visiting grandee, Odili is resentful, despising the Minister and the 'silly ignorant villagers'. He is still contemptuous when the Minister emerges from his Cadillac and passes among the dancing villagers, clothed in 'damask and gold chains' and waving his fan 'which they said fanned away all evil designs . . .': ignorant Chief among ignorant people, Odili thinks, but his hostility is soon blown away:

'You are Odili.'
'Yes, sir.' Before the words were out of my mouth he had thrown his arms round me smothering me in his voluminous damask. 'You have a wonderful memory,' I said. 'It's at least fifteen years.'

Before long Odili has agreed to visit Nanga in the capital and to accept his help in arranging an overseas scholarship. That evening he defends his new patron: 'Churchill never passed his School Certificate' (Chapter 3). Odili has been 'a hero in the eyes of the crowd'; his headmaster has praised him for the first time; he has been remembered, recognised, warmed and flattered. The presence of a beautiful girl in the Minister's entourage has attracted him too. It is an old truth that personality and personal relations make politics something more than a science. Charisma is harder to resist today because principles and protocol are so uncertain. Odili thinks that he may have been applying inappropriate standards in judging the Minister's professional ethics. But he is vague about what standards might apply. Nanga has learned the cant of modern political campaigning: 'Don't you know that minister means servant? Busy or no busy he must see his master' (Chapter 2). But he speaks as a master in a culture where servants know their place. When a colleague, Chief Koko, is served OHMS ('Our Home Made Stuff') instead of imported coffee, the cook is in danger of his life until Koko learns that he has not been poisoned.

Another area of uncertainty which preoccupied novelists of the 1960s surrounds the quarrel. Odili brings his girlfriend to spend the night at Nanga's house and the Minister installs her in his absent wife's bedroom. Then he sits working for an hour, so positioned that he blocks Odili's access. When at last her young man reaches Elsie's room, Nanga is there before him. She has the habit of crying out 'in the heat of the thing' the name of her most recent lover and Odili soon hears her screaming for him. The thought that she wants to be saved from her ravisher lasts only a moment; then Odili leaves the house in defeat. Next morning his long-suppressed conscience is freed by his resentment. '"What a country!" I said. "You call yourself Minister of Culture — God help us. . . . You are just a bush . . ."' He is lost for the word (Chapter 7). The Chief is apologetic. Odili has in fact spoken of Elsie as 'just a good-time girl'. Achebe's handling of the incident is reminiscent of Kingsley Amis in its narrative skill, and in its comic vision of a sexual free-for-all among characters for whom honour is remembered only when convenient. Many of the scenes at Nanga's house introduce American and English characters and demonstrate Odili's doubts about European and African standards. Both cultures are undecided about sexual ethics, each sometimes finding in the other pretexts for 'permissiveness', without forgetting good manners, and restraints which were more forceful in the recent past in Africa and in the West.

Later in the story such difficulties of transition appear to be peculiarly African and to resemble divided loyalties to be seen in the English literature of earlier periods. Is a girl to marry the man her father chooses for her? Is a son to submit to a bigoted father, or teach him the way we live now? Family bonds are beginning to weaken in Africa, it might be argued, as they weakened in Europe several generations ago. But Achebe makes it plain that the causes, effects and implications are different now. As the later chapters of *A Man of the People* follow the private lives of Odili and the girl he marries (against a picture of the state's decline into anarchy and military rule), we see that African society is not involved in catching up with European emancipation, but in facing the risks which attend the pursuit of a wider personal freedom, in the context of its own modern history.

Having quarrelled with Chief Nanga, Odili seeks revenge. Besides fighting him in politics he means to take his girl, the lovely Edna, first glimpsed in Chapter 1. But Nanga has paid her bride-price and her school fees; she belongs to him, and her father is pleased to have so powerful a future son-in-law. 'This is the time to enjoy an in-law, not when he has claimed his wife and gone away. . . . He will bring and bring and bring and I will eat until I am tired' (Chapter 9). Such a time and such an in-law is what fathers of daughters dream about. 'It is not so much that I want to be called a minister's wife but a matter of can't help', Edna writes (Chapter 11). When Nanga has fallen and Edna is united with Odili she admits that the girls in her college were laughing at her; she had no wish to be second wife to an older man who was, for all his money, 'bush'. Tales of this kind are told by dozens of modern African writers, perhaps most shrewdly and entertainingly by Guillaume Oyônô-Mbia. Since, as in Achebe's version, the girl's family is usually reconciled to the new suitor and prepared to accept the new bride-price, the question of family authority is not fully faced; the young men of letters who illustrated the problems involved naturally awarded the girls to suitors of their own kind. *A Man of the People* grants Odili one clear victory over Nanga, and some relief to its unhappy ending; Achebe also sets the story of Edna in relation to unhappier affairs.

Odili's father supports his candidacy in Nanga's constituency because he shares the Minister's views of politics as a career: 'he took the view . . . that the mainspring of political action was personal gain' (Chapter 11). He is pleased when Odili acquires his Party car and distressed when he refuses Nanga's bribe. But Mr Samalu's loyalty is firm. He is removed from his POP office and his taxes are reassessed; but when asked to dissociate himself from his son's folly, he won't. Odili, who has long thought the old man a rogue, is astonished. 'But our people have said that a man of worth never gets up to unsay what he said yesterday', his father tells him (Chapter 13). 'I thought to myself: you do not belong to this age.' Today's men of worth, Odili has found, have no such sense of honour — not even the 'high-minded' Max. Odili's own standards have been dirtied by the game. Mr Samalu's words affect our reading of Nanga's charge that Odili has betrayed friendship, emphasising the duplicity of his earlier behaviour as a guest. The narrator admits on this occasion that he was baffled and had no time to consider: 'I had never really been close enough to my father to understand him'. Mr Samalu as the spokesman for traditional values is suddenly more impressive. The principles of 'our people' are taken more seriously as a test of the narrator's facile 'modernism' in the later stages of the novel.

Like so many contemporary heroes Odili has aimed for an isolated, individual integrity, 'a certain amount of autonomy'. His fondness for Elsie shows how he conceives it: 'I can't pretend I ever thought of marriage . . . Elsie was such a beautiful, happy girl and she made no demands whatever' (Chapter 2). He sometimes feels jealous, none the less. Meanwhile he disapproves of his father's accumulation of wives and children, and so lives beyond his means; offended by hard words from a son, the old man has sworn to take none of his money. The freedom Odili expects in his dealings with Elsie is that of many English heroes of the 1960s, in Amis or Iris Murdoch: a freedom taken for granted by many of his generation in the Europe he wants to visit. He notes complacently that 'I don't mean to go there for the white girls — you can have those out here nowadays' (Chapter 2). They, like Elsie, have a certain amount of autonomy. *Those* is the key to Odili's contemptuously possessive view of them; as so often in Achebe the tone conveys his meaning. Edna's touching 'a matter of can't help', when she is prepared to obey as a daughter, is unemancipated, but the tone helps to make us believe she will be good for Odili.

Autonomy is also what Nanga wants. 'If you like I can bring you six girls this evening,' he promises when trying to appease Odili after the quarrel. That is a typical remark, not just because it offers a bribe, but because he presupposes his power to fix anything and anybody. He is astonished that Odili should be such a fool as to quarrel with him. Having taken control of the villages which elect him he is largely a free agent in politics, managing local supporters and foreign capitalists but responsible to neither. The scale of his freedom is part of his appeal to Odili who challenges him in the same sphere, entering the elections with Party money and an optimistically free conscience. Nanga wants autonomy for the sake of his fleet of coaches; Odili wants it partly for his concept of what the people need, and partly for revenge. For both it is desirable in itself. Their clash leads to anarchy, and then to military rule and the curtailment of freedom for either to belong to a political party.

Odili agrees to the arming of his bodyguard because of threats from 'hoodlums and thugs calling themselves Nanga's Youth Vanguard or Nangavanga, for short'. These activists take literally their aim to 'annihilate all enemies of progress' in order to 'project true Nangaism' (Chapter 11). Odili's windscreen is broken by stones. He is to learn to keep away from elections in future, Nanga warns. At the Chief's Inaugural Meeting Odili is beaten unconscious. Recovering on Election Day, he finds that his Nomination Paper, intercepted by the Nangavanga, never reached the Electoral Officer. That night Max is killed for standing against Chief Koko. Eunice, his girlfriend, kills Koko. Fighting breaks out, and spreads when Nanga pays off his private army and they terrorise the countryside, sacking markets. Other gangs join in. When the army takes control, jailing the government, Nanga is caught disguised as a fisherman. Political parties are abolished until further notice. Most of these events are reported briefly and without comment. Achebe spares us the details of violence which African novelists of the 1970s tended to put on show. Democratic politics quickly turns to banditry, without fuss on Achebe's part.

The novel makes plain that this is neither a 'reversion to barbarism' nor a recycling of colonial experience with Nanga as a black colonial. The circumstances are new. Achebe properly reiterates the charge that British interests are behind Chief Nanga's campaign. Defending his deception of Chief Koko, Max explains that British Amalgamated has contributed £400,000 to POP election funds, and the Americans 'have been even more generous' (Chapter 13). Max's finances come, as a rival investment, from the Eastern bloc. The fight between his bodyguards and Koko's which results in anarchy is seen in relation to larger hostilities. The political activities of *A Man of the People*, as much as the private lives, belong to the 1960s. Barbarians and colonials have had their opportunities. Those of Nanga, Odili and Max take different, contemporary shape.

It became a commonplace of the 1960s to speak of 'a loss of faith in the political class': that is to say, in politicians. The elderly councillor at the CPC meeting knows what the people want: their 'share' of the 'National Cake', lest the next village take too much. Any politician knows that. It is an outlook which almost demoralises Odili who cares for the Nation. At the CPC meeting where Max denounces POP and PAP as privileged élites there is resigned amusement, a general hope of sharing in any privileges to be had, a shrewd suspicion of the speaker, and a sense of helplessness. Apathy of this kind is a mixture of scepticism about human nature, communal self-defence and helplessness. Men of the people everywhere depend on it. 'We are ignorant people and we are like children', says the councillor who proclaims the doctrine of 'our share' before everything. He is deferring to Max's higher education. There may be British politicians who take the same view of local councillors, although the councillors are less likely to admit it of themselves. Expertise in the management of modern states increasingly divides governments from the governed. Most people today are subject to the slogans of Nangaism or CPC. 'True Nangaism' and its 'projection' belong to a political style first pinned down by Orwell. Odili's pessimism and anger at the end of the novel were shared by many of Achebe's African readers and by readers elsewhere. One of the novel's messages is that men of the people should be received with intelligent suspicion rather than with songs and dances. Few political novels of recent times make that truth so plain, or convey so well the power of 'the great' to bemuse the sharpest into forgetting it.

Things are plainer here because Odili's country is so much poorer, materially and in the institutions of a nation state. Where villages are waiting for water supplies and the promise of electricity, the corruption of a Nanga is more vicious in its effects. Where the educated class is small and young, controlling him is more difficult. Where considerable economic power lies beyond the country, and where much that is modern is also foreign and new to most people, comparison with richer states, it can be argued, is patronising and liable to obscure the facts of underdevelopment. But since African countries are not developing towards the present general state of any 'advanced' region of the world, but are involved, at many kinds of disadvantage, in a history which it is to be hoped will lead to better conditions of life than those of West or East today, it is perverse to ignore what is contemporary in their predicament. Achebe's novel brings it out. He obliges African and foreign readers to see all his characters as men 'of this age'.

At the end Odili expresses an Achebean regret that the nation cannot function with the united, traditional ease of the community. This is half of what he has in mind when he decides that his father does not 'belong to this age'; he is also prompted by depression into the classical thought that virtue has gone from the world. Of course Mr Samalu is as much a man of the age as Odili; he has adjusted to the times and surrendered less of his village culture. If he cannot contribute to the Government's overthrow, nor can Odili. Throughout the novel the narrator's pessimism is offset by the vigour, sense, and vitality of the people. Achebe's liking and respect for people and skill in catching their voices warms what might have been a chilling novel. Mrs Nanga thinks herself too 'bush' to go to America, but she could hold her own anywhere. She says all there is to say about embassy parties: 'What can you enjoy there? Nine pence talk and three pence food. "Hallo, hawa you. Nice to see you again." All na lie lie' (Chapter 3). 'Bush' wives are not alone in having thought on those lines; few have ever put it better in such short space. Arguing with Odili, Mr Samalu is spiritedly ironic: 'Not that you ever say anything to me. Why should you? Do I know book? Am I not of the Old Testament? . . . Let me finish.' (Chapter 11). Edna's father warns him: 'My in-law is like a bull and your challenge is like the challenge of a tick to a bull.' (Chapter 10). The variety and energy of the novel's language reflects a self-confidence and articulacy in the people which foreign readers may well envy, thinking of the common state of spoken English in most parts of Britain and America. Nanga's ability to handle different strains of English is part of his dangerous charm: 'Every goat and every fowl in this country knows you will fail woefully.' he tells Odili. An honest Nanga would be formidable.

For some critics the novel shows that the old and true African life has been hopelessly corrupted, so that the best in African culture belongs to the past. David Carroll writes that 'the story of Josiah the trader must be seen as a parable which anticipates the final destruction of a way of life which had been celebrated with pride, affection and concern throughout the novels'.[17] It is Josiah who 'has taken enough for the owner to notice'; he stole a blind man's stick to help him blind his customers. Nanga's magic has worked better, as David Carroll points out; the village can condemn Josiah but Nanga has blinded them. 'He has stolen from the constituency its traditional ethic,' David Carroll continues, 'What was once their strength has become their weakness, for this man works in the sphere of national politics where they can neither understand nor control him'. This brings out very well Odili's insights at the end of the novel. But Odili has always underestimated the resources and intelligence of the villagers. David Carroll considers that Achebe sometimes abandons the 'dramatic function' of the first person method and uses Odili to express his own views.[18] Odili is often cruder in his judgements than the author intends us to be; but he is not a fool and some of his conclusions are sounder than others. Odili is more convincing as a character because he is muddled in his views. In the course of the story he comes to a more respectful view of community life than he expresses in his narrative: 'primitive loyalty I call it,' he says of a colleague's support for Nanga as a fellow villager, in Chapter 1. His own support is to be more sophisticated. Meeting primitive loyalty in his father, he is grateful. He remains detached, however, in telling his story: 'personally I don't care much for our women's dancing', he says on the first page. His concern with decent conduct of the national government often takes on the appearance of a wish to Europeanise; his own language often sounds rather sourly British. His final remark of all, that Max died a good death since he was avenged by someone he loved, without her having to be paid to do it, conveys his own bitterness. The dramatic function of the narrator is preserved to the end. We need not consider his assessment, however shrewd, to be the last word. It might be said of Achebe, as Henry James claimed of himself, that he never has a last word. His world is 'like a Mask dancing'.[19] Several vantage points are wanted to see it whole.

Although village culture no longer provides the kind of intimate social discipline needed for the nation, it can still affect conduct at crucial moments, as when Mr Samalu supports his son, or when Odili is distressed by Max's modern legalism over the POP bribe; it is still alive in this age, and such incidents make us feel how lively it can be. In Nanga and Koko the acquisitive, status-seeking aspect of life in Achebe's novels of older Iboland has found itself fresh opportunities. Other traditional values are not ruled out because the world has changed. A Minister can choose between enriching himself and providing for his people, however wicked the wider world, even when the community is not present to enforce its will. The public honesty expected by the old Ibo way of life coincides with the more rigorous standards which progressive Americans have recently tried to introduce into their own public life: perhaps it is common sense. 'Koko had taken enough for the owner to see', Mr Samalu explains to Odili when the government has been disgraced. These are not Achebe's last words, although they are given prominence at the start of the last paragraph and are words we shall remember. Embittered by Max's death, by his own failure, by the general condemnation of the former regime by people who would not support him, Odili is struck only by the contrast between the force of the words in village conditions and their weakness in the state. He fails to notice that proverbial wisdom has been applied for the first time to a leader of the national government. Although it comes too late this time, it is a citizen's judgement. Odili's conclusion is a diatribe; Achebe's novel is far more subtle and full of life than that. It ends by showing that Mr Samalu, a traditional villager who profited from colonialism, now belongs to our age — although his son has always been unwilling to admit it.

Achebe, among others, has attacked the Ghanaian Ayi Kwei Armah for writing a first novel too modern for present-day Africa. *The Beautyful Ones Are Not Yet Born*, he objected (at Harvard in 1972), is 'a sick book' aiming at a modish existential misery for which Africa is not yet ready.[20] Armah's central character, whose consciousness is reflected by the narrative, is certainly not a typical Ghanaian; his morbidity would be unusual anywhere. But Achebe sees his wretchedness as an unwelcome literary import belonging to a stage of Western civilisation which Africa has happily not yet reached:

> Presumably European art and literature have every reason for going into a phase of despair. But ours does not. The worst we can afford at present is disappointment. Perhaps when we too have over-reached ourselves in technical achievement without spiritual growth we shall be entitled to despair. Or, who know? We may even learn from the history of others and avoid their particular fate. But whether we shall learn or not, there seems to me no sense whatever in rushing out now, so prematurely, to an assignation with a cruel destiny that will not be stirring from her place for a long time yet.[21]

Many English novelists and critics would agree with Achebe's distaste for the literature of despairing alienation, Kingsley Amis's 'Legion of the Lost': 'all those characters you thought were discredited, or had never read, or (if you were like me) had never heard of: Barbusse, Sartre, Camus, Kierkegaard, Nietzche, Herman Hesse, Hemingway . . . The Legion of the Lost, they call us, the Legion of the Lost are we, as the old song has it'.[22] But while Amis thinks that English literature in the 1960s has passed this company by, Achebe identifies Jean-Paul Sartre and existentialist fashions with modern literature in the West and claims that Africa has not yet reached this painful stage in the history of civilisation. He finds fault with Armah not for aping a certain trend of earlier writing, but for going in pursuit of a modernism from which Africa is so far still immune: 'Armah is clearly an alienated writer, a modern writer with all the symptoms. Unfortunately Ghana is not a modern existentialist country. It is just a West African state struggling to become a nation. So there is enormous distance between Armah and Ghana.'[23] 'Alienation' and 'existentialism' stand for ideas and literary manners which have interested a minority of writers all over the world, even in England, and in Africa. But the conditions in which it arose, including the first impact of nineteenth-century scepticism upon Christian culture, have changed everywhere. Such 'down-to-earth' observers as Amis and Achebe were always likely to mock at the high-minded pessimism to which this kind of view of the human condition often leads, and might now regard it as old-fashioned: a counterpart to the breezy self-confidence which afflicted simpler-minded imperialists. Achebe compares Armah's 'icy distance' from Ghana with that of Cary's description of Fada in *Mister Johnson* and suggests, in sarcasm, that Africans seeking 'a modern alienated stance' may 'end up writing like a white District Officer'.[24] That seems unlikely.

The words of the title, which the hero sees painted on a bus at the end of the novel, are comparable with other wry legends on mammy wagons. Achebe himself quotes elsewhere 'no telephone to heaven'.[25] They are reminiscent too of a dreamy, idealistic tone common in America in the 1960s. The slogan on the bus surrounds the image of a flower. As for the unsparing details of physical squalor and the theme of black integrity, they too may owe something to Armah's time at Harvard. But the novel's subject is poverty and its temptations. It is poverty which isolates and unmans the central character — not the existential *angst* which commonly attacks the prosperous. If Armah has been affected by Western writers their influence has helped him to survey conditions of poverty-taunted-by-wealth, which are widespread in the contemporary world, and which are at their most acute in Africa.

The poor have always been so, but the experience of poverty is relative and therefore changeable. Unoka's debts and lack of titles are painfully shaming to young Okonkwo but such a man in an African village was able to prosper if he chose, through honest hard work. The majority of Europe's poor in the same period had no such option and lived with the signs of spectacular wealth all about them but beyond their reach. It is in the contemporary world that urban poverty has started to seem shameful, given the new insistence on freedom of opportunities, even in cities of the Third World where opportunities for the uneducated are so limited. E. M. Forster remarked in *Howard's End* that the novelist is not concerned with 'the very poor', who call for the poet or the statistician. His poor clerk in that novel belongs to the English 'shabby-genteel' who lived on the fringe of the middle classes and on 'the edge of the abyss'.[26] Their fears and humiliations, which appeared in Forster, in Maupassant and in Dickens, were confined to a minority in the particular conditions of nineteenth-century Europe which no longer obtain anywhere. Armah is not concerned with the very poor of Africa, but with a state of mind which is produced among the poor in modern cities and most painfully in the cities of Africa. If the poor of Victorian London had little hope, and the shabby-genteel more fear than hope, the 'disadvantaged' of today are tantalised by the prospects of immediate enrichment which press so close and hard upon them. Workmen discussing the success of an acquaintance in Chapter 9 of *The Beautyful Ones Are Not Yet Born* are hurt by their own failure.

> 'He is only a small boy . . .' 'Two cars now . . .' . . . 'you will think I am lying, but he was my classmate, and now look at me' . . . 'Ei, and girls!' . . . 'Contrey, you would do the same . . .' 'True . . . money swine.' 'Money swine.'

The novel's central character suffers, although less crudely and directly, the same sense of deprivation.

'The man', who is never given a name, works as a railway clerk on a very small income which he might supplement by taking bribes from contractors, except that he is an honest man. His family have scarcely enough to eat. Home is poor, dirty, and made more depressing by his wife and mother-in-law who nag him about his failure to do better, and about Koomson's success. 'His Excellency Joseph Koomson, Minister Plenipotentiary, Member of the

Presidential Commission, Hero of Socialist Labour' was the man's classmate at school. Through the Party he has risen from the dockyards to a villa in the upper Residential Area, equipped by the State Furniture Corporation with the latest of everything. The man himself is troubled, as he admits when he visits the villa, by envy and self-doubt. He confides in a friend, Teacher: 'I am asking myself what is wrong with me. Do I have some part missing? Teacher, this Koomson was my own classmate. My classmate, Teacher, my classmate. So tell me, what is wrong with me?' (Chapter 5) They started, the man feels, as equals. He had hopes of going to the University, but marriage made that impossible. Koomson has pushed ahead. Teacher diagnoses: 'You cannot lie very well, and you are afraid to steal'. Koomson is corrupt, and so is the rich 'small boy' the workmen speak of, and so — the novel implies — are most of those who have succeeded in Nkruma's Ghana. Most will take a bribe or filch from work. The book shows too how this indiscipline is fostered by poverty in the absence of socially agreed principles and in the presence of such alluring temptations to *consume*.

When the man admits to his wife Oyo that he has refused a bribe she taunts him:

> No perfume, no car, no 'things'. 'Like Estella Koomson?'
> 'Yes, like Estella. And why not? Is she more than I?'
> 'We don't know how she got what she has', the man said.
> 'And we don't care.' The woman's voice had reverted to its flatness. With a silent gesture she sent the children back inside. 'We don't care. Why pretend? Everybody is swimming towards what he wants.' (Chapter 5)

Oyo's moral frailty flatters her voice and gestures the children away. That everybody does the same is an old excuse but the circumstances are those of today. Estella has everything. 'Is she more than I?' French perfume and a car are Oyo's rights, and readily to be had if her husband were not an honest fool. The principles of Christianity and of Socialism, which might have replaced in consumer society the older African codes of fair dealing have, it seems, little force, here as elsewhere. Oyo jeers 'Onward Christian soldier' at the man. Koomson elsewhere confides that 'the old man' does not really believe in Socialism. Envy undermines, given the profusion of material benefits to be seen, for instance, at Koomson's house.

This is Ghana, not England, although English readers are unlikely to feel that there is anything backward about Oyo's outlook, rather the contrary. The novel shows how it is that dishonest policy has come to be the most effective in post-independent Africa. The demoralising effects of colonialism are illustrated, as in most novels of this kind, with Armah's own examples of acts of callous violence, and with his exceptionally good evocations of the paralyses and bafflement of the late colonial period which the prospect of independence turned into eager and ill-founded hopes. Production remains overseas. The electronic toys in Koomson's house are all imported and the Minister drinks only Scotch whisky. Although the sale of foreign drinks is forbidden, such laws can be evaded. When the man takes a new kind of taxi it turns out to be a Toyota and the driver remarks that 'it seems everybody is making things except us. We Africans only buy expensive things' (Chapter 11). Meanwhile, as Robert Fraser has pointed out in answer to critics who accuse Armah of ignoring the economic facts of Ghanaian life, the railway system helps to convey materials abroad.[27] The man is reminded of how certain chiefs exchanged people for trinkets at the height of the slave trade. Trinkets are within everyone's reach today. Before Independence 'the white man's gleaming bungalows were so far away, so unreachably far, that people did not even think of them in their suffering' (Chapter 6); for those whose thoughts strayed in that direction there were stories of dogs on guard. Today 'the gleam' comes from the spotlights of a grand hotel, built 'an insulting white' on a hilltop above the town, perhaps 'to draw the love of a people hungry for just something such as this' (Chapter 1). The Atlantic Caprice Hotel beckons to all and poverty within the gleam of its lights is a peculiarly shameful kind of suffering, acutely felt where normal life is so drab; Armah understands that very well. The cinema shows 'new fashions in dress and in murder' (Chapter 4), and in much besides. 'Is there anything wrong with some entertainment now and then?', Oyo pleads. The latest fashions in entertainment are on sale at the Atlantic Caprice.

The man's lack of a name irritates Achebe because it reminds him of 'the best manner of existentialist writing'.[28] Robert Fraser is reminded of Everyman.[29] Anonymity might better suggest the manner of parables — 'there was a man who . . .'; or the one just man who would have saved the Cities of the Plain. Armah's man is untypical. He is not living in Sodom, but he feels as though he were. He is obsessed with dirt as a metaphor of corruption, and the narrative reflects this obsession. Oyo dreams of Estella Koomson's 'clean' life, and he tells her: 'Some of that cleanness has more rottenness in it than the slime at the bottom of a garbage dump' (Chapter 4). The dirtiness of his own milieu, to which he is so sensitive, reinforces his obsession; he dreams of the streams of childhood where 'the water coming from the hills was always clean', and in his most depressed moments he thinks that contact with mankind must always sully such cleanness. 'Keep your country clean by keeping your city clean', he reads on a poster in the first chapter; he is conscious everywhere of physical and moral pollution. The man's mind is sick, with poverty and defeat.

The mind of the novelist is agile and enterprising, and perhaps over-eager to accumulate images of corruption and decay; it is a young man's first novel. Armah is aware of what a modern critical seminar can do with 'levels of imagery' or 'themes and symbols'. Critics have rightly admired his handling of light and darkness in relation to Plato's Cave of Shadows. There are passages which give the impression of exercises in creative writing, especially those in which the vaguely portentous figure of Teacher appears. But the sad, passive figure of the man, exasperating and touching, gives a meaning even to Teacher. The man is no intellectual; he lacks mental energy; he broods more than he thinks. His education ended with a Grade II School Certificate; nowadays he has neither time nor money for reading; his bookcase holds old school texts, and a family of mice. Failure to reach the University has left an 'ache' whenever he recalls the 'white beauty' of the unfinished college buildings at Legon. The austere, pretentious hermit Teacher fails to supply an unsatisfied need for a life of the mind. The man's poor library contrasts with Koomson's luxurious trinkets from Europe. Fraser calls the man 'a victim of history'.[30] Armah persuades us that his character is trapped by present circumstances, not only in a dull job and a poor home, but also in a mental life which cannot escape the narrow consciousness of opposites, dirt and cleanliness, the light and the dark, gleaming imports and grubby home.

The moral fable works better because it takes social conditions into account. Koomson wants to acquire fishing boats, but socialism is 'a nuisance' because 'fools will start throwing slogans at you' (Chapter 10), and he proposes that his first boat be in the man's name. The man can see little good in the arrangement but his wife and mother-in-law like to be associated with the Minister; even talking about him soothes them. The man allows his wife to sign the papers. When a coup puts a stop to this government, Koomson flees to the shelter of the man's home. He has been swaggeringly ostentatious while rich and powerful; now he is broken, and he stinks with terror. The man helps him to escape, through the latrine, of course, whose normal use Koomson disdained on a previous visit. Scattering bribes on his way, the old classmate escapes on his boat. Although the novel ends gloomily as the man watches a policeman taking a bribe, and then reads the comment provided in the title words, Koomson in defeat is an effective picture of Armah's central theme. He is quickly bereft of his riches, but they never really belonged to him; he too is a poor man, although he has for a time manoeuvred himself into a post of wealth and power. His swagger was always pathetic. 'I am glad you never became like him', Oyo whispers to her husband, stressing the fable. Koomson and Oyo have been demoralised. The man's predicament helps to show why.

The man is the gloomy creation of a melancholy writer. Armah's characters in later books lack resilience and are prone to mental breakdown. Like his character's the author's high-minded fastidiousness leads him to polarise experience. 'There is something so terrible in watching a black man trying at all points to be the dark ghost of a European', the man tells himself. Armah's racial integrity is a strength, but he frets. The man next wonders what will happen to the soul of an African child who is christened 'Mike'. Chinua Achebe tells us that he was christened 'Albert'; his soul and sense of humour are none the worse. Like Victoria, he writes, he lost his Albert.[31] The bright new machines to be seen at Koomson's can create the frustrated 'longing' felt by the man's children. Such products also provide a harmless though noisy pleasure even for the poor, but Armah would not let us know it. To say that pleasure in the more expensive trinkets can soon wear thin might seem just the taste of a grossly over-provisioned society. But when the man, who plays with his children and plainly loves them, judges that the heartless Koomson's daughter has been raised to a higher pitch of living by her bicycle, it is hard to agree. Children want more than bicycles. 'But in *The Beautyful Ones Are Not Yet Born* these are trifling matters. Achebe and Soyinka offer more complete and satisfying modern African worlds; but Armah's narrower more painful work is no less African and no less modern.

4 Stories, Themes and Impressions in Recent African Fiction

'Joseph was now a tall youth in a neat uniform of khaki shirt and shorts. He held Sembene Ousmane's novel, *God's Bits of Wood*, in his hands but he was not reading much.'

In the last chapter of Ngugi wa Thiong'o's *Petals of Blood* (1977), Joseph is brooding on strikes and revolution, first at school 'to put to an end the whole prefect system', and afterwards in the world. Sembene Ousmane's *Les bouts de bois de Dieu* (1960) is a Senegalese novel, well worth reading, whose theme is solidarity under oppression. For Joseph it serves as an emblem and, if he reads it, perhaps as a handbook on strikes. Novelists of the last ten years have been increasingly urgent and polemical in presenting the topics which have been most acceptable in the realm of African fiction: politics, education, money, the white man. Others follow *The Beautyful Ones Are Not Yet Born*, of which there are traces in *Petals of Blood*, in creating an impression of poverty without and desperation within. Some lose sight of what a novel is, allowing theme and impression to get the better of the story; and Ngugi's Joseph is reminiscent of many student readers for whom a novel is a prestigious container of relevant themes rather than a compelling narrative in which themes can be questioned. But the best novels are still, without seeming any more old-fashioned in method than in content, stories which put the contemporary world to the test of their authors' observation.

Ngugi's latest volume of essays is *Writers in Politics*. The book argues for African literature in African languages, since 'to choose a language is to choose a world', and European languages have been a distraction to African writers who should be engaged with the peasants and workers in a revolutionary effort. This aim is expressed in the spirit and terms of Fanon; it is the 'struggle against exploitation by an alliance of the imperialist bourgeoisie and the *comprador* bourgeoisie to end all forms of exploitation, oppression and domination'; Ngugi has no doubt that such an end is possible.[1] *Petals of Blood*, written in the same conviction, is a more ideological work than his earlier fiction and it is the novel by which he would wish to be judged as a writer in English. (*Devil on the Cross*, 1982, was first composed in Gikuyu.) Although Marxian formulae and slogans are far less intrusive than in the essays, the book is polemical. Passages in novels where the author argues a case which might have been left to the reader's judgement or inserts facts which might have been kept for an essay can seem inartistic for several good reasons, but in themselves they are, like the excremental imagery favoured by Ngugi and Armah, beyond criticism, given the variety of taste and opinion among readers today. Large, loose, complex novels can accommodate some self-indulgence by the author in pressing opinions and in conveying information which the strictest application of artistic criteria would have eliminated in revision. Balzac is given to asides in which he supplies esoteric facts apparently because he happens to know them; Balzac is so compelling that the reader is scarcely disturbed.

Petals of Blood is none the less a work which confirms D. H. Lawrence's opinion that where a novelist is possessed by an ideology his talent may subvert the argument: 'the novel walks away with the nail'.[2] The hero's father is a devout Presbyterian and a rich conservative, tough with his workers. Ngugi's anger at the thought of such a man coarsens the narrator's irony into sarcasm. 'They the workers nearly all had one thing in common: submission to the Lord. . . . There were of course some who had devilish spirits which drove them to demand higher wages and create trouble on the farm.' (Chapter 2). A few lines later he recounts an incident from the hero Munira's youth in which religious submissiveness is very tactfully observed. After his first sin with 'a bad woman at Kamiritho' Munira fails to confess at church because he fears the faithful will not believe him; instead he makes a match-box-model of the prostitute's house, burns it with cowdung, and is afterwards 'at ease with himself and peaceful in his knowledge of being accepted by the Lord'. During the night a barn takes fire from the smouldering sacrifice and he feels as if his father knows this, which adds 'to his consciousness of guilt'. The transition from the caustic anti-clericalism of the essays to the inquiring imagination of the early novels is striking in that passage, and in many others. Polemical intentions flaw certain sequences, obstructing the author's intentions. But the novel remains very good, and more than just a picture of Kenya today.

Petals of Blood aims to show us Kenya as Balzac aims to show us France. It is often reminiscent of nineteenth-century fiction — English and Russian (the novel was finished in Yalta). It opens in 'present-time' in the manner of a modern detective story. Four characters are visited by police investigating the murders of three prominent brewery directors who have 'helped to build Ilmorog from a tiny nineteenth-century village . . . into a modern industrial town that even generations born after Gagarin and Armstrong will be proud to visit' in the words of the sensational *Daily Mouthpiece* quoted at the end of the first chapter. We are returned to the nineteenth-century village at the start of Chapter 2.

> But all that was twelve years after Godfrey Munira, a thin dust-cloud trailing behind him, first rode a metal horse through Ilmorog to the door of a moss-grown two-roomed house in what was once a schoolyard. He got off and stood still, his right hand akimbo, his left holding the horse, his reddish lined eyes surveying the grey, dry lichen on a once white-ochred wall. Then, unhurriedly, he leaned the metal horse against the wall and, bending down, unclipped loose the trouser bottoms, beat them a little with his hands — a symbolic gesture, since the dust stubbornly clung to them and to his shoes — before moving back a few steps to re-survey the door, the falling-apart walls and the sun-rotted tin roof. Suddenly, determinedly, he strode to the door and tried the handle while pushing the door with his right shoulder. He crashed through into a room full of dead spiders and the wings of flies on cobwebs on all the walls, up to the eaves.
> Another one has come into the village, went the news in Ilmorog. Children spied on him, on his frantic efforts to trim up and weed the place, and they reported everything to the old men and women. He would go away with the wind, said the elderly folk: had there not been others before him? Who would want to settle in this wasteland?

If the iron-horse were a horse we might be in Wessex, Loamshire, or a small town of exile far from Petersburg. The paragraph catches the lonely moment of arrival, set in time against the years which have brought spiders and cobwebs to the abandoned school, and the coming years in which Munira is to cycle through Ilmorog; the quiet decay of the place, and the awkward opening of a door, the children spying and the old folk shaking heads while the stranger trims and weeds — atmosphere is created in a style which is no less effective because it is familiar. Curiosity is stirred as it must be: there is a story behind the question of *who* would come here, and the narrative soon moves further back in time to tell of Munira's failure and retreat to Ilmorog. In the same pages Ngugi begins to place Ilmorog in its Kenyan history. In the fields the women sing of 'another horseman long ago when Ilmorog was truly Ilmorog', sure in their own culture and mocking the new man with a knowledge of how strangers come and go; there is a slow change to be pondered in peace which recalls rural scenes in older novels. But this is a novel of the 1970s and the scene is only twelve years back from the new Ilmorog admired in the astronaut age.

The leisurely description of Munira's arrival, written as though in the confidence of hundreds of leisurely pages to come, follows a first chapter which is as brisk as any thriller. The novel's first sentence is: 'they came for him that Sunday', and the arrests that follow are mostly presented in dialogue. 'It's nothing much Mr Munira. Just routine questioning'. The stories of Ilmorog and its characters' lives are developed, in conventional style but with a contemporary freedom from traditional plot and plain direction, within the framework of a *roman policier*. The combination of genres is unlikely to disconcert many readers, although Eustace Palmer, a fastidious reader, objects that the mystery's solution is melodramatic and 'takes a remarkably serious work back to the level of the detective thriller'.[3] Dickens could make a serious work out of a detective thriller but a Victorian novelist would have been unlikely to juxtapose separate modes in the manner of contemporary 'fabulators'. Ngugi is certainly not impressed by 'fictiveness' but he is not inclined to defer to other peoples' traditional literary decorum, and he knows that their present decorum does not expect it. Introducing Gikuyu and Swahili diction, songs, sayings and lore, he writes, as C. B. Robson's *Ngugi wa Thiong'o* shows in detail, an English which can be vigorously independent within its own world, appropriate to an African novel.[4]

Many passages remind us of Ngugi's affection for Dickens and George Eliot and show how an abrasively progressive novel can still make good use of styles and devices which have worked for over a century. The narrative can move with the assured fluency of Victorian prose: 'But all that was twelve years after Godfrey Munira . . . first rode an iron horse through Ilmorog'; and this power is sometimes lent to the characters. Munira at his gloomiest and the young radical Karega at his most eloquent can be imagined conversing with Jude the Obscure. Some of the English names label their characters more blatantly than would now be likely in a British or American novel except in burlesque: Fraudsham, the Reverend Hallowes Ironmonger. Elsewhere dialogue, and narrative which reflect the thinking of characters who are much less highly educated than the author, are convincingly and at best tenderly done. The children in Munira's primary school discover flowers with petals of blood.

> 'No, you are wrong,' he said, taking the flower. 'This colour is not even red . . . it does not have the fullness of colour of the other one. This one is yellowish red. Now you say it has nothing inside. Look at the stem from which you got it. You see anything?'
> 'Yes,' cried the boys. 'There is a worm — a green worm with several hands or legs.'
> 'Right. This is a worm-eaten flower . . . It cannot bear fruit. That's why we must always kill worms in. . . . A flower can also become this colour if it's prevented from reaching the light.'
> He was pleased with himself. But then the children started asking him awkward questions. Why did things eat each other? Why can't the eaten eat back? Why did God allow this and that to happen? He had never bothered with those kind of questions and to silence them he told them that it was simply a law of nature.

But if this reflects reading of George Eliot or Hardy, it belongs to a different sort of novel. Ngugi would agree with Terry Eagleton's comment on Lukács's praise of critical realism: 'what Lukács is calling for, then, is essentially for the modern age to move forward into the nineteenth century'.[5] His praise of George Eliot in *Writers in Politics* is tempered by a complaint that her 'intellectual and moral conflicts do not arise out of an awareness of a changing world' and he means that her work is not committed to the cause of the proletariat in the manner of socialist realism.[6] The children's posers are not truth in the mouths of babes as they might have been in a Victorian rendering of the scene (or in L. P. Hartley). They are opportunities for Munira, who is not enlightened enough to use them, to give lessons which are taught by the novel as a whole. The flowers, for Ngugi, are symbols of the blooming of independent Kenya and a tribute to the Mau Mau dead; the new nation is rotten with worms and kept from the light of political understanding. In society things eat each other because of the class struggle; and God will not help.

Petals of Blood asserts that Kenya is part of a world changing from post-colonial capitalism to revolutionary socialism. In its 'present-time' Munira is in prison and further imprisoned in religious enthusiasm arising from despair at what capitalism has done to Ilmorog, and expectation of the second coming of Christ. The headings for Parts 2 and 3, 'Toward Bethlehem' and 'To be Born' from Yeats's 'The Second Coming', help us to interpret his religious misconception as a reaction to the advent of a new political age. The workers of Ilmorog are mobilising; the heading for Part 4 is 'Again . . . *La Luta Continua*'. Munira's religious conversation enables Ngugi to attack the present state of the world apocalyptically, and to urge the inadequacy of religion at the same time; incidentally it frees the part of his imagination which is stirred by Biblical language and Christian imagery.

It is a strength of Ngugi's Marxism that he always keeps history in view. He shows Ilmorog as a tiny twentieth-century village which remembers a happier nineteenth century when people herded, and revered the land, until the settlers came; a colonial period ending in armed resistance; and the recent departure of the young people to Nairobi where the new authorities, occupied in business ventures with Western partners, ignore the village as far as they can. The newspaper phrase 'a tiny nineteenth-century village', which is the novel's first reference to the old Ilmorog, indicates the official attitude which the effect of the novel is to repudiate. The blasé education officer under whose authority Munira works in the primary school, and the Member of Parliament who flatters himself that his constituents are 'a happy contented lot' scorn Ilmorog's 'pastoral' appearance, and neglect it because development is so exciting in the cities. When the Trans-Africa Road comes to turn the village into a boom-town the interests of its people are ignored and their condition is worse than before. Ngugi captures the pastoral integrity of the dusty impoverished village proud of its past, which sensible assistance could have improved, and the callous brashness of the New Ilmorog. His case that rural Kenya is a vital part of the country after Uhuru, whose conditions deserve neither dismissal in terms of 'nineteenth-century backwardness', nor unplanned conversion into a copy of a twentieth-century 'new town', makes his story most persuasive. A truly contemporary version of the place would not resemble the deserted village or the new town. But even readers who are already sympathetic towards it may be disturbed by the political alternative which the novel proposes, because Ngugi is so truthful in showing how his ruthless managerial characters outmanoeuvre the vulnerable, decent characters of whom they take advantage.

Munira twice appeals to his education officer, Mr Mzigo, for assistant teachers. Being without a car, he cycles to town on the iron-horse. Unwilling to help, Mzigo implies on the first visit that rural life and honest poverty may have compensations:

> Do you have good roads? You know these damned cars — a real nuisance, the true black man's burden — believe me, Mr eeh, eeh, — Munira — a bicycle is so much less trouble.
>
> (Chapter 2)

Many think so in London, and in some African cities, but Mzigo's design is transparent. He is rightly very sure of himself on his own ground. Munira has been so harassed by lorries on the bush roads — 'let the cycle suckle the udder of the lorry' — that he is angered by the official 'pomposity' and comforted by thoughts of bucolic Ilmorog. Guillaume Oyônô-Mbia has ridiculed the simpler tactics of bureaucratic self-defence. His villagers picture official life naïvely: you sit in a room breathing European air which comes out of a metal box, and you tell the people who are queueing outside to come back next month. There are subtler methods to combat Acting Headmasters who have to be admitted, and Munira has already been put in his place. In this scene we share the character's impressions of the 'specklessly' clean office with neat in-tray and out-tray signalling efficiency, three 'enormous' inkwells signifying the size of the tasks and responsibilities undertaken, and a map on the wall which signifies administrative power: there Munira's school, and the fields in which he gallops his horse in pursuit of reluctant pupils, are reduced to a drawing-pin. Appeased with offerings of chalk and writing books, and given permission to recruit for himself, he goes home. Like Munira one is less frightened in such places than made to feel the futility of opposition. Next time Mzigo fends his visitor off with simple but effective ruses. He speaks again of the roads and 'these damned cars'. 'Damned' is slyly defensive; it speaks of Mzigo's normal sphere among equals, all inconvenienced by fleets of cars; and it is a word the teacher cannot use back. Then something better than chalk is offered:

'I'm sorry not to have been to your school yet: but I'll be coming shortly. Any good roads yet? I dont need to tell you about these damned cars. Anything to wet my throat? By the way, congratulations. You were before only an Acting Headmaster. It's now confirmed. You are the new Headmaster of Ilmorog Full Primary School. Congratulations again.'
'I am touched by the honour', Munira said, actually thrilled inside.
'It's nothing,' said Mzigo. 'Your own dedication.'
'But I could do with a few more teachers. At least one . . .'
'Teachers?' (Chapter 5)

Invited, as he is leaving, to join Ilmorog's MP in a cultural tea-drinking (which turns out later to be part of a nationwide capitalist plot to induce loyalty) the new Headmaster leaves 'glowing with pride'. 'Ilmorog had given him greatness. Hoyee!' The need for new teachers is forgotten. Munira is a mild, unsuccessful, lonely man, nervous of people and afraid of his pious, powerful father. He is very susceptible to the gifts of status which please most people. It is in the official's casual manipulation of the small man's self-esteem by means of skill with voice and tone that Ngugi is most effective. Harping on 'any good roads yet?' — the good road is a symbol of modernity throughout Africa — is more a ploy than lazy-mindedness. Mzigo seems more human, and harmless, because of his tag; he is quaint, something of a 'character'. Used to the phrase, one smiles at him. He is matey, 'anything to wet my throat?'; a colleague, 'Congratulations'; and a superior who speaks performatively, 'you are the new Headmaster'. The only real moment of the interview is when he says 'Teachers?' Its shock has been carefully cushioned. Mzigo is deft without glibness; his is a dry not an oily art; otherwise we might have despised Munira. As it is we see that he is a gull but we cannot quite feel superior. Who in his position would altogether resist 'new' in 'the new Headmaster', which makes Munira feel an illusion of change?

Mention of Ilmorog's MP prepares for the scenes in which his constituents confront Mr Nderi wa Riera in Nairobi, in Chapter 6. Drought reduces the village to desperation, and its people trek to the capital to plead with their 'son'. Nderi is not a Kenyan version of Achebe's Nanga: he lacks the Chief's infectious fun and high spirits, and he is almost past troubling himself with the role of 'son', although 'there was a time when Nderi wa Riera was truly a man of the people'. Nowadays he is busy with directorships in foreign-owned companies, and he banks on Ilmorog's remoteness and bushiness to let him prosper in peace. He has become increasingly 'sensible' about the people's need to face the realities of capital investment for development, and although he champions 'Black authenticity', denouncing Christian names and blond wigs, Ngugi sees this as a good cause borrowed to camouflage a smart selfish politician's betrayal of fundamental black interests. Nderi sees in the presence of Munira and his friends nothing but a plot to embarrass him. Because he miscalculates, this is to be one of his failures. When he goes out to address the throng he dissipates the initial goodwill by talking of self-help and traditional songs to people who have been starving; when stones are thrown he fetches the police to arrest the ring-leaders. A noble communist lawyer saves the Ilmorogians with a fine court performance; charitable gifts are followed by promises of development schemes. Nursing his annoyance Nderi plans revenge on his enemy the lawyer. The satire is pungent, if predictable; those who can read *Petals of Blood* can presumably read the Nderis of this world in their broad outlines. But Ngugi is especially good at showing how close, in what is for Nderi an impossible situation, the politician can come to charming intelligent but uneducated characters.

> 'My name is Nderi wa Riera.'
> 'We know you.'
> 'I used to be called David Samuel. But I asked myself: why should we abandon our names for these foreign ones? Ha! ha! ha! I know a friend, black as the soot on a cooking pot, who calls himself Winterbottom.'

There are many such small tributes to Achebe as this borrowing by Nderi. The needless introduction is a hook for the routine display of African integrity which looks flimsy to the reader but impresses the old Ilmorog farmer Njuguna, a delegate with Munira; he has not read *Arrow of God*. '"This was indeed a sensible man in Parliament", he thought'. That is after the brave solidarity on the road, the saddest moment in the eighty-page account of the march to Nairobi although far from the most painful for the marchers. Mzigo exemplifies the deftness of an administrator who knows his country schoolmaster. Nderi does not really look at his constituents because they can be so easily managed with familiar routines, and because he automatically suspects a conspiracy by his parliamentary rivals. Nderi shows the crudeness of power on a large scale.

The Trans-Africa Road which transforms Ilmorog, and which should have brought unity to Africa, becomes a destroyer — an agent of the foreign investors who mean to exploit the access it offers them. In overcoming the weakness of the past which was lack of communications, the road removes what is now the only defence for such villages as Ilmorog against the designs of capitalism. In Chapter 11, which describes the development, we are meant to remember Mzigo's phrase, 'any good roads yet?'; the effect is trenchantly ironic. Roadless Ilmorog was 'nineteenth century'. On the Trans-Africa Road it suddenly turns 'twentieth', or ('generations after Gagarin') 'twenty-first' century, and is even more displaced from its claims on the present. What happens is neatly figured in the fate of the donkey belonging to Abdulla the lame trader. Old Ilmorog has been suspicious of this unfamiliar animal and the people are tempted to sacrifice it during the drought, but the donkey is essential to Abdulla as his second leg. When an aeroplane surveying for the road makes a forced landing in the donkey's field the winged horse proves fatal where village superstition was merciful. The donkey turned out to be a modest, useful addition to Ilmorog which could have used more such improvements, however disturbing at first. But its death represents modern Nairobi's impatience with what is really valuable to people. After good service on the march, the donkey was impounded for fouling a street in the capital. It is finally sacrificed to the road and the oil companies who have other means of transport while the Ilmorog people live in a shanty quarter of the new town, known as New Jerusalem.

New Ilmorog is no New Jerusalem (Blake, at whose 'Sick Rose' the worm-eaten petals hint, is quoted at the head of Parts 2 and 3) and it is more dreadful than the old Jerusalem which the Biblically minded Ngugi perhaps has in mind in associating the donkey with sacrifice. Foreign-based banks and Nairobi businessmen own the new buildings and factories. The final sections of the novel give a clear picture of the usual vulgar and inhuman consequences of rapid industrialisation. The brewery manufactures for local consumption a noxious spirit, Theng' eta, named after a traditional drink which gave men visions and barren women babies. The true Ilmorog is impoverished. The heroine Wanja who had been a brave and enterprising, although vengeful, girl throughout the story, is demoralised when her mother dies of grief after the confiscation of her land, and her own bar is closed down. She returns to prostitution, which she had renounced to come to Ilmorog, and becomes rich, as anyone can, it seems, who is bright and unscrupulous. The songs of old Kenya are replaced by the harlot's cry. The young Karega, who has been Munira's assistant at the school, sees in modern socialism a way to restore older and healthier systems of production. Convincing himself that he must try to save Karega from Wanja, Munira sets fire to her brothel where Mzigo and two other directors of the brewery are killed. Meanwhile the workers, roused by Karega, are chanting slogans, ready to strike.

In all this the novel exposes the recalcitrant realities behind Nderi's facile version of a 'free enterprise' philosophy. Considering the novel as, among other things, a political analysis, a 1970s reader might have been reminded of Amadi's remarks (quoted above) about the need for gradual re-education in social discipline after the colonial turmoil, because although Ngugi provides vivid portraits of villains who represent 'this system' and of heroes (such as the lawyer, Karega) who resist it, the scheme of his argument is often so simplified that it defeats its own ends. Ngugi's great narrative power, in the events which follow the marchers' arrival in Nairobi for example, fails to compensate for his evident design on us in representing whole social categories by individual samples. The marchers, exhausted and needing help for a sick child, call on a rich Nairobi clergyman who is as hypocritical and unhelpful as any bad parson in Trollope, Dickens, or Richard Graves. But whereas their satirical targets are to be seen in relation to an idea of the true pastor, Ngugi's people decide to avoid all clergymen in future and he implies that all African clergymen are now rogues, which any reader – however unsympathetic to Christianity – knows to be untrue. At another house Munira and his friends are locked up while the capitalist householder Kimeria, whom Wanja has known before, forces her to submit to him by threatening to call the police. (Kimeria is to be one of Munira's victims at the end.) Only when the group find a communist lawyer are they properly received. Even a responsible sermon (and that genre has certainly influenced Ngugi) which reallocated the roles would hardly risk such blatancy of purpose. The most anti-clerical socialist might be provoked into remembering a capitalist or a clergyman with imagination or generosity or an eye for real need. This section of the book could be used to illustrate Lawrence's point that realism in novels requires a fairness to experience if the reader is to be persuaded at all. Neo-Marxist criticism has recognised that. Even more damaging to the novel's political case is Ngugi's skill in portraying the tenacious pursuit of power in his 'worms' (Mzigo, Nderi and others). There is nothing to indicate why they should not flourish, and the decent characters be obliged to oppose them, under a different system. Mzigo's bland managerial flair and Nderi's deployment of stale party rhetoric belong to men who will profit from whatever system is there. But a novelist can do more than show what such people are like; he can show the false assumptions by which they and (as is to be seen in Nuruddin Farah's fiction) their ideological opponents elsewhere in Africa modernise their country and themselves. The bad roads keep Mzigo away from Wanja's bar, where he might have 'wet his throat' among Kenyans less 'modern' than those at his golf club, until it is too late to see what Ilmorog in the 1960s has really been. He is as sadly trapped in his speckless office as Nderi, once a darts player and man of the people, is in his directorships. Ngugi does show, although he does not fully analyse, where the outlook of such characters is mistaken in his treatment of their schooling — the subject he knows best.

A major theme of *Writers in Politics* is the need to Africanise Kenyan education: African languages and literature, history and culture must come first; English and studies of the world situation should proceed from there. Ngugi sometimes overstates: 'that the central taproot of his [the European] pupil's cultural nourishment should lie deep in his native soil is taken for granted. This ABC of education is followed in most societies because it is demanded by the practice and the experience of living and growing.'[7] Putting the case like this reminds us that the central taproot of the best

English education over the centuries has lain in the native soil of Italy and Greece. But it is true that colonial education presented English language and literature as though they were the equivalent for Africans of classical studies in Europe, as the basis of civilisation rather than a modern culture in a different part of the world. In Francophone colonies French culture was imposed with even greater confidence in its classical status. In the circumstances of Africa after Independence, African culture taught by Africans must have a central place in the humanities, and the teaching of African literature is valuable in combating the false assumption to which students are constantly exposed that the real modern world is elsewhere, and that Africans must imitate other peoples' modernity. 'Literature and Society', the first essay in *Writers and Politics* has two epigraphs, of which the second is from Fanon's lines beginning, 'If we want to turn Africa into a new Europe'. The first is from Mao Tse-Tung: 'ignorant of their country, some people can relate tales of ancient Greece and other foreign lands'. Ancient Greece is a foreign land for everyone. The disservice of foreign teachers in Africa has been in presenting the tales of their own lands as though they are to Africa what ancient Greece has been to Europe.

In *Petals of Blood* education is second only to politics, and it is treated as a topic. In Ngugi and in most African fiction, argument about education has counted for more than exploring how schooling is experienced. Even in Dickens, who can remember so well what it is like to be at school, there is, as John Carey has recently demonstrated, a tendency for the author to 'forget', so that although we may believe in Doctor Blimber's school we do not believe in little Paul Dombey.[8] Education in fiction might be more entertaining and revealing if novels were written by children. The topic is partly treated through prolonged reminiscences of schooldays at the prestigious Siriani, an establishment which appeared in earlier novels, from which Munira and Karega have been expelled for taking part in protests. Eustace Palmer summarises Ngugi's approach accurately:

> The purpose and content of imperialist education is throughly scrutinised and its relevance to the African situation questioned. It is presented as an oppressive, irrelevant, and racialist system obviously geared towards perpetuating white domination and instilling into the pupils a respect for British institutions and

attitudes. Cambridge Fraudsham, the eccentric headmaster who terrorises his pupils and eventually provokes student riots, is the embodiment of this educational process. But his successor Chui, an African who in his student days has been victimised by the oppressive imperialist system and might therefore have been expected to effect changes, turns out to be more British in his attitudes and policies than Fraudsham himself.[9]

The pupils rebel against Chui and he puts down the rebellion. Student insurgency has a strong appeal to Ngugi's imagination and emotions. The thought of ending the prefect system for ever stirs him; and he seems to condone ending classes in English grammar. Professor Palmer, who has perhaps suffered from an over-enthusiastic spirit of revolt among his own students, is judiciously reproachful of that.[10] Teaching good English in a country where English is needed (these rebellions took place thirty years ago) is arguably less imperialistic than neglecting to do so. Eustace Palmer ends by objecting that Karega, as a student leader, did not know what the pupils really wanted, and that 'Ngugi ought to know'.

Palmer is right; Ngugi has misrepresented the case against imperialism's cultural front. But critic and novelist fail to see what was wrong. That Fraudsham terrorises his pupils (cold showers at five, and so on) is only to be expected. A British schoolmaster of Fraudsham's type — which he represents at its most clownish and narrow-minded — would have been very likely to do so, in Kenya or in England. That he and his African successor expect good English teaching is only their duty. Eliciting respect, although not veneration, for British institutions and attitudes is presumably not wrong in itself, in an English or a Kenyan headmaster. (There can be few more generous or moving tributes to France in modern literature than that from Camara Laye, no friend to imperialism, in the Introduction to his last book.)[11] But Fraudsham and Chui are classical-minded, with British civilisation in the place of the classics; they teach an alien culture as though it were the necessary foundation for the Kenya in which their pupils are to be leading citizens, and this is imperialism. When challenged by his pupils (in Chapter 6) Chui quotes them words of authority:

> . . . O, when degree is shak'd
> Which is the ladder to all high designs,

> The enterprise is sick! How could communities,
> Degrees in schools and brotherhoods in cities,
> Peaceful commerce from dividable shores,
> The primogenity and due of birth,
> Prerogative of age, crowns, sceptres, laurels,
> But by degree, stand in authentic place?
> Take but degree away, untune that string,
> And hark, what discord follows!

'These', says the Headmaster, 'are the words of a great writer'. They are the views of Ulysses, of course, rather than those of 'a great English poet', although Shakespeare certainly feared riots, knowing what commonly happens to writers ('tear him for his bad verses'). The opinion expressed was only one of many available options in the Renaissance. To quote it with the semi-mystical authority of Shakespeare as an eternal verity is preposterous when teaching young Africans in the 1940s, and Ngugi's anger at the use of English lore as a sure guide to truth appears in other scenes. Mzigo tells Munira the story of Robert the Bruce and his spider, urging him to return to his kingdom of Ilmorog school in the same spirit of independent resolve. That is one of the truly funny moments in a gloomy book. This use of what Shakespeare, looking down on the Middle Ages, called 'base authority' continues today throughout the world and probably supplies a natural need. Its practice in Africa, with tags and tales taken out of their contexts in another culture, would be laughable except that it is symptomatic of the essential falsehood: that a supposed chasm in African history, between the Middle Ages or the Stone Age and today, must be filled in with European experience. Chui should have quoted *Troilus and Cressida* in its proper place, the class on Shakespeare. Had Ngugi made this plainer he might have allowed himself to create more interesting or more sympathetic characters than Fraudsham and Chui, and so have strengthened his analysis of where the teachers of his own youth misunderstood their role. It would have been possible to show the necessity for Africans to study Africa first, without provoking objections from any sensible reader.

Munira is one of the novel's strengths. As Palmer and others have pointed out he has evolved from characters in the earlier novels, Njoroge (*Weep Not, Child*), Waiyaki (*The River Between*) and Mugo (*A Grain of Wheat*). As a man who feels defeated, after expulsion from school, domination by his father, and general fear of the world, he goes to teach in a lonely school, as many do, for peace, purpose, and a small safely circumscribed authority. Inside the walls of his classroom he is sure of himself; he fears the open fields, where the bolder Wanja is at home. His lusty affair with her, and his jealous meanness when Karega takes her from him, are compatible in his complex personality with the religious obsession which overtakes him, and with his humane decency. The passage already quoted in which he relaxes while confidently instructing the children, and then panics when their questions are out of his reach, is part of the touching, true picture of a man who is in his entire approach to life a teacher out of his depth. Thoughtful but half-educated, hurt into frailty but admiring the strong, and baffled by events in the new state of the country, he is exactly the man to shrink into fundamentalism, watching for signs of the Last Days because the present days are beyond him. Perhaps he burns down Wanja's house because he burned the matchbox-house long ago: or perhaps not. We have liked and grieved for him. In a 'tiny nineteenth-century village' he might have learned to grow; he is destroyed in Ilmorog. Through his fate Ngugi achieves his most forceful indictment of developments in Kenya, and also one of the best pictures of a schoolmaster in recent literature.

Elsewhere in East Africa there is bewilderment in different circumstances.

> 'Gulag or no, you are doing well. I don't see why it is you who puts a neck out. Why you? Where are the others? Why must you carry the standard? Why must you be its bearer?'
> 'I am no bearer of anybody's banner. But I feel humiliated. I feel abused, daily, minutely. A friend of mine is in for anti-Soviet activities. But where are we? What era is this? Is this Africa or is this Stalin's Russia?'

It is the Somali Democratic Republic during the Russian presence. In the Prologue of Nuruddin Farah's *Sweet and Sour Milk* (1979) Soyaan, the second speaker, is dying. Soyaan is an economic adviser to the Presidency and a dissident, the cause of whose sudden death from 'complications' is not to be too closely inquired about. The novel is, like *Petals of Blood*, an attack on foreign interference in an African country, and as in Ngugi the fraudulence of the African stooges is methodically demonstrated. In this case they are directing a reign of terror, under cover of socialist slogans, while serving the interest of an outside power. The novel is not anti-socialist − the regime is seen as fascist; but it is anti-Soviet. The irrelevance of Western and Eastern concepts to Somalian or African progress is frequently asserted by the more thoughtful characters, and the novel is a plea for modern Somalia to develop itself. If Ngugi protests in effect against the supposition that Kenya is in the situation of England in the 1830s, Farah protests explicitly against the reduction of Somalia to a state resembling Stalinist Russia.

A *Guardian* reviewer (quoted in the Heinemann blurb) commented that Farah can be effective 'while moving on an ordinary story', as though that were remarkable today. Farah's novel has a story in which Soyaan's twin Loyaan investigates his brother's recent life and subversive activities, his death, and the use which is made of his name afterwards. Loyaan is told that 'Soyaan is from this day onwards state property and will be treated as such' (in Chapter 7). Soyaan dies repeating Loyaan's name, but it is officially given out that his last words were LABOUR IS HONOUR AND THERE IS NO GENERAL BUT THE GENERAL. His life is recreated, in Orwellian fashion, as that of a hero of the revolution, while the authorities try to trace his disloyal writings. Ironies are heavy throughout: the East Germans are said to have built an underground 'super-prison' as 'aid'. At the end Loyaan is to be deported, perhaps to go as a diplomat, via Moscow, to Eastern Europe. The last line brings a knock on his door.

Although the main purpose is to portray this species of political corruption, the novel is most interesting in its treatment of education, which is a related topic since the regime must try to re-educate an Islamic population in an alien doctrine. 'There is no general but the general', perverts the Islamic profession of faith, and there are many such exploitations of the incongruity of an 'Islamic Marxist−Leninist state'. Schoolchildren sing praise-songs to the general and old men mingle them with their prayers. The epigraph for Part 2 is from Wilhelm Reich: 'in the figure of the father the authoritarian state has its representative in every family'. The authoritarian father of traditional Somalia is a model for the head of state; his power rests on tribal consent and he fears tribal leaders of his own generation more than young intellectuals. One of the novel's ironies is familiar from novels satirical of capitalist abuses: that the cause of 'progress' is most profitable to people who have little schooling.

The twins' father Keynaan supports the general's scheme to rewrite his son's history. Education has caused a startling divergence in outlook between father and sons. The difference and conflict is figured in an incident from childhood. The twins possessed a ball which they have illustrated 'from their fantasies' as a globe without frontiers; it is the round world they have learned about at school, and the world as they dream of it. Their father had been taught that the world is flat, and he resents their new idea; when he finds his sons quarrelling over the ball he punctures it and tears it in two. 'I don't want you to believe everything these whites teach you. I want you simply to get some kind of certificate so that you can get jobs as clerks with the government. Just that.' Discussing their view of their father Soyaan has said, Loyaan remembers, that to know the world to be round gives 'a perspective of an inclusive nature − more global; our views are "rounder"' (Chapter 6). They think Keynaan's outlook 'exclusive' and as dull as his flat world. He needs flatness for his conception of God as a 'towering mountain' before which man is powerless, and of himself in the family as the 'Grand Patriarch'. That is a world-view in which the general is acceptable; in the twins' he is not.

A consequence of Keynaan's view of the universe is that he despises and frequently beats his wives and children. Women, he teaches the twins, are for sex and childbearing, and nothing more. Their new idea cannot be torn in two, however, and they oppose him by educating their younger sister. True to their fantasy globe they tell her stories from China, India (Tagore), Iceland (sagas), and Arabia (the *Nights*). 'They fed her small brain on figures round, complete and open ended. . . . She was like them − except she was a girl. *The world is an egg and it awaits your breaking it*' (Chapter 7). Beydan, second wife to Keynaan, had no illustrated ball as a child, Loyaan reflects, and so no world to dream of. The plight of women in Somalia was the subject of Farah's first novel *From A Crooked Rib*, and the manner in which traditional assumptions among women obstruct their emancipation is a theme of this. Loyaan prefers Koranic teaching, which is more enlightened in regard to women's rights, to his father's conventional rural prejudices: the general, it is noted, disregards the Koran, neglecting the rights even of his equals. But Soyaan's child is Marco, born to an Italian–Somali, Margaritta; and the twins' mother Oumman reacts flatly: 'I don't want Soyaan's name linked with that Christian' (Chapter 4). 'Marco': 'now what kind of a Muslim name is that?' Loyaan coaxes her into a 'rounder' tolerance: Margaritta chose the name, and a mother is more to a child than a father — she has always said so. His mother is soothed, and she ends by smiling at the name Margaritta.

Such happier moments are rare. Brooding on Prague and Budapest, Loyaan decides that if the world is round it is 'awaiting a hand to break it in half like a rubber ball'. Margaritta is writing a thesis on National Security Services in Africa and South America, for the University of Rome. She oversimplifies in conversation: 'Africa: a text book reproduction of European values and Western thinking'; and 'we see Africa "taken back" to an era she has lived through before.' (Chapter 8) In the novel we see a new era in which technically up-to-date security service methods are supervised by foreigners while illiterates fill the ranks in a system of oral reporting which has reminded Soyaan of Dionysius of Syracuse, whose prisoners were kept in a cave which 'whispered' their secrets by a trick of acoustics, and served as an 'ear' for the tyrant. The fears of an autocrat are the same in ancient Sicily or modern Somalia, but security methods change. The advantage of the general's oral method, his foreign advisers have shown him, is that no files need be kept. It is the incongruity of the new situation which the general exploits. A sense of incongruity inspired the title of Soyaan's secret 'memorandum' on the security system, 'Dionysius's Ear'.

Incongruity is kept in mind because the novel's title is reinforced by short prose-poems at the chapter heads, in many of which an infant denied mother's milk is feeding on poisons. How is a child, Loyaan wonders, to be nourished today? Colonial education provided sour with sweet milk. At school where the twins learned of a round world they were also taught they they 'had no history', but were brought into the world by Arab and later by Italian intervention. Trained in Italy for a modern role, Loyaan has become a dentist; but since bad teeth are unknown in Somalia he will have to wait until development has spoilt the nation's diet before he can be useful. The general does not fear the young, Keynaan tells his son, because they have 'no ideology' to fight for. Nuruddin Farah does not endorse that view as Ngugi would have wanted. Loyaan is baffled. Farah claims to have been influenced by Joyce. The narrative follows Loyaan's thoughts and sensations, if not in a Joycean stream of consciousness at times with an artful intimacy. But main points are plainly made:

> *What am I? Who am I? Whom am I dealing with? What century is this? Of what era must I partake fully, actively?* Must he fully and actively belong to this century of technology, of SAMs, MIGs and satellites and KGBs and CIA espionage networks, or to one of Beydans and Qummans, one of wizardry and witchcraft and hair-burning rites of sorcery? (Chapter 10)

He remembers the quip, which he attributes to Clemenceau, that America passed directly from barbarism to decadence, and he wonders if that could be said of Africa, or of other parts of the Third World. Then, in a passage characteristically sensitive to the sufferings and stamina of ordinary lives, he looks at Beydan pregnant and worn by a hard life, and he dismisses the sophistry. It is not 'a question of a generation linking or dividing persons in this continent', but of what cultural 'strands' actually reach the individual: 'a question of how cultural discontinuities had woven Solomonic arabesques of difference between any two persons'. It is because the humbler characters, the women especially, are so tenderly observed that Loyaan's rejection of the nonsense about 'barbarism and decadence' is effective. Those terms may best be applied to elements which are irrelevant to most people's lives. Beydan dies in childbirth, and Loyaan awaits deportation; Beydan's baby is named at the end, Soyaan. *Sweet and Sour Milk* offers him only frail hope of a change for the better, in the underground resistance to 'any superpower' which his father supported. But the last scene in which the women, including Margaritta, attend to the child and Keynaan offers the evening prayers — figures dignified because they are now intimately familiar — persuades us before the knock on the door of the unhelpfulness of superpowers (the Russians had gone when the novel was written) in the present state of Somalia.

Ngugi and Farah impress and disturb by the hurt sense of deprivation in their descriptions of ordinary African life and this sharpens their satire on the irresponsible exercise of power. Some novels of the 1970s are devoted to scenes of poverty. Meja Mwangi's first novel *Kill Me Quick* tells of the misfortunes of two unemployed youths for whom there are no prospects in modern Kenya. His second *Carcase for Hounds* is a story of the Kenyan Emergency. *Going Down River Road* which followed in 1976 could only be read as a novel about poverty. Mwangi records the squalor of cheap lodgings, poor eating-houses, bars, dance halls, brothels, and the conditions of life at a building site where most of the characters work.

> There is something malignant about shanty huts. They go up in smoke at dawn, spring to life again by twilight. One just cannot keep them down. The Council knows this. Char them as many times as you like and they mushroom back just as many times. Sticks, wire, paper and iron sheets is all it takes. The shanty house is reborn, maybe a bit frail, but quite potent and once again a health hasard. (Chapter 19)

The burning of the huts (at the close of Chapter 18) and their reconstruction next day is told with a calmness which reflects the residents' perseverance, and capacity for good humour. Council 'charrings' are treated almost as a game because prompt action can repair the damage. At work and about the city there is no scope for initiative among labourers, and the result is demoralisation. Daily routine involves feuds and brawls; drink, drugs, and girls take most of the workers' pay, although some has to be sent to wives in the country to prevent their coming into town. By an ironic ploy which is no less well justified because it is obvious, the multi-storey building under construction is to be called 'Development House'. Mwangi's English rendering of the dialogue, which mixes British and American slang and bawdy, is exactly right: as inanely coarse as the characters' circumstances. Foul language in the narrative reflects the characters' speech and so does the brisk, very simple present-tense narration full of physical impressions:

> Onesmus wallows in the dust, trying to get up. Ben stamps on the fleshy belly, slips and stands on the dust. They roll under and out of the truck tearing and bashing at each other. Ben frees himself from the other's vice grip and thumps him on the mouth. Onesmus gasps. The other hands applaud. One deems it a noble idea to douse the battling snarling bulldogs with a bucketful of water. (Chapter 9)

The odd words 'deems' and 'noble' do not belong to any identifiable narrative voice; they might be Ben's. Such a description almost descends to the lowest kind of popular writing. But there is no hint of excitement: fighting in the dirt seems futile beyond comment. Without nuance, the writing shows the figures with a bare realism sometimes achieved in the present-day cinema. Social criticism throughout is confined to Ben's reactions and those of his friends, and is otherwise implicit. The Council, the rich, the police, Indians and whites, are 'bastards'; but, in this lower depth, so is everyone except 'buddies'.

No attempt is made to attract sympathy for the characters except in the implication that they have been brutalised by their way of life. Ben, the central figure, is boorish and more a victim of his own folly than of 'society'. A former lieutenant, he has been cashiered after selling a mortar to a criminal gang. This incident is one of many in which we feel the absence of guidance from a narrator. A gangster talks the young officer into selling a gun:

> Ben shook his head sadly. 'It's all so easy to say it. But the damned thing is in the armoury.' He shook his head almost regretfully. 'The place is guarded day and night.'
>
> Mbugua sipped his drink, and fiddled carelessly with the trump card. 'You go on tactical exercises', he dropped, his mouth still. The devil had thought up everything. Except a few serious points.

The only serious point that occurs to him is that he does not go on exercises alone; Mbugua explains that he can bribe his platoon. This idea gradually sinks in. The lieutenant is so slow-witted, here and throughout the story, that he can hardly be held responsible for his actions. His personality is no more attractive. He is a womaniser and a misogynist, aggressive and spineless. He takes charge of his girl's young son when she abandons them, but this is a grudging, passive undertaking, and he is unfit to look after the child. Ben is in every sense a poor man.

The novel cannot be read as a moral work, or a story with characters. Incidents are connected but their banality and the participants' lack of character are what the author means to show. His point of view is set within a milieu where there is almost no moral consciousness, or even respect for life: lorry drivers are willing to 'run people over' for a small fee. African culture has been destroyed here; hospitality is barely recognised; women and children are a nuisance. *Going Down River Road* deprives itself of many of fiction's richest resources but relies on one most effectively: it is realistic. In some of the most sinister passages the infant 'Baby' is seen to be growing into a teenage criminal, through insult and neglect. An African magazine quoted in the publisher's advertisement says that 'our time and place is what this novel is all about': it could almost have been set in a European or American city because development in Nairobi has reduced Mwangi's people to an alien kind of poverty. This is and ought not to be a part of contemporary Africa.

Conditions are worse in the cities of South Africa, and are often said to be unpropitious for creative writers — they certainly are in that so many are banned, imprisoned or exiled. Nadine Gordimer, quoted in the next chapter, has noted how hard it is to imagine life across the colour-line and how hard to avoid producing fictional propaganda. Alex La Guma has overcome both difficulties. His work is justly praised in Adrian Roscoe's *Uhuru's Fire: African Literature East to South* (1977). Acknowledging him as one of the finest living writers in English, Roscoe praises the short stories of *A Walk in the Night* above his novels, because La Guma's ability is 'to choose a core idea or situation and work it out in the tightest, most organic way'.[12] The short novel *Time of the Butcherbird* published after Roscoe's book, in 1979, shows commitment arising from broad sympathy, an artist's control of one complex situation, and writing of high quality.

Up-country in South Africa the salesman Edgar Stopes is obliged to spend two nights in 'a bloody one-horse town' while waiting for his car to be repaired. The garage will be closed tomorrow like every other business because the Dominee is to hold a special service to pray for an end to the drought. Hannes Meulen, a parliamentary candidate from a long-established farming family of the district, is also staying in the town. Shilling Murile has arrived, after years in prison, meaning to kill Meulen in vengeance for his death brother; Meulen and a crony tied up Shilling and Timi Murile — a pair of 'baboons' — one night and Timi died in his bonds; Shilling assaulted the crony and was jailed, while Meulen was fined. Chief Hlangeni's sister, the indomitable Mma-Tau, is organising opposition among the people who are due to be transported to a Bantustan to clear the way for a mine. The

English Stopes spars in conversation with the Afrikaaner Meulen. The Dominee prays and preaches. Mma Tau sends the sheep to the hills; her people stone the police, and follow. Shilling Murile kills Meulen and Stopes who chances to be there. In the city the people are marching: they too sense the time of the butcherbird. On a smaller scale than Ngugi, La Guma surveys the background through memories and reminiscence, and sets the present violence against the history of war in South Africa. His sympathy is with the black community, but he observes the urban English and the rural Afrikaaners with more pity and curiosity than anger. La Guma offers a determined version of things to come: the angry young ex-prisoner shoots the Afrikaaner with his own weapon, and incidentally the other white man; then he joins his people in the hills. He asserts, too, a present reality against an illusion of fading credibility. There is, as in many South African novels, a strong sense that all communities are sealed off together by their peculiar common history from the rest of the world.

That is an illusion. However widely foreign sanctions are publicised, South Africa is economically unignorable. The outlook of conservative Afrikaaners is not unique, but only in South Africa is it found in the ruling class of a large, powerful nation. The problem of South Africa is that a seemingly anachronistic world-view is a fact determining all contemporary life. South Africa can resist innovation but it is in the world of the 1980s and will in one way or another change accordingly. Meanwhile Hannes Meulen remembers his father who believed his land to be a heritage gained 'through the sacred blood of the ancestors and the prophetic work of God.' 'They had come into this land like the followers of Joshua.' Hannes has joined the national party which is closest to his father's faith, and he tells himself that it is his turn now to hold the land that God has given; the current drought is nothing new. The Dominee sees the drought as a warning. His sermon at the heart of the novel explains that God is punishing corruption in the cities. There are girls who 'defile their purity by wearing revealing clothes'; there are exhibitions of lewd paintings. Serious charges of decadence, drug-taking, and suicide among the young, are jumbled with old-fashioned puritanism. What seems to have shocked the Dominee most is a story of a woman dancing near-naked in a night-club with a snake — 'the symbol of evil'. *'Woe unto Nebo! for it is spoiled.'* Miscegenation, he goes on to say, is the surest spoiler of civilisation; the congregation is impressed.[13]

Such sermons can be heard in North America, and in North Africa, but their conception of a 'true way of life' is usually hemmed in by somewhat more liberal men in power. The Dominee, who feels himself caught between African barbarism and Western decadence, expresses views which help to support the ruling party in South Africa. Stopes looks down on Afrikaaner fanaticism, but he and his circle consider themselves the guardians of civilisation and would agree with Meulen's prospective father-in-law who asks 'what can be done with a people who a century ago had not discovered the wheel?'[14] The Stopeses represent a drab version of the Dominee's decadence; his wife is dreaming at home about how to be rid of him. Chief Hlangeni's people, meanwhile, are stirred by a resolution as old as the Dominee's but more likely to be realised today. They will not be moved from the land of their ancestors. Their ability to adapt in order to succeed is firmly denoted by the fact that they are led by a woman, while the chief feels diminished by white authority, as though clasping 'at the cloak of old dignity that was wearing thin'. The irony that rain-making ceremonies are often cited as evidence of primitivism in tribal custom is not lost on Mma Tao.

Her speeches affirming that 'the land is ours' carry an authority which is corroborated by the old shepherd Mandonele who is associated with the land in passages of evocative writing which dwell on its harshness and 'cruelty'. Older disputes over the land are introduced in recollection. Hannes Meulen's grandfather relives the scene at Spionkop when the Boers fought the British and his friend Karel was killed. He recalls too the killing of a Bushman hunting party during his boyhood, and one dead body in particular: 'the little sightless eyes, a necklace made from pieces of ostrich shell about the limp neck'.[15] These images are fused in memory, so that Karel wears the necklace. Next day Hannes Muelen is killed and La Guma's horrific description of the shattered head recalls the earlier scenes. The final pages contemplate the land geologically; in time the earth moves and changes. The precariousness of all human order is appropriately brought to mind.

What may follow the time of the butcherbird is not Alex La Guma's concern, understandably. The Afrikaaners' outlook is false to the country they govern because they refuse to admit that it is a multi-racial society and not what their ancestors took it to be, a veld given by God to be defended from the British and cleared of

Bushmen. The novels of Ngugi, Farah, and Mwangi show that whatever follows will go wrong if it fails to recognise what South Africa really is and has been. The issues raised by La Guma's story are grave, and to some it would seem impertinent to praise his art. But he orders his people, against the background of the land they fight for with a mixture of pity and design — Coleridge's passion and power — which gives authority. Fictional realism here is a contemporary and urgent art.

5 Outsiders? Nadine Gordimer and Laurens van der Post

'South Africa is a country of black men and not of white men. It has been so; it is so; it will be so.'[1] This is Trollope in *South Africa* (1878) when the white tribes had already been there for over two centuries. There are two emphases in the simplification: one is upon black-and-not-white, and Trollope objected that even alleged 'friends of the negro' would not accept blacks 'in partnership'; the other is on past-present-and-future, and that too remains a slogan with special resonance in South Africa. Both the novels considered in this chapter foresee the impending likelihood of bloody revolution. Verwoerd answered the Trollope view, as Prime Minister in 1953:

> If the native in South Africa today, in any kind of school in existence, is being taught to expect that he will live his adult life under a policy of equal rights, he is making a big mistake. There is no place for him in the European community above the level of certain forms of labour.[2]

It is a claim to control of participation in what the present and near future has to offer, based on the assumption, seen in the last chapter in remarks by characters in Alex La Guma, that modern civilisation belongs to Europeans. To demonstrate that it does not has been a primary objective in the fiction of some of the best white South African novelists including Nadine Gordimer and (in a very different manner) Sir Laurens van der Post.

Protest against oppression among white South African writers is not new, and has not been effective. Thomas Pringle, who published *African Sketches* (1834), a book of stale Augustan verses, made an honourable start to South African literature, and his sentiments are often repeated today in modified language. Nadine Gordimer has observed that 'he foreshadowed the contemporary South African liberal view — obliquely comforting to the white conscience, but none the less true — that any form of slavery degrades oppressor as well as the oppressed':

> The Master, though in luxury's lap he loll
> . . . quakes with secret dread, and shares the hell he makes[3]

In fact he *stated* what has become a contemporary liberal South African view, which is none the less true for having been expressed, in other contexts, by Shakespeare, Milton, Blake, and — closer to Pringle's sort of poetry — by George Crabbe. What is particularly characteristic of contemporary South Africa is the idea that liberal (and Godless) dissent is a form of privilege which obliquely contributes to oppression; in one view it lends respectability to the ruling caste ('there is decent opinion in white South Africa'); in another view, it fosters an illusion that changes of heart can alter political realities. Nadine Gordimer poses another problem for the liberal novelist:

> Black or white, writing in English, Afrikaans, Sesuto, Zulu, even if he successfully shoots the rapids of bannings and/or exile, any writer's attempt to present in South Africa a totality of human experience within his own country is subverted before he sets down a word. As a white man, his fortune may change; the one thing he cannot experience is blackness — with all that implies in South Africa. As a black man, the one thing he cannot experience is whiteness — with all that implies. Each is largely outside the other's experience-potential.[4]

'All that implies' is the key phrase. South Africa (the words mean more and less than a country) is not an internal matter. Given a state which is beyond the effective reach of satire, beyond even the indignation of a black Swift were one to appear, a quiet, persevering, intelligent dissent is the best policy for a white novelist. As robust humanists well aware of the intellectual challenges to their humanism, Nadine Gordimer and van der Post, among others, have composed fiction with a respect for life which reveals the inseparability of lives in modern South Africa. In the novels considered in this chapter each creates a fictional present which relates to the present as they know it. If they write for the outside world, their readers are unlikely to be detached from the worlds they create. Nobody today is far enough away to feel apart from their country.

Nadine Gordimer's *July's People* (1981) is set in a future close to the time of writing, which might have come into being by publication date. Her state of affairs has certainly existed in the mind: South Africa is in revolution. The strikes of 1980 have led to riots, attacks on buildings, marches, occupations, and mass arrests. White Rhodesian Selous Scouts and other experts at containing terrorism fly in from various parts of the continent, and all is quiet for a time. Then there are 'the transformations of myth or religious parable': 'the gunned shopping malls and the blazing, unsold houses of a depressed market . . . the burst mains washing round bodies in their Sunday-morning garb of safari suits, and the heat-guided missiles that struck Boeings carrying those trying to take off from Jan Smutts Airport'.[5] Liberation forces arrive (plausibly or not) from Botswana and Zimbabwe, Zambia, Namibia, and Mozambique. Cubans attack by air. Freedom fighters from Soweto and other townships range the land. America hopes to airlift out its citizens and, perhaps, 'Europeans'. In Johannesburg Bam Smales, an architect, and his wife Maureen possess a yellow shooting-brake or 'bakkie', a second vehicle for holiday outings in the bush. In this they escape, guided by their servant July, with three small children and a few provisions. When the novel begins the Smaleses are hiding in a village hut, among July's people.

The relationship between July and 'his white people' changes and Maureen, brooding about her former servant, decides: 'the present was his; he would arrange the past to suit it'.[6] In fact since July enjoys only a partial emancipation, and since the civil war lasts throughout the novel, it is hard to say whose the present is. The Smaleses' radio reports inconclusive fighting throughout the country; rocket attacks on one side; 'Colonel Mike Hoare', leader of a 'crack commando', on the other. Besides the Afrikaaners and the black insurgents, there are white liberals such as the Smaleses, and black supporters of the regime such as the local Chief; and there are the people of July's village who have little interest in the radio news. In these groups we see what the recent past has been: how they have shared a period within several interpenetrating cultures mutually damaging, in grossly brutal, and in almost imperceptible ways. Any reporter can record the brutality, although few so coolly and concisely. One distinction of this book is the accuracy with which the subtlest corruptions are analysed.

The Smaleses have tried to live by a trust in humane, liberal standards. The usual muddles in their views are quickly exposed by an author who knows all the varieties of suburban radicalism. They have always admired Castro, 'from a safe distance'. They have partly hoped for what the majority of white people consider the worst that can happen. 'They joined political parties and "contact" groups in willingness to slough privilege it was supposed to be their white dog nature to guard with Mirages and tanks; they were not believed'.[7] Emigration would have been a dishonourable 'evasion of the issues', and inconvenient because of exchange controls on their 'growing investments'. They have not learned African languages (or discovered in fifteen years as his employer that July's name is Mwawate) and Maureen regrets (though her husband forbids her to 'fish' in those waters) that it's always those who take it for granted that Blacks are inferior who speak their languages. The Smaleses' only real interests, reasonably, lie within the professional, suburban family life which can be enjoyed with a free conscience in Canada — where they considered transplanting themselves. Nadine Gordimer exposes but does not ridicule the ineffectuality of their earnest, decent principles. Rowland Smith, commenting on her *The Late Bourgeois World*, has written of 'the ghastly fact that humane values themselves are part of South African liberals' privileged status'.[8] The Smaleses have wanted the regime to reform to avoid Civil War; they regret the persistence of 'rural backwardness', including pro-government chiefs; and they want July's domestic services without the shame of degrading him. Their misfortune is only that a South African white suburb is not the middle-class district of some Canadian city, where they would have been at home.

Having escaped instead to July's village they are so far from home that they gradually lose their sense of reality, in a South Africa which alarms them most because it has no use for them as temporary villagers or as friends. At first they are curiosities although their whiteness is a disappointment on close inspection; later, they are accepted as familiar oddities, and Maureen feels that her family are 'their creatures' like their animals. The whites know nothing: the white woman cannot tell leaves a cow would avoid from those which are nourishing for children. Maureen, from whose point of view most of the novel is presented, hopes that July's wife will 'accept her as a woman', and she works among the village women. The result is that she is disliked and resented. Bam misses the usefulness on which he has always depended for self-esteem. July takes over his truck; and although his gun makes him useful for a while, he loses that to a young man who goes to join the fighting. 'A man with nothing', he then loses his nerve. Maureen feels that her real husband has somehow remained 'back there'. She cannot believe in him out of context, and other beliefs are shaken:

> The humane creed (Maureen, like anybody else, regarded her own as definitive) depended on validities staked on a belief in the absolute nature of intimate relationships between human beings. If people don't all experience emotional satisfaction and deprivation in the same way, what claim can there be for equality of need?[9]

Love-making, it now seems, needed the clean privacy of a suburban bedroom; she and Bam abstain in the hut. As she is compelled to slacken hygienic and dietary rules for the children's health and to adjust to raw physical conditions throughout everyday life she tells herself she is in another 'place and time' — that is why, she decides, she cannot read her one novel *I Promessi Sposi* for the usual pleasure of vicarious living in a different time and place. She and Bam become 'her' and 'him' to one another. Away from 'normal life', they cannot relate or keep their personalities intact. July's total dependency on them is reversed by the end.

One is tempted to object that real people would be more likely to unite in adversity: that Nadine Gordimer underestimates the tenacious adaptability shown by the most unheroic individuals; that she understands her characters without loving them (or hating them) and that they therefore lack substance, and leave us indifferent to their fates. There is evidence here for Dennis Brutus's view that she 'lacks warmth, lacks feeling, but can observe with the detachment, with the coldness of a machine' because South Africa 'dehumanises' even the artist.[10] What she coldly observes best in *July's People* makes the shallowness of the Smaleses' relationship more convincing. July has been about their house for fifteen years and Maureen — especially — has accommodated him to her creed which has been meaningless to the servant who has his own criteria of human dignity. In the village she discovers that her courtesy at home throughout the years has been the source of his deepest resentment. He has had his own room, across the yard, where his friends and his mistress have been received (his wife remaining in the country). His privacy has been respected by what is called in another context 'the chivalry of the suburbs', a form of politeness which has not been understood. Now Maureen begins to fear him — it is the first time in her life that she has been afraid of a man. The point is not that he ought to be frightening as a man, but that this mildest of figures — 'You like some cup of tea?' are the words with which he opens the novel — can turn out to be formidable. When July's 'private' life, that which he shares with his people, becomes reality for the Smaleses its long invisible presence among them, ignored for so long, emerges and threatens all their assumptions, undermining their sense of identity. As Maureen confronts her servant their past relationship is constantly reviewed in her mind. It is not that her liberalism is made to seem false, but that his being there has challenged it with implications about the whole of South Africa which she has never understood. Mwawate's has been a real but silent presence which is shattering to her composure when she begins to hear him speak with confidence.

The poverty of human relations in Johannesburg is heard throughout the novel in dialogue. There is a poorer language in South Africa than appears anywhere in the book; Maureen remembers it from childhood in a Western mining region — 'the bastard black *lingua franca* . . . whose vocabulary was limited to orders given by whites and responses made by blacks.'[11] July's English, after so many years, remains pitifully broken. It lacks the vigour and expressiveness of the pidgin which is a living language in West Africa. This is a toneless communication system. July speaks the English of his employers with a very restricted vocabulary, and imperfect control of the verbs. 'Nice' is almost his only word of approval, serving him in scores of contexts where another adjective is wanted. Maureen tactfully chooses to speak his English: 'Why didn't you tell us before, if the polite thing — if it's nice to go and see the chief?'[12] She has always 'translated' her own English into 'concrete vocabulary', avoiding the word 'dignity', not because she thinks he hasn't any, but lest the term be 'beyond his grasp of the language'.[13] Within this servant's register she has tried to preserve his dignity, banning words like 'boy' which are taboo among the educated, but imposing her notion of his dignity on their conversations. He reverts to 'boy' as an undisguiseable technical term for his form of employment, and insults her with a statement of fact when she appeals to their civilised mistress—servant relationship:

> Fifteen years
>   your boy
>   you satisfy

This is 'the one thing there was to say between them that had any meaning'.[14] Having had no relationship with the Smaleses beyond the conventions of 'master'—'boy', and baffled by their distant fastidiousness, July has preferred to confine his English to a set of commands and responses, more highly developed than the 'bastard' tongue of the mines, but not essentially different. The absence of value words (other than his synonymous 'nice' and 'good') is the clue to their neglect of one another. 'Big' is an indicator of prestige which he resorts to in argument with Maureen.

> The master he think for me. But you, you don't think about me, I'm big man, I know for myself what I must do. I'm not thinking all the time for your things, your dog, your cat.[15]

Maureen angrily retorts that Bam is not his *master*, and he asks if he is not to be paid this month, aggravating her annoyance, and concludes, 'Africa people like money'. He intends not an irony but a rejection of all claims except the contractual. Whether a French employer of an African *'boy'* who briskly imposes *le français correct* and never pretends to be more than a demanding but just *patron* is less injurious is beside the question. Maureen's humanism is not absurd in itself although it has never reached July except to demean him.

Ngugi has alleged in *Writers and Politics* that English is the most racialist of European languages used in Africa.[16] One may disagree with his evidence from derogatory senses of *black* which is a pejorative term in some African languages and in French, presumably from association with night rather than with pigmentation. French, especially in *'pied noir'* argot, is more resourceful than English in racial abuse. But many varieties of current English, finely honed by our taste for exclusive linguistic communities – school, regiment, club, set – and for irony, limit its use as an educated *lingua franca* in areas where French (and, it is said, Portuguese) are less rebarbative. Nadine Gordimer catches the polite insult – to go to the other extreme of African society – in her scene on the President's lawn in *A Guest of Honour*. Miss Harrison whom President Mweta has inherited with the former Governor's house ('she did the flower vases, things like that') interrupts a moment of presidential family fun.

> Miss Harrison's clear Englishwoman's voice sailed in: 'Children – I wonder who's been borrowing my *sécateur*? Do *you* know Mangaliso? I should think Mangaliso might know, wouldn't you Telema?'
> The children dropped to earth, cut down.[17]

They cannot catch her tone. Even the President's understanding is tested by his friend Colonel Bray's nuances, and Bray cannot put at ease, for all his goodwill, the young schoolmaster he meets when he starts work as an educational adviser. July could never have talked to the Smaleses.

The novel does not try to persuade us that they are worth talking to. They are quick to detect falsity in the diction and voice of the radio newscasters who speak of 'containing' trouble, in the phrases from 'back there' – 'counter-revolutionary pockets' – which they now find meaningless, and in each other's feebler speech habits. Maureen likes to recall, for example, small pomposities in Bam's cocktail party conversations of the past. Nadine Gordimer is good at producing the shades of playful sarcasm which such a couple need to reduce friction and regulate mutual respect. Irritated with it herself, she complains at one point: 'this kind of repartee belonged to the deviousness natural to suburban life'.[18] But suburban deviousness can be less dull than the Smaleses' conversation – in which catastrophe fails, in the whole novel, to produce one joke, although a thin self parody is natural to them:

> 'I used to think, one day I'd like to see where he lived, to make the trip home with him. I knew it would never come off.'
> 'No . . . the sort of thing that sounds fun . . . it was pretty impossible, then.'
> 'In that way.' In her pause he said nothing. 'You know.

Combining it with a shooting trip for you. In the children's holidays. Bringing all the camping stuff. The portable fridge. What'd I imagine?'. . . .
'Walking in here with presents for them, all lined up clapping their hands together in greeting. Telling the kids, this is *his* home, this is how he lives, see how cleverly July builds houses for himself.'[19]

Hers is a weary, defeated self-satire, conscious of how fifteen years have burdened them with July and July with them. If it offers no prospect of a happier coexistence — July's people have been lucky to escape the campers — it concentrates in its desolate tone the burden of the whole novel, that their smart suburban villa and his home have never really been apart, for all the pretence.

Another novelist might have seen a crude justice in the Smaleses' having to learn what poverty is like, or have been tempted to a Shakespearean view of reversed roles. Any work which shows the stripping and levelling of too-well-accommodated man can sometimes put *King Lear* in mind. Bam and Maureen are reminded that they are forked animals: away from the suburban bathroom, they smell; hair sprouts on Maureen. But they have little interest let alone satisfaction in returning to nature, except for the pleasure of becoming drunk on meat for the first time in their lives when Bam shoots wart-hog — it might have been their discovery of what feasting means. There are no philosophical consolations for them, or for July's people. Nadine Gordimer can see their dependence on material provisions through their pretences about 'real concerns of life' which, they take it, July cannot understand. Her satire on the suburban is as effective as that in any of the countless suburban novelists of our time. But her chosen situation shows human possessiveness, movingly, as both silly and inescapable. July lolls on the bakkie with pride of ownership like any new car-owner. The novel is very attentive to the way that physical possessions define people's lives. The bakkie and the gun dominate the consciousness of all the characters. They are of course crucial things. Without the bakkie the Smaleses cannot escape; its bright yellow paint may, if seen by guerrillas, betray them. To July it represents new freedom and status, and a simple pleasure as he learns to drive it, and speaks English for once almost freshly. 'You know I'm turning round already? I'm know how to go back, everything'.[20] The gun is a hunter's weekend toy, but to the local Chief and to Daniel who takes it to go to war it is the only weapon available for defence or for spoils during the troubles. Its disappearance completely unmans Bam: he turns despairing on his face before the children when he loses it. These are to the Smaleses the last sizeable fragments of their normal life, images to which they cling. Robert J. Green has observed of *The Conservationist* that it 'revolves obsessively around images' and he uses the term 'Imagist' of her art.[21] The keys to the vehicle, which July takes in charge, are a recurrent obsession for him and for the Smaleses. Holding the keys was July's right by office at home and he still feels entitled to it, although the balance of power has shifted his way. As he and Maureen quarrel over whether she resents his having the keys, the dialogue in which the word *keys* is reiterated reflects almost incidentally the larger struggle for the keys of state, while making pitiful the yearning for ownership which neither can acknowledge. The keys pass from hand to hand and for all his loyalty and her goodwill they cannot help injuring each other.

The children's indignation over property is a further trial to the Smaleses' fairness. Victor takes an orange-sack that was 'lying around' and the rope-maker who unravels and replaits the bags calls for compensation. 'Victor was angry with a white man's anger, too big for him. "He mustn't say I stole. I just took stuff that gets thrown away"'.[22] Nothing is thrown away here. The rope-maker is paid, rands still have value. When Bam has set up a tank to collect rain water Victor protests that 'they' have learnt how the tap works. '"Ow, dad, it's ours, it's ours! – "' '"Who owns the rain?" The preachy reasonableness of his mother goaded him. "It's ours, it's ours."'[23]

A plain point is the contrast, blatant everywhere in the novel, between African poverty and European abundance. The sadness and futility of the child's 'it's ours' is Nadine Gordimer's note; it is hard to say whether her picture of superabundance in the Smaleses' life of expensive toys creates a less melancholy impression than the absence of any but the simplest tools among the villagers. July's people are the poorest of Africans, impoverished by the absence of most of their men working in the mines and in domestic service; the Smaleses are rich by Western standards. The extremes of encumbered affluence and near-destitution give the cluster of characters the air of a microcosm, and the novel that of another 'fable of our time'.

No representatives of the government or the revolutionaries appear in the novel except for official voices on the radio, and the young Daniel, a minor figure, who assures July that there are to be no more taxes or licences. When he goes to the war with his clenched-fist salute and Bam's gun, we have no sense of a 'creative struggle of the masses' but only the feeling that he, like all the novel's characters, is likely to be killed before long, without quite knowing why. Maureen is more startling than anything in Manzoni's seventeenth-century Italy. She lays her novel aside:

> No fiction could compete with what she was finding she did not know, could not have imagined or discovered through imagination.
> They had nothing.
> In their houses, there was nothing. At first.[24]

African possessions here must be searched out in the dark of a hut: ochre bands, animal tails, traces for oxen, a piece of cowhide, a hoe, a pile of rags, grain in baskets, mats for use as table-tops or as bowls. Among these small useful things are second-hand treasures from the Smaleses' house. July requires his wife to lend back the 'beautiful' pink porcelain cups which have been a gift from his employers. Maureen notices fragments of her property which she has never missed, a pair of scissors and a gadget for removing the dry cleaner's staples without risking one's finger nails. The incongruous coexistence of modest necessities and specialised luxuries, talismanic in the village perhaps, is matched in the Smaleses' new home. They are reduced to one suitcase. They have one bed, a Primus, a basin, a tin of milk-powder and an electric motor-racing track smuggled here by the child Victor for whom it is a talisman. The villagers own so little that they cannot litter, Maureen notes. 'Back there' July and other servants of the large white houses profited from the surplus of a society which can hardly help littering the world. July's bag, marked AEROLINEAS ARGENTINAS, a relic of one of Bam's trips abroad, is a reminder of the surplus of 'the modern world'. He has a used carpet for his room, and chairs, and pictures no longer needed in the house. July's wife is struck by his white people's present destitution. There they had rooms for everything — he has told her — hot water made like the lights in town, a machine for washing clothes, hundreds of books . . . 'Now you tell me *nowhere*'. To her they are monarchs in exile.

To the Smaleses it seems they have been plucked from normal life, and set in a world stranger than the fiction of the past. The novel shows how close these modern worlds of the city suburbs and the distant hamlet have been. The 'Boss Boy' plaque is a telling image. The 'beautiful' pink cups and saucers and the staple-extractor are, among the mud huts thatched with grass, at once ridiculous and touching things.

Each community is struck by disintegration in the other. Seated before the Chief Bam is conscious that the chair is coming apart and surreptitiously he tightens screws his thumb working 'automatically' where previous thumbs have had no such instinct to repair. The children's toy car is dismantled by the youngest villagers, each prizing a fragment of it as his own. The walls of houses rot away, Bam the architect notes, and are allowed to do so, the mud being used to build again among another cluster of rocks. In July's possession the bakkie, Maureen tells him, will become another wreck: 'She told him the truth which is always disloyal . . . it'll be there, July, under the trees, in this place among the old huts, and it'll fall to pieces while the children play in it. Useless.'[25] In more technologically developed regions of the country things are falling apart apocalyptically. Houses blaze in the suburbs. Official buildings are blown up, aeroplanes shot down, shops and houses looted (even by Maureen, stealing medicines before leaving). The radio brings news of destruction at intervals, so that the mud huts look relatively permanent, until the station is silenced. Bam wonders if the Afrikaaners are destroying installations sooner than surrender them to the Blacks. July wonders whether there will be anything 'back there' to which to return. Allowing for Nadine Gordimer's high reputation, an additional reason for the prominent reviews the novel received in England may be an appeal in the fantasy of 'civilisation's collapse', so common a subject of popular fiction. With the power to build rapidly goes not only the power to destroy even more quickly but also, perhaps, an urge to do so which July's people would not understand. However that may be, the novel does not admit that any general group of people has less respect than others for the good uses of arts and science.

The background of apartheid is recalled in images of prison especially; and in memories of Maureen's early life among the mines of Western Areas. One passage recreates her happy, easy relationship with Lydia the housemaid with whom she shares fizzy drinks and chocolate, and the secrets which matter to schoolgirls and housemaids. They are photographed together on the street one day, to Lydia's satisfaction; they are never sent the copy they hope for, but Maureen finds the picture, years later, in a book about South Africa, with comments:

> White herrenvolk attitudes and life-styles; the marvellous photograph of the white schoolgirl and the black woman with the girl's school case on her head.
> Why had Lydia carried the case?
> Did the photographer know what he saw, when they crossed the road like that, together? Did the book, placing the pair in its context, give the reason she and Lydia, in their affection and ignorance, didn't know?[26]

July's people have known little of *Herrenvolk* attitudes and life-styles, but life in his village (or strictly, hamlet) has been affected by the world beyond.

Two coldly observed African figures add to the complexity of the novel's picture of present interests. July's chief has been astonished by the collapse of his own conception of South Africa today. When he summons the Smaleses, Bam expects that they are to be told to move on, but what the Chief wants is a white man's explanation of why white rule has failed him. He appeals to history. Revolution is unprecedented. Who, after 350 years, is 'blowing up the government'? He has heard about 'Russias' and 'Cubas' and he knows of 'Sowetos' — they will take his land and cattle. He means to fight and hopes to practise with Bam's gun. Bam thinks that the government may, as a last resort, arm 'their homeland rulers', and he protests: 'the whole black nation is your nation'; moreover 'I don't shoot people'; there follows 'a short disgusted snort from the black man; a backwash of laughter.'[27] The Chief can be encapsulated in phrases from 'back there' — 'counter-revolutionary pockets' — but he makes it seem likely that the civil war will be complicated into more than a struggle between black and white. The Smaleses fear for July who may be killed for having sheltered them.

The other, more impressive figures are July's wife and mother. His wife, who toils among the women in the weekly effort to bring up their children in a community where the men are mostly absent or demoralised, is curious about the whites — July's people to her — although unable to imagine her husband's other life. His mother regrets the loss of her house which has been lent to the Smaleses; she wants to reroof it when the grasses are ripe for thatching. Modern warfare means nothing to them, but they have a stamina which moves Nadine Gordimer, at moments, to warmth. As July explains about the war his mother interrupts to complain that he has killed the wrong fowl. The small preoccupations of a countrywoman are irrelevant to the grand designs of history, whatever they may be at present. The novelist cannot say. But she puts more trust in the patient endurance of the African women than in the various species of militancy. Reflecting on the role of the bakkie, bought for fun, in the Smaleses' escape. she makes a comment which might be remembered when we hear July and his wife discussing their possible future in the village when the war is over.

> In various and different circumstances certain objects and individuals are going to turn out to be vital. The wager of survival cannot, by its nature, reveal which, in advance of events. How was one to know? . . . The circumstances are incalculable in the manner in which they come about, even if apocalyptically or politically foreseen, and the identity of the vital individuals and objects is hidden by their humble or frivolous role in an habitual set of circumstances.[28]

July's People ends with the arrival of a helicopter; without knowing if it means rescue, or death, or some unforeseen development, Maureen runs towards it, on the final page. In these circumstances nothing is predictable. The recent past has been 'possessed' by no one group although many have thought they had the present under control.

Laurens van der Post's *A Story Like The Wind* (1972) combines, among other things, a tribute to what the author has most admired in the traditional rural life of the African peoples he knows best, with an interpretation of the present state of affairs, observing (and here sharing certain assumptions with Nadine Gordimer) the limitations of white liberals who cannot prevent the approaching revolution. It is a remarkable reworking of various types of African fiction written from a European point of view: an adventure story, a novel of childhood, and an anthology of myths, legends, and memories. Its sequel *A Far-Off Place* (1974) suffers because the Buchanesque adventure is overdeveloped, but the components are well balanced in *A Story Like The Wind* which I shall treat as a self-contained work, referring to the sequel only for clues.

Few writers are more inclined to label present-day cultures as 'medieval', 'Homeric', or 'prehistoric'. Van der Post was a friend and student of Jung and he is Jungian in his use of 'civilised' and 'primitive'. The three peoples of this novel, Bushman, Matabele and European, represent for the author three ages of Mankind. (He always equates 'the twentieth century' with 'the spirit of Western man'). It could be argued that he presents his Africans in states of traditional cultural 'purity' because he consigns them theoretically to limbo. But a reading of the novel creates the opposite impression; and we should be willing to push aside the Jungian formulations preferring the book's effect to the implications, because van der Post is least interesting as a systematic thinker, and most talented as a story-teller.

Each of the novel's three cultures contributes stories of its own, and each is presented according to the criteria of the culture itself. The educated, liberal Europeans are analysed, especially in the person of Pierre-Paul Joubert, by reference to a culture which sees itself to have failed. Joubert represents the enlightenment and the failure of the best of his own people. The Matabele are in possession of a sounder, more circumscribed way of life. Matabele characters, especially 'Bamuthi, are seen as examples of what the Matabele admire, as in their stories of courage and virtue. Xhabbo, an ideal Bushman, presents himself to François by means of his own lore. In this remote setting, which the author's introduction tells us is not 'photographic', each people is independent, until 'the twentieth century' overtakes them all. As for the boy François who learns from them all, his integrated modern world is a memorable version of what our time might have had, and might still have to offer. The most urgent appeal to the Western reader, many will think, is the book's interpretation of the failure of European civilisation in Africa. This is made in the person of a very 'modern' European.

In a farmhouse in the heart of Southern Africa a civilised and progressive white African is dying of exhaustion and despair. Pierre-Paul Joubert is an active, imaginative liberal intellectual. He could lecture to applause in any English or American university.

But Joubert, in the opening chapters of *A Story Like The Wind*, is no Kurtz; it is not the heart of darkness which is killing him, but the contempt and indifference for his ideals among his fellow white South Africans. Although he does not know it, his attempt to create a new South Africa in miniature is already doomed; armed insurgents across the border are preparing to destroy it. But he is already conscious of his failure and has lost the will to live. Years ago he resigned from a government career in protest against *apartheid* and turned to farming in the hope that he might create 'a tiny model of the non-racial Africa he had visualised', as an example or a proof that life could be 'put right' by peaceful and constructive means. He has failed to convert anyone.

Pierre-Paul Joubert, also known as Ouwa, comes from an old-established South African family of French descent. His Huguenot ancestors came from Europe in the seventeenth century in the hope of making 'a better world'. There was still room in Southern Africa for him to try again, in the 1950s. South of the Victoria Falls and east of the desert, on an ancient road running across the continent and near the Amanzim-tetse River he found an ideal place unclaimed for farming, and proposed to a neighbouring Matabele chief that they form a partnership to develop the land, sharing the profits which might come from marketing products south by rail. The project succeeded. Joubert and the Matabele headman 'Bamuthi have become allies and friends in prosperity. Further claims are established in the names of 'Bamuthi's kinsmen. Joubert has brought up his only son François in accordance with his principles. Pierre-Paul had learned Amaxosa in childhood; François learns Sindabele, and Bushman from his nurse. He calls 'Bamuthi 'old father' and regards the Chief and the senior kinsmen with the same awe and love felt by his friends among the Matabele boys. 'Bamuthi is at home in the Jouberts' farmhouse, Hunter's Drift; they are at home among the Matabele kraals – especially François.

European reactions are predictable. To the white South Africans who visit or know of Hunter's Drift, the scheme is outrageously liberal. It constitutes 'letting the side down'. The relatively enlightened Sir James Monckton, who comes hoping to build a farm himself with hired labour, is shocked when 'Bamuthi, in hunting costume, strolls into the room. Earlier visitors, who have seen François performing a war-dance before his toy soldiers as a Matabele king dances before the battle, ask how Pierre-Paul can allow his son to grow up like 'a white kaffir'. The pressure of disapproval from his own community is more painful than he is willing to acknowledge. François becomes indifferent to European Africa.

Pierre-Paul is worse troubled by the objections of visitors from abroad who find his approach paternalistic and his system feudal. These critics can be as rude, and as unrealistic, as the racialists. A group of missionaries from the World Council of Churches inspect Hunter's Drift after Joubert's death and — in the last chapter — show no understanding of what he attempted. 'Could they have found anything in the twentieth century quite so feudal and so wicked?' 'In the twentieth century' is telling; they cannot have travelled much. 'Paternalistic' is ironic because this father is somewhat hesitant about his own role within his family. It is unfair since 'Bamuthi is his partner not his protégé. 'Feudalism' is the European label for the structure of society within 'Bamuthi's kraals, which has remained, in this far-off place, traditional. The Chief's benevolent authority reflects that of every father, and since the farms are preyed upon daily by wild animals, automatic obedience to his summons is vital. Solidarity in Matabele life does not resemble feudalism. Put more intelligently, however, the objections might have weight. Joubert has created a useful alliance between two peoples — 'Bamuthi's and his own small circle — who co-operate for mutual benefit without the racial tensions suffered elsewhere; as a demonstration that these can be avoided, it is admirable. But the alliance is an example which cannot be imitated except in such hazardous, arduous and rewarding conditions as those of this frontier. The Matabele way of life, very well suited to Hunter's Drift, would not normally be feasible today. In many respects the alliance is not a partnership on equal terms since 'Bamuthi depends on the Jouberts for modern techniques of science and economics, although he is learning these. But this unrepresentative and, for everyone involved, privileged enclave cannot survive, given the present state of the continent. Pierre-Paul's demonstration has come too late. His Utopia cannot be separated from the rest of Southern Africa, and his good intentions will lead to the destruction of all 'Bamuthi's people. Although he is unaware of the insurgents, he knows 'instinctively' (as van der Post would say) that his life has been wasted.

The novelist endorses his attempt, although he criticises his approach, and that of liberals like him, and sees in Joubert's death the tragedy of his country. It is François who realises, after his mother and friends have been massacred, that his father and the guerrillas have been on the same side against a common enemy, although their methods have been so different. In Chapter 6 of *A Far-Off Place* he overhears a conversation between two European advisers to the insurgents and comes to this conclusion:

> He remembered with a pain which blurred his eyes with tears that all the many dear friends as well as brutal enemies who had been killed in the bush in the last forty-eight hours were not the first casualties in this particular war. His father, Ouwa, was the first. He had been the first, as far as François knew, to take up this cause and the first to die, killed by the common enemy of all three of them. Yes, he had to admit it; Ouwa, the Scot and the Frenchman had the same enemy and were on the same side. That was the irony of it. Ouwa himself had been murdered, as he saw it, by the people the other two called 'the tyrants of the south', killed simply by turning their backs on Ouwa, rejecting him irrevocably because he had recognised error in their way of life and was trying to put it right in the only fashion that life could ever be put permanently right.

That fashion, 'Bamuthi and François's 'Uncle Mopani' have taught him, following Matabele and European wisdom, is patient and circumspect, like the elephant. But life has gone so wrong in Southern Africa that the solitary example of Hunter's Drift is offensive to both sides in the impending war and it perishes, caught between them.

François is made to look further into the reasons for Ouwa's death as the author searches the white South African state of mind. Colonel van der Post has written more directly elsewhere about the apparent mindlessness of racialism. Two concepts recur in his reflections on apartheid which are present in *A Story Like The Wind*. For him the word 'childlike' is an extreme compliment when applied to a mature and well-adjusted adult. He employs it in the novel for the idealised figures of the white hunter Mopani and the Bushman Xhabbo: both have retained in maturity the trust and sympathy of a child. Children have to be *taught* to despise people of another race. 'Childlike' contrasts with 'childish' which means ignorant and foolish, and which conveys in this context the irrational rage induced by insecurity which can occur in adults. 'Childlike' has for this author a background in William Blake, in the Bible; and in the respect for what is childlike in their own children, matched by stern impatience with what is childish, in such peoples as the Matabele and the Bushmen. The other concept is African and found in the greeting, which François prefers to European formulas, 'I see you, indeed I see you'. In those words François feels recognised as a person and admitted to fellowship. Recognition of 'presence' is a principle throughout *A Story Like The Wind*, and its sequel.

These concepts can be seen in passages from Laurens van der Post's second book on the Bushmen, *The Heart of the Hunter* which incidentally provides evidence of the novel's background in the author's experience and of the commitment which inspires his critique of racialism. Returning from the meetings with Bushmen in the Kalahari the author is struck by the behaviour of a white South African stationmaster who finds two non-white members of the expedition sitting on a railway platform bench which is reserved for Europeans. The man is driven frantic with rage. Since the station is outside South Africa he can be stopped, and he leaves, head in hands, 'with the melodrama of despair' (Chapter 7).[29] When the author crosses the border he is soon made aware that he is 'truly home again'. Driving past a suburb he sees a crowd of small boys in prep. school caps and blazers shouting encouragement as the biggest of them beats up a coloured child, whose grandfather stands by 'with averted face on which there was an expression of acute hopelessness and shame'.[30] Having a good Kalahari stick at hand, the author intervenes. After the rescue the old man explains that the attack on his grandson was unprovoked. The boys' behaviour, the writer reflects, was worse than ordinary childish bullying; we remember the stationmaster. Recalling the maturity, combined with a 'childlike' charm of trust and good manners, in the people of the Kalahari we feel the unpatronising force which van der Post can give to that complimentary word.

Another passage of *The Heart of The Hunter* records the conversation of an intelligent and humane South African judge who admits that he does not 'see' Africans in the streets in the way that he observes Europeans — speculating about their lives and occupations. Van der Post writes in Chapter 9 'The Black Out':

> I told him that what appeared particularly sinister to me was that psychologically we did not see the black and coloured

people in Africa at all. I said that vision was complete only if we saw reality with both the outer and the inner eye. Not doing so, we commit the error of the one-eyed vision of which Blake accused the scientist. Our trouble was that we saw the African only with the outer eye and not through the eye of the heart as well. I believed one did not know human beings really until one saw them that way as well — in other words, knew them also through a kind of wonder they provoked in one.[31]

That may seem elementary but it provoked a new degree of self-awareness in the judge, who then admitted his blindness in the Blakean eye of imagination. The greeting 'I see you' reflects a more observant culture, unknown to the judge.

Returning to van der Post's scrutiny of racial prejudice in *A Story Like The Wind*, we find these concepts illustrated. When François dances before his troops of clay he is childlike, and not immature, in expressing his apprehension of a soldier's gaiety and honour, disciplined by the dance rhythms and movements learned from a warrior-people. The offended visitor is merely childish. Sir James is childish, although he feels superior to François, when he resents 'Bamuthi's presence which the boy takes for granted. Pierre-Paul is more mature; but although not childish, he cannot value the childlike in others or in himself. Courtesy prevents him from smiling at times at the 'childlike' Mopani who is no fool. And although he co-operates with them in practical matters, he yields to the feeble-minded banality that 'Africans are just children' in a spirit which is the opposite of the author's tribute to Mopani and Xhabbo. The two words English affords are one to him.

The novel connects that shortsightedness with his failure to 'see', in Blake's or the African sense, the Matabele and other peoples of the region, despite his tolerance. His principle is firm and good; but it is only reasoned, and he suffers 'psychological blindness'. Van der Post exploits the verb 'to see' when he writes of Pierre-Paul's seeing specialists in South Africa for a diagnosis of his *malaise*, and of François's and 'Bamuthi's wish that he see the great wiseman of their district, uLangalibalela who is famous as a *seer*, looking into and beyond a man's condition. There is frequent play on the word. Coaching François when the two go alone to see the wise-man, 'Bamuthi provides the correct greetings:

> Of course you must begin, 'I see you, indeed I see you' but then you must immediately go on to say also, 'But you will be here

tomorrow when I have gone and can no longer see you, to see me and things that I cannot see for myself.' (Chapter 6)

If he replies that he has seen them since they left their kraals, that will mean he is already at the heart of their matter. François has realised that Ouwa would scoff at a consultation of this nature, but he takes a sample of his father's hair. uLangalibalela divines what is wrong: a man cannot live if his people have 'turned their backs on him'. Pierre-Paul's people have turned their backs and the government has bewitched him. The doctors in the south tell Joubert that he is tired and needs a rest by the sea. Had he seen the witchdoctor he might have found relief in a truer diagnosis and, possibly, a cure in coming to respect a different culture.

There is no apparent cure for the general situation in the country, and nothing can save Hunter's Drift from destruction. Van der Post is concerned with the state of mind of the liberal white South African, a proper leader of opinion, who shares responsibility. The failure to 'see' people links Joubert with the judge and with a white class of intelligent and progressive-minded people, not only in the South but across the continent and throughout the century.

Ouwa has been a teacher and an education officer, twice a Director of Education, and he has believed in teaching as the only means of creating a 'new Africa'. His conception of learning is entirely European and progressive. Some of his views are sensible. He recognises that too many hours are normally spent in the classroom (to provide teachers with a livelihood) and he sets François only two hours of study each day, besides nightly Bible-reading and occasional lectures on the possible influence of Latin on Sindabele. He fears the conformist influence of modern schools. He believes in good discipline. It is a modern outlook, free from 'modern' errors; we are meant to respect him. He teaches, however, a pronounced rationalism which he prizes as the 'modern' alternative to African muddle. When François observes that a landscape is sad, Ouwa tells him that the sadness is only in himself; neither Mopani nor the author would have corrected him. Such insistence excludes Pierre-Paul from a recognition of other means of apprehending and reasoning, present in fact in his culture as well as in cultures in Africa, although the novel classes them as African. This is seen as a tragic limitation, in him and in the 'twentieth-century' approach to the world.

Van der Post identifies a psychological maladjustment in the rigorous European rationalism in Ouwa. His love for François embarrasses him and he masks it with banter which can be playful or sarcastic. François knows the love behind the teasing but he would prefer a less schoolmasterly reserve. It may be that Calvinism has inhibited Ouwa, but it has not warped Mopani who is warmly affectionate towards François. Progressive thought enables Joubert to rationalise his shyness. He and his wife Lammie decide that their child must be allowed a measure of independence lest his 'urgent little spirit be driven underground' (Chapter 3). They avoid the possessive term 'son' and François uses their nicknames instead of 'father' and 'mother'. Van der Post comments in his Prelude to *A Far-Off Place* on their wish for their son to be 'another little person' — a disturbing phrase — that

> the consequences of such an approach to their one and only child are as profound as they are subtle in the evolution of François's character. Although Lammie's love of her son is never in doubt, it is hard to know whether the dignity implicit in such a concept is not conferred on François too soon, and that he might not have welcomed a little less honour and somewhat more immediate and less conceptualised love.

An unusually 'complete' love between Ouwa and Lammie, intensified by their joint defiance of their own community, often makes François feel excluded. After her husband's death Lammie is still absorbed in him; knowing this, she fears the 'feminine possessiveness' of her love and protects François from its influence. Politely distanced, François responds warmly to the spontaneous ('primitive') affections of his nurse Xoba and the cook Ousie-Johanna, of 'Bamuthi and Uncle Mopani. These are good mentors, but their inexhaustible wisdom and guidance threaten to stifle the spirit his parents have resolved to set free. Psychological planning defeats its own objectives. Xhabbo, whom François rescues from a lion-trap, rescues him from dependency, by offering a precious friendship between equals, and by giving the boy a 'secret'. It is through the secret friendship that he and Nonnie Monckton, who brings another kind of friendship, escape the insurgents. Ironically François has kept his knowledge of their movements a secret, but the portion of his life which is committed to Xhabbo has helped him to grow, guided by his parents, 'Bamuthi, Mopani and the rest, but ultimately independent.

Although the African characters are not explored through individual psychology, they are observed with such sensitivity that we can see the Jouberts from the point of view of African culture. It would be interesting to know more of 'Bamuthi's private thoughts about Pierre-Paul and François, and uLangalibalela's impressions of the white boy; that is outside van der Post's scope. But 'Bamuthi's fatherliness towards François — whom he seems to think both neglected and spoilt — reflects on what is unsatisfactory in Pierre-Paul's character, on how his good intentions go awry in his parental as well as in his public role. Leading François through the bush with a sharp eye out for elephants, snakes, and 'men of the spear', 'Bamuthi is an adventure hero (and no deferential 'native'; he is in charge). But as he switches from genuine anger to unashamed, tender and constructive sympathy when François comes home hours late and bursts into tears, he makes us think again about Pierre-Paul and about the culture the Jouberts represent. He has a further role in the novel's praise of Africa. The adventure story is rarely at odds with the other dimensions of *A Story Like The Wind*. But there is no need to apologise for the adventure itself.

The plot is simple. François finds Xhabbo and shelters him in a cave known only to Bushmen until he is sufficiently recovered (in remarkably few days) to return to the desert. There, he senses, his people are in danger. Bereaved, François provisions the cave, ready for his return. The Jouberts go south in search of doctors. François and 'Bamuthi consult uLangalibelela. Ouwa dies. Sir James arrives with his daughter Nonnie. Other more sinister strangers are about. Fourteen months later Xhabbo returns to warn François of the approach of an army (apparently from a base in Angola). This force sweeps through Hunter's Drift killing everyone except François and Nonnie who take refuge in the cave. (In *A Far-Off Place* they eventually escape across the desert to rescue at the sea.) There are many incidental episodes, especially of hunting and journeying. *A Story Like The Wind* is one of those adult novels which can be enjoyed (with some skipping) by younger readers. If the narrative excitements and comradely romance, as well as the poetry and humour, are meant to appeal to the young in all of us, there is a corner of van der Post's imagination which is possessed by the spirits of Rider Haggard and John Buchan, and even English readers who retain an affection for those tall stories may be bored at times. The scene in which François stalks the insurgent band is melodramatic, like it or not. In *A Far-Off Place* there are many incidents which leave one uneasy, not because they could never happen, but because they happen in stories which are much cruder in their distinctions between right and wrong than Laurens van der Post.

An adventure story requires an outer world; the geography of this novel is physically vast and humanly varied. It is partly constructed from memories of childhood. In *Jung and the Story of Our Time* the author has described something of his childhood (he was born in 1906) in a large farming family on the high veld, sleeping out almost always under the stars, and discovering Mantis with his nurse who worshipped it after the Bushman faith. Van der Post excels at recreating the landscape and natural life of the world he first knew, and his sense of adventure there. In *The Heart of the Hunter* he writes of what he heard, from his grandfather and others at the farm, of Southern Africa in the nineteenth century. 'In this and many other ways I have only to stretch out my hand, as it were, to touch a day 120 or more years old.'[32] The 'Testament' to *A Story Like The Wind* is extracted from a statement left by a mid-nineteenth-century Bushman convict. Taking a long view of his country's past, the novel sees its peoples caught together in history. Behind the individual lives of people of all cultures we sense the presence of tradition and custom. The Matabele people of the novel, we are told in the Introduction, 'are not representative' but serve as conductors for 'what is representative in African man'. The author had visited a Matabele clan, relatively unaffected by modernity, 'still telling their stories in the ancient way. Theirs was one of the voices I had in my ear as I wrote.' Another is that of the Bushmen. As in an epic there is an oral background – 'the spoken word I once had from their burning imagination'. The Jouberts are not typical either. Xhabbo is the author's tribute to the Bushmen whose precarious survival in the Kalahari he had publicised in books, film, and lectures. It might be objected that van der Post's Matabele, whatever burning imagination he has found in countrymen who perhaps saw the Romantic in him, are glamorous versions of what some foreigners consider 'real Africans', to be visited on safari. Reproving a critic who praised Ekwensi's 'real Africans' in *Burning Grass*, Chinua Achebe wrote: 'one sensed that a

Lagosian or an African from Nairobi might be deemed less real than a Masai or a Tuareg, surely a matter of social taste and not of literary criticism!'[33] Of course they are equally real. Adventure stories have misrepresented Africans for over a century. The genre requires characters who are exceptional and usually simple. In *A Story Like The Wind* the African characters are both, but they are heroes by the criteria of their cultures.

All the major characters, Jouberts apart, are heroically predictable, fit for their adventurous roles. Warrior spirit, in 'Bamuthi, stirs van der Post's imagination. All the proper adjectives apply: stern, demanding, resourceful, reliable, brave, pious, compassionate, courteous Bamuthi lives nobly and dies fighting for the kraals of his people. His great war-shout 'To me!' is 'equivalent to a knight's':

> It was a shout of all that stood for courage in man, who, however great the inducement to fear and no matter how hopeless his cause, maintained his stand to the point of death. As such it was the purest human sound François had ever heard. Everything in him responded to it and urged him to go instantly to the man who had uttered it. (Chapter 11)

'Bamuthi is said to be 'Homeric'. Van der Post's is the spirit of Maldon and Agincourt, and of Hornblower in Rosas Bay.

A sketch of Ousie-Johanna would recall the redoubtable kitchen-lady who sustains adventurers in countless tales, the cook to whom, for all her scoldings, anyone would wish to come home after a week in the bush. She is worthy of her art and worth mollifying. ('A thin lot of good that will do' is her style of disapproval.) Xhabbo is the ideal companion for a boy-hero. As much of a man as 'Bamuthi and even more ready for anything, he is François's size and accepts him as an equal. When Xhabbo leaves and François is desolate, there is still a rogue elephant to be shot, out with Uncle Mopani, truest and most African of white men. These people are cast for adventure but in each case their heroism is the expression of the character's own culture.

Laughter and weeping are cultural signs. In contrast to the Protestant inhibitions of the adult Jouberts, the older African customs are mature. A Matabele boy is brought up to weep easily for others but not for himself. That code is illustrated (and not criticised). 'Bamuthi's dismay when François breaks down in Chapter 4 is not a special trait in the Old Father but a feature of the 'fine art' to which the Matabele have brought the care of children. 'Indeed they felt guilty even if they saw a small child in tears and . . . François had hardly ever heard a Matabele baby cry' (Chapter 4). That tenderness does not preclude a flogging for neglectful herd-boys; afterwards none of them, believe it or not, has a tear in his eye. For other occasions one learns 'to string the beads'. 'Bamuthi weeps for Pierre-Paul although Lammie preserves a responsible calm. Laughter is therapeutic too, and has its occasions. To comfort François 'Bamuthi takes him to his kraal for a session of riddles; the smallest of the Chief's daughters can raise a laugh against his slowness in this game. Nobody can laugh like Xhabbo and his people (except, van der Post thought, C. G. Jung). He can be wholly possessed by laughter. Pierre-Paul's defeat, consumed by melancholy, is contrasted in the opening chapters with the Bushman's refusal to despair. His own and his nation's peril are lost in laughter when François suggests that his leg mangled by the lion-trap, may take a week to heal. Hearing it, one would give anything to laugh with such 'glittering' abandon (Chapter 4).

The Bushmen live on the brink of extinction, and their laughter is as strong as their resolve. Whatever the antiquity of its sources, delightful for the author to contemplate, it may have been lent quality by the trials of recent centuries; courage in Xhabbo is a desperate need. In the settled Matabele, hardiness is wanted for daily living. 'Bamuthi's war-cry sounds Homeric but it is not that of an island kingdom's warrior caste; normally it summons herdsmen to repel a marauding lion, as in Chapter 3. Any Matabele man who fails in the virtues which are so impressive in the Chief is 'divided' or bewitched. 'Bamuthi is the very man with whom to make a week's journey through dangerous country to consult a witchdoctor. The author means to say that his Matabele are men for such work, as no doubt he knows. Ousie-Johanna is equally a woman of her time and place. A Xhosa widow, she spars with 'Bamuthi, recognising in him 'the voice of male authority but growing 'militant at the slightest hint of what she regarded as the male's universal compulsion to be obstinate' (Chapter 6). Her feminity is that of a culture in which roles are adjusted to allow considerable female resistance to the recognised authority of men. The *données* of a particular social discipline are as deeply planted in her as in 'Bamuthi.

They talk an English which is persuasively Sindabele, pithy with proverbs and loan-words, formally dignified, often indirect and laconic. Garrulity is not for men. 'More talk now will just be wandering in the belly of a bullock', 'Bamuthi warns in Chapter 3. Eloquence is taught, and so is attention to strangers' words lest the people be deceived. Pierre-Paul is interviewed at length before his proposed alliance is accepted. Matabele women have their own ways with words and 'Bamuthi is sometimes worn into compliance. Nuin-Tara knows when to be quiet. Bushman, which clicks with 'crackles of electricity' on Xhabbo's lips ['X' represents a click], is rendered in a mixture of idioms from that language and features of Tudor English. The result is readable and it conveys the writer's pleasure in a way of life richer and stranger than most. Nonnie's upper-class schoolgirl's chatter brings out the gravity and colour of François's English, a rare idiolect unpretentiously improved by his reading and by his African languages. François has learnt something of Mopani's caution, summed up in his favourite *ja-nee*, 'yes-no'. Between them words are often unneeded; a 'faster communication' is possible whose meanings words would 'blur'. For them as for the Matabele what is unsaid counts for much. Van der Post's Africa understands the uses and the dangers of talk.

To say so is the right starting-point for an account of the 'mystical', 'meditative' or 'visionary' dimension of van der Post's fiction. The essence of François's education in *A Story Like The Wind* is the African conception of *presence, recognition, seeing*. Without that, conversation is less than real.

Presence, from Wordsworth to Yeats, is a Romantic term; and van der Post's sense of what it means to Africans is Romantic, as is his conception of 'the poet' whom he recognises in Africans. 'Bamuthi, Pierre-Paul observes, 'could give the average Poet Laureate a few lessons' (Chapter 5). Van der Post finds Blake in the story-telling of the Bushmen and would say that Blake was alive to 'the Bushman in himself'. Failure to see people 'with a kind of wonder' is his diagnosis of apartheid. Seeing people and the world with wonder is the strength of his own poetic imagination which is always Romantic in feeling in *A Story Like The Wind*, but usually shaped by African habits of mind.

To name is to acknowledge. European fiction shares with African custom a respect for the magic of names. 'What does it mean, François?' asks Nonnie when they first meet; 'Luciana' means 'Bringer of light'. Xhabbo takes for granted that names must fit. His own, borrowed from the Victorian convict who supplies the Testament, means Dream; 'there could be no other name for me'. François shares the author's reverence for dreams and dreamers. Xhabbo renames him 'Foot of the Day' because he came at dawn to rescue him; 'foot of the day' is the Morning or Evening star, and a praise-name among Bushmen since the stars are great hunters. François is known as 'Little Feather' to the Matabele; his father is 'Great White Bird', a compliment from them, and an allusion to a Hottentot story, we learn in *The Heart of the Hunter* akin to the allegory of truth in Olive Schreiner.[34] 'Little Feather' has become slightly irksome to François but it suits the author's view, learned from the Bushmen, that the smallest things, even a feather on the wind, may be the most worthy. Other names are complimentary among the more practical Matabele. 'Ouwa' is 'old wagon' because he bears many people. Mopani is named for the evergreen, apparently ageless Mopani tree. Nuin-Tara, 'Daughter of a Star', is an 'exalted' Bushman name. Animals are admitted to fellowship in being named, and the lions whose roars are heard nightly at Hunter's Drift have their names, as for François have crocodiles, and baboons — creatures whom 'Bamuthi is accustomed to salute with 'I see you'. 'Hintza' commemorates a Chief of the Amaxosa, distinguished in the War of the Axe. The second syllable of his name has to be dropped since it is a Bushman assault command which he knows by instinct. The Bushmen had *tsa* from the stars whose hunting cries are audible to them. 'Bamuthi's weapons have Sindabele names, conferring power. The assegai *n-Simsela-Banta-Bami* is 'He who digs for my children'. His club *Igumgehle* is 'the Greedy One'. The spear has fed many generations; the club is a glutton for enemies. For 'Bamuthi (as for John Cowper Powys) weapons have life and character. Even resting places in the desert have these, for the Bushmen, and are named accordingly.

'Bamuthi, Mopani, and Xhabbo teach François to 'read' the world about him. 'Bamuthi sees spirits of ancestors or wizards in living creatures, which can be inconvenient, as it is when he almost succumbs to a snake-bite because the mamba who bites him is an ancestor, calling; none the less, he always *looks* at the world. Mopani's bushcraft is both practical and mystical. The Bible is the only book Mopani has read. Since he has read it all he can hardly be thought uncultured by contemporary standards, but his deepest culture resembles that which the Matabele boys acquire from their duties in guarding the herds. They read 'the hieroglyphic code of which the Europeans had lost the key' (Chapter 3). Mopani sees every sign of life; nature to him is 'allegorical'.

Symbolism is another way of reading nature as van der Post is well aware: 'world without and world within . . . are expressions of one another.' (Chapter 5). The novel's symbols arise from African cultures. Xhabbo's cave, for example, which François keeps supplied for the Bushman's return, and which at the novel's close is his only remaining home, corresponds to a vacancy in the boy's life; and for the author it is a secret, lost place in the human spirit. It is also a Bushman shrine. The mantis, as a symbol of the infinite in the tiny, serves the book's vision of how the slightest event or change of heart can have momentous consequences. Mantis is also the Bushman god. World without and world within reflect each other in myth before the novel's art creates symbols, from a rogue elephant, or from 'the way of the wind'. The elephant 'Uprooter of Great Trees' whom François shoots in Chapter 5 is both awesome and destructive. Drunk on the fermented fruits of the marula tree the animal is threatening to rampage through houses and gardens. It is remembered at the close when 'Bamuthi is dead with all his kraals. Elephants stand for wisdom because they move slowly and perspicaciously, when not drunk or maddened. The insurgent army, it is asserted, disobeys, with its reckless killing, a rule of life. Both aspects of the elephant are present in myths. To the Matabele the elephant is a great lord, housing a powerful spirit; its peaceful presence is a blessing. To the Bushmen it 'played the same role as the one-eyed giants in François's Greek legends . . . It was always threatening the life of the innocent and small' (Chapter 4). In this role it is combated by Mantis in one of the tales. The wind blows rain and life to the land and stories like the wind restore, through myth and literature, the life of the mind. In Bushman belief the wind takes the last footprints of men from the desert and blows their spirits together as clouds. Old Koba has taught François 'that clouds and the spirit of human beings were interchangeable and went into one another's making, before birth, during life and after death' (Chapter 4). That is to make presences of the clouds. The author came to his rendering of man in nature as to his humanism, by way of such teaching.

Since the heifer Night and Day which François offers uLangalibalela combines black and white markings she might be taken for a symbol of the alliance of races at Hunter's Drift. But such rare animals are especially revered by the Matabele. 'François could still remember the great cry of happiness and wonder which had gone up in the cattle kraal at the end of the garden when it was announced that a calf of this miraculous combination of black and white had been born.' (Chapter 6). Van der Post explains in *The Heart of the Hunter* that he had this belief as a child; now he sees it as a reflection of an African (rather than Christian or Romantic) sense that 'every living thing shares in the process of creation'.[35] Night and Day is an appropriate offering. In so far as her colour scheme hints at racial harmony, the offering is not good enough.

One of the attractions of van der Post's work is his willingness to take risks. He presents without a trace of embarrassment scenes which most serious novelists would shirk from fear of sentimentality, and we accept them because we come to respect the narrator. With all his foibles, the story-teller has charm and authority. One reviewer grudgingly called the story 'moving, and even noble'. Towards the end of *A Far-Off Place* we are told that 'there is implicit in all [Europe] a strange envy for what is true and noble' (Chapter 15). Laurens van der Post, at least, is utterly free of it. His admiration for such a dog as Hintza, such a boy as François, such a witchdoctor as uLangalibalela, irradiates his writing: all are noble, although their imperfections are watched with intelligent, amused, sympathetic alertness.

The effect of the style is difficult to illustrate because the writing is so expansive; its unit is a long paragraph. The sentences are exploratory. Fluent, rhythmic, evocative, assertive, they have never quite finished with what has to be said. Even in descriptions, one bird cry will produce a dozen more as memories flood the page. There is a love of how things are done — a leg bandaged, a leopard skinned — which gathers every detail into writing that can be crisp but is rarely concise. In reflective passages, explanations seek to be exhaustive. Irony is present in the story but not in the style, which seeks to share as full and clear an appreciation as can be achieved. Nothing is too small or commonplace to be worth appreciation. The narrator is intrigued by a sunset, a jackal, a Sindabele word, a saddle-fastening, a passage of Scripture, or a herbal soup; and he considers these as thoughtfully, shrewdly, and wonderingly as any larger matter. We grow aware of an unusually open mind and the writing creates its own authority. We normally resist the sentimental, the whimsical and the banal because they enclose the mind with triteness. Van der Post does not skirt these dangers in his story; he disarms them. Nothing is trite to him.

A related quality in his work fortifies the simplest ideas with a pressure of feeling and conviction. Killing from necessity, 'Bamuthi and Mopani teach, is justified; reckless killing is not. The story abounds with examples of both kinds. François admires a group of bustards: 'a touching innocent sight' (Chapter 4); then he shoots them for the pot. The insurgents show their error by slaughtering more game than they need. It is disregard for life in detail which the writer condemns and his minute, loving attention to every form of life supports his judgement on the expedient elimination of Hunter's Drift. A simple and today most unpopular idea in which the wise-men of the story coach François is that creation in human affairs as in nature must grow slowly. Another is that there may be more in heaven and earth than 'modern' philosophy knows about. François admits Xhabbo's claims to powers of perception Pierre-Paul would not acknowledge. A 'tapping' within Xhabbo, as within all Bushmen warns him of remote events. uLangalibalela returns Night and Day on the eve of the telephoned message that Ouwa has died at the Cape. Harley Street would have been less confident of a dream's validity; and less scrupulous about returning an unearned fee. Elsewhere in the novel people find omens in the stars and among the birds. Few African writers have treated this aspect of traditional culture with such an intelligent blend of good-humoured scepticism and imaginative open mindedness. Whether or not we think there is more beyond life than we know, we are likely to be persuaded, at least while we read, that there is more within it.

Van der Post has what might be thought a simple faith in storytelling; for him it is vital in the growth of cultures and of individuals. The Bushman convict's Testament regrets that 'here in a great city . . . I do not obtain stories'. The epigraph to *A Story Like The Wind* sums up the notion from his statement which offered the title: 'The story . . . is like the wind. It comes from a far-off place and we feel it.' There are aspects of African history, the Introduction observes, which can only be transmitted 'in the way Africa itself excelled . . . through stories, myths and legends'. He describes how he and the other fifteen children of his family were in touch with Africa's past through stories 'before the slanted Calvinist spirit of our society could convert us into sour creatures of disapproval and acid judgement'. 'All the fairytale characters of my childhood were not the pale faces of the breed to which I and my family belonged but the yellow, copper-coloured and black indigenous peoples of the land'. European and African history and literature merge in François's mind as in the author's memories, and he too sees the lives of the people around him in relation to their ancestries; and so escapes the worst of Calvinism. Recognition of the power of story is declining today in all cultures, the author believes, and his novels are written in the hope of its renewal in all of us.

No species of cultural development has diminished the appeal of the oldest stories. Van der Post's is reminiscent of epic in some of its conceptions and procedures: the physical immensity of its setting – with the whole continent as a background; legends and gods (Mantis appears, to give counsel in Xhabbo's cave); journeys and conflicts; meetings between races; formal speeches; and, most of all, idealised characters who represent Virtue – the old virtue which authors of literary epic always tended to think in decline in their own day. But whereas epic celebrates the omnipotent, the African and especially the Bushman is the hero here, in the sense that the Roman is the hero of the *Aeneid*. Van der Post's Introduction to *A Story Like The Wind* speaks of advancing the 'honour' of Africans in other societies. In *The Heart of the Hunter* he remarks on how the insulting terms 'kaffir' and 'massarwa' (for Bushmen) damage the sense of honour: 'I am certain that no one will ever understand the complex and desperate situation in Africa unless he understands first that at bottom it is an affair of honour'.[36]

Van der Post is probably best known for his commitment to the Bushmen of the Kalahari. His films, books and lectures have made theirs an honourable English name throughout the world and have helped to preserve a way of life which most people of all other races have considered due for extinction. The Bushmen are few and it might be argued that there are more urgent issues in South Africa. But van der Post sees in them the most desperate losers from a prolonged history of conflict in Africa: 'I could not separate the process which had exterminated the Bushmen from the one which set white and black at one another's throats'.[37] The Bushmen also present a test, since they dislike modernity and wish to live apart from it. Indeed, all contact with 'the twentieth century', we are told, is poisonous to them. They are the most extreme instance of a people consigned to limbo in the cause of a limited conception of 'the twentieth century world' and its needs. More than any African people they have been badly treated because they were 'prehistoric'. Whatever they are, *A Story Like The Wind* affirms their vitality and their right to enjoy it.

6 Afterword

African writers are unlikely to allow their work to slide into mere formalism but they are increasingly captured by the idea of subjecting or sacrificing 'the novel as art' to a cause for the public good. What is 'commitment' in fiction, and what effect do novels have on their readers?

Wole Soyinka spoke on this subject after his release from prison in 1969:

> There are no binding laws of commitment . . . Each individual discovers sooner or later his own level and areas of commitment. If I had a choice I'd rather be a writer with no social commitment. That is by far the most comfortable form of creativity . . .
>
> I am incapable of any peace of mind under certain social situations.[1]

Soyinka, Ngugi, Laye, Amadi and La Guma, have all been prisoners of conscience or prisoners of war (as, incidentally, has Laurens van der Post in the Far East). Exile or apprehension of arrest can become a condition of mind. No one free from it would wish to challenge commitment in writings other than fiction. The theme of Soyinka's prison book *The Man Died* is that the man dies who is silent in the face of tyranny.[2] Ngugi's *Detained*[3] and Amadi's *Sunset in Biafra* also convey the humiliating absurdity of imprisonment — and their authors' courage. In each case the novelist chose to write a work of record. The physical horrors of prison and war are very difficult to convey in fiction; only a few great novelists have ever succeeded. Commitment to opposing tyranny should not necessarily take this form. Soyinka's second novel *Season of Anomy* (published in 1973) treats the lawlessness of Nigeria in the previous decade of coups, army rule and war. It could be considered a huge prose-poem in which images from nature and myth are orchestrated around scenes of atrocity. Soyinka cannot write badly even when he seems to be trying to damage his style with verbosity. *Season of Anomy* is horrifying; but the horrors of this century are known to his readers, and in detailing carnage the neutrality of the photographer offers more than most creative writers can hope to achieve. The danger in accumulating descriptions of savagery, as we see in Armah's *Two Thousand Seasons*, is of rendering them banal. The fact that there are strict limits to what novels can make real confirms the fact that realism is selective not photographic. Contemporary writing often forgets the powers of restraint. A raised fist can produce a more violent impression in fiction than a catalogue of killings by mutilation. This kind of commitment is usually self-defeating.

Petals of Blood confirms the observation made by generations of novelists that although theirs is an argumentative and talkative genre, a novel's purpose must be to create an impression rather than advance an argument. Impression, as in *Time of the Butcherbird*, can have the force of argument, and Alex La Guma's novel is good because he impresses; everyone knows already what he is arguing. *Going Down River Road* persuades without preaching that this is how things really are. Most readers of novels also read competent journalistic polemic in large quantity and most of it is quickly forgotten. There are scenes in Ngugi, Mwangi and La Guma which linger in the memory, but the more a passage appears to be contrived to persuade us by illustrating an interpretation of the world, the less likely it is to do more than confirm opinions already held. In *Time of the Butcherbird* the killing of the Afrikaaner is a token of the author's attitude. The most moving passages are those in which he and the Dominee are seen objectively and with a degree of pity, as men trapped in a culture whose own imaginative vision has worn out.

Racialism arises from an impression which is simply false, and here a novelist's commitment can take its natural course of reflecting reality. *A Story Like The Wind* is a useful as well as a good book because it dispels the illusions behind the South African use of the word 'kaffir', at least for so long as it is read which means for many enjoyable and memorable hours. Van der Post is arguing that the most persistent form of racialism is that which identifies one race with progressive wisdom and another with pupilhood; Pierre-Paul and 'Bamuthi are planned to illustrate the interpretation; we may well feel that the white man's death is just a ploy and that the black man is too good to be true. But little resistance is provoked because the story's total impression is true to the author's experience of life.

Christopher Ricks's theme in *Keats and Embarrassment* clarifies the question of literature's usefulness: 'one of the things for which we value art is that it helps us to deal with embarrassment, not by abolishing or ignoring it but by putting it to good human purposes'.[4] The world has become a stage for embarrassing encounters of a kind which are most acute in Africa, and no longer only across the colour line. Alberto Moravia meeting the charming girl in copper rings in a Kenyan shop is embarrassed, and he 'abolishes' the feeling by assigning her to prehistory. The anachronistic survival of such people embarrasses some African governments, whose representatives occasionally recall an old enemy of embarrassment, Dickens's Podsnap, who 'had even acquired a peculiar flourish of his right arm in often clearing the world of its most difficult problems, by sweeping them behind him'.[5] Podsnappery today will not see what is 'not modern'. When Ngugi's Ilmorog becomes an embarrassment the big men of Nairobi abolish it by false modernisation. Novelists serve a good human purpose by treating this kind of awkwardness as truly as possible. Odili in Achebe's *Man of the People* is usefully embarrassed when his father ceases to seem a stereotype from another age. The villager's robust vitality in Nanga, still present although corrupted, embarrasses the smug Odili on many occasions, showing us what Odili is slow to see, that the Minister possesses other qualities than the sophistication wanted for international cultural conferences. Ricks's definition of his theme continues: 'art, in its unique combination of the private and the public, offers us a unique kind of human relationship freed from the possibility . . . of an embarrassment that clogs, paralyses, or coarsens'.[6] Soyinka is acutely aware of embarrassment and of how Sagoe shuns it; the scene in which Faseyi is embarrassed by his backward English wife would be painful, in life, causing guests to edge away across the room. In *The Interpreters* it is funny and human. The backwardness of a Chief Winsala would embarrass any young intellectual looking for a job; in the novel the Chief's 'bush' habits of mind are pleasing, and we are reminded that a Board anywhere can include one drunken rogue. Throughout these novels the writers' commitment to showing how things really are works against the Podsnappish evasions which have abetted so much disastrous misdevelopment and will continue to do so.

When the students in Nairobi hear about Ilmorog, they write papers on 'uneven development' caused by neocolonialism; it is not clear whether Ngugi approves of this as correct analysis or scorns it as ineffectual theorising. 'Uneven development' is the subject of *Understanding History* by the American Trotskyist George Novack.[7] In his view there is a scientific law of 'uneven and combined development' which was derived by Trotsky from Marx and Engels. Societies develop at different rates; 'lower' and 'superior' stages of development in separate societies can merge to cause sudden advances, with further types of uneven development. He employs his law to explain difficulties in Russia since 1916, in the cause of a Marxist analysis of history. The phenomena are unmistakable. Examples in Novack's essay include the Vatican's use of television; the interaction in America of advanced capitalism and social theories current centuries ago; and the co-existence in Britain of a House of Lords, medieval in origin, nineteenth-century capitalism, and left-wing trade unions. Britain has experienced combined development under American and European influences; Africa is everywhere subject to stronger outside influences and so in Novack's words to 'combined formations which have a highly contradictory character and exhibit marked peculiarities'.[8] One merit of Novack's book is that he sees the modern as adjustment to recent innovations: what is characteristic of modernity is neither the bishop or mullah, nor the television, but the bishop or mullah on television; in the case of television bishops there are marked peculiarities, but their order has been liable to seem anachronistic for most of its history. Considered in human terms such a theory is insulting. Nobody wishes to be regarded as a 'hybrid formation'. Novack's lowest 'states' of development – 'hunter-gathering', 'higher agricultural barbarism', 'slave-civilisation', and 'feudalism' – account for most of Africa in the nineteenth century. Marx's 'historic purposes' make a limbo of most of the world. Edward Said's recent *Orientalism* which demonstrates how vocabulary used to describe another culture 'censors' it, points out that Marx's human sympathy succumbed to the effect of large collective terms applied to whole tracts of mankind. The novelist's business is to restore human sympathy by showing the people who are really there.

English novelists are usually alive to the ease with which people adjust to the intermingling of mature and recent institutions and phenomena. A pair of committed characters in a novel by Iris Murdoch will affably discuss whether Christian Platonism or Marxist Leninism is more out of date; even such sharply opposed positions have a common background in the history of ideas. A novelist attuned to George Steiner's 'post-culture' who began to write realistically of modern England would discover that many people lag behind it. But the urge to feel securely modern appears everywhere in the West: in our attitude to the Victorians, for example, with whom we share many of our beliefs, more or less well adjusted to post-industrial, post-modernist conditions; 'nineteenth-century' is often used in England and America as a term of disapproval for features of modern culture which seem to intrude on modernity. Containing Africa within the designation of past periods helps to bolster the illusion of our own consistent and predictable progress. A demoralised and 'masochistically' self-critical Western culture is often presented as if in monolithic opposition to a 'primitive' but 'soulful' black world. Both civilisations are more complicated, and more human in the way they live now.

When contemporary Western novelists write about Africa they tend to be disadvantaged more by Novack's sense of the hybrid than by ignorance or racialism. But John Updike's *The Coup* succeeds, even in the dangerous mode of comedy, because he does not presuppose any more dignified disposition of affairs elsewhere. Updike is amused by all that is inappropriate in the American and Soviet presence in his 'ancient desert kingdom of Kush'. The oracle he sets talking in one of the best scenes of the book is a grotesque travesty not of African oracles but of latter-day imperialist communications. The severed head of the deposed king is captured by Soviet agents from the scene of his execution and filled with microelectronic equipment. The narrator, President Felix Ellelloû, makes his way to the cave near a tourists' lodge where the head is rumoured to be issuing critiques of his regime; entry ticket costs fifty *lu*. There he listens to the attack on himself:

> 'Just as nostalgia leaks into his reverie, while he dozes above the drawing-board of the People's Revolution so vividly blueprinted by our heroic Soviet allies, so traces of decadent, doomed capitalist consumerism creep into the life-fabric of the noble, beautiful, and intrinsically pure Kushite peasants and workers.'

I felt the hand of a hack writer had intruded these phrases into the tape and exclaimed aloud the Barber word for still-fresh camel dung. My neighbours in the throng shushed me angrily, having been thus far held fascinated by the head's analysis of our internal difficulties. . . .

The head was concluding, its lips visibly out of sync, 'This has been a vision vouchsafed to me in Paradise, where the veil is lifted from the eyes of men. It comes to you courtesy of Soviet technology. Thank you for your attention. Feel free to wander about the cave, only do not touch the pre-historic Saharan art work, which the moisture of your breath is gradually eroding.

(Chapter 5)

Meanwhile the pro-Soviet Ellelloû has been deposed by a pro-American rival and a boom town is under construction. The Soviet, American and popular–Islamic styles in the oracle's discourse meet in the realm of the electronic; the severed head is an appropriate symbol. There is nothing whole or loving in the activities of the Powers and their puppets. Nowhere in modern fiction is the pointlessness of misconceived co-operation more effectively exposed. The only Kushite characters are the rulers and their entourages. The people go about their lives as best they can, unserved as yet by what alien facilities may have to offer. Updike does not imply that the people are irrelevant because backward, but rather that there are civilisations today which cannot easily be replanned from above, whatever the foreign 'blueprint'. The truth of Fanon's lines about Europeans who wish to make a new Europe out of Africa is celebrated in comedy in *The Coup* – but the Europeans turn out to be less competent than Fanon envisaged.

Notes

The place of publication, unless otherwise stated, is London.

CHAPTER 1

1. The notion that African fiction has been new in content and old in form has been assailed by various studies, including those of Charles R. Larson, David Carroll, Eustace Palmer and Eldred Jones referred to in the following chapters; it persists none the less, and a symptom is the word 'materials' which implies anthropological field-work to be written up as fiction.
2. Interviewed in *Lire*, April 1979, p. 36. 'Soljénitsyne' said Barthes, 'n'est pas un "bon" ecrivain *pour nous*: les problèmes de forme qu'il a résolus sont un peu fossilisés par rapport à nous'. Barthes needed, of course, to shield '*bon*' with quotation marks.
3. See especially George Watson, *The Story of the Novel* (Macmillan, 1979).
4. Wole Soyinka, *Myth, Literature and the African World* (Cambridge University Press, 1976) p. x.
5. Chinua Achebe, *Morning Yet on Creation Day* (Heinemann, 1975) p. 9.
6. Watson, *Story of the Novel*, p. 11. The example of an African pupil recognising Lady Catherine is given in the next few lines.
7. A student made this objection to Mr Knightley (in *Emma*) in an examination script in 1973.
8. In the Preface to *African Literature Today*, ed. Eldred Jones, I (Heinemann, 1968).
9. Dylan Thomas called it a 'bewitching, tall, devilish story' in his *Observer* review, 6 June 1952.
10. Mikhail Bakhtin, *Problems of Dostoevsky's Poetics* (1929, 1963) trans. R. W. Rotsel (Ann Arbor: Ardis, 1973) p. 99.
11. See Robert Scholes and Robert Kellogg, *The Nature of Narrative* (London: Oxford University Press, 1966).
12. *Three Suitors, One Husband; and Until Further Notice* (Methuen, 1968) is Oyônô-Mbia's English version of plays composed in French.
13. E. D. McDonald (ed.), *Phoenix: the Posthumous Papers of D. H. Lawrence* (Heinemann, 1936, 1961) p. 538.
14. David Carroll, *Chinua Achebe* (Macmillan, 1980) p. 183.
15. This idea is to be found throughout V. S. Naipaul, *Among The Believers: An Islamic Journey* (Deutsch, 1981).
16. Achebe, *Morning Yet on Creation Day*, p. 24.
17. Albert Moravia, *Which Tribe do You Belong To?*, trans. Angus Davidson (Frogmore, St Albans: Panther Books, 1976) pp. 43–8.

18. Ibid., p. 54.
19. Ibid., p. 57.
20. Ibid., pp. 135–9.
21. Ngugi wa Thiong'o, *Writers in Politics: Essays* (Heinemann, 1981) pp. 15–16.
22. Zdzislaw Najder, 'Conrad's Casement Letters', *Polish Perspectives* 17 (1974) 29; quoted in Ian Watt, *Conrad: In the Nineteenth Century* (Berkeley, Los Angeles: University of California Press, 1979) p. 160.
23. Joseph Conrad, *Heart of Darkness*, ch. 2.
24. See, for example, the persuasive explanation in these terms in Carroll, *Chinua Achebe*, pp. 1–5.
25. Ngugi, *Writers in Politics*, p. 67.
26. Ibid., p. 19.
27. Ibid., p. 20.
28. Karl Marx, *Surveys from Exile*, ed. David Fernbach (Harmondsworth: Penguin, 1973) pp. 306–7, 320.
29. Frantz Fanon, *The Wretched of the Earth*, trans. Constance Farrington (Harmondsworth: Penguin, 1967) p. 254.
30. Achebe, *Morning Yet on Creation Day*, p. 45.
31. Ngugi wa Thiong'o, *Homecoming: Essays on African and Caribbean Literature, Culture and Politics* (Heinemann, 1972) p. 43.
32. See Placide Tempels, *Bantu Philosophy*, trans. Colin King (Paris: *Présence Africaine*, 1969).
33. Soyinka, *Myth, Literature and The African World*, p. xii.
34. Elechi Amadi, *Sunset in Biafra* (Heinemann, 1969) p. 13.

CHAPTER 2

1. Charles R. Larson, *The Emergence of African Fiction* (Bloomington and London: Indiana University Press, 1971) ch. 2.
2. Ngugi, *Writers in Politics*, p. 76.
3. Carroll, *Chinua Achebe*, p. 31.
4. Larson, *Emergence of African Fiction*, ch. 2.
5. Watt, *Conrad*, pp. 112–15.
6. In his profile *Chinua Achebe* (Longman, 1969).
7. 'Introduction' to William Plover, *Turbott Wolfe* (1965) pp. 9–55.
8. M. M. Mahood, *The Colonial Encounter: A Reading of Six Novels* (Rex Collings, 1977) p. 62.
9. Carroll, *Chinua Achebe*, p. 30.
10. Translated from the Arabic by Desmond Stewart (Chapman and Hall, 1966).
11. Eustace Palmer, *The Growth of the African Novel* (Heinemann, 1979) p. 173.
12. Ibid., pp. 182–3.
13. Camara Laye, *The Guardian of the Word* (Fontana, 1980) p. 19.
14. Ibid., p. 21.
15. Soyinka, *Myth, Literature and the African World*, p. 124.
16. Larson, *The Emergence of African Fiction*, p. 223.

Notes

17. Ibid., p. 201.
18. Adele King, *The Writings of Camara Laye* (Heinemann, 1980) pp. 56–7.
19. See Ahmed Sefroui, *La boîte à merveilles* (Paris: Seuil, 1974).
20. In Amis's *The Green Man* (Cape, 1969) the hero discusses the issue of his soul with God.
21. See King, *Writings of Camara Laye*.
22. Ibid., p. 53.
23. Karega in *Petals of Blood* (Heinemann, 1977) p. 305.
24. See King, *Writings of Camara Laye*, pp. 43–4.
25. John V. Taylor, *The Primal Vision: Christian Presence Amid African Religion* (SCM Press, 1963).

CHAPTER 3

1. Larson, *Emergence of African Fiction*, p. 257.
2. Eldred Jones, *The Writing of Wole Soyinka* (Heinemann, 1973) pp. 162–3.
3. Ibid., p. 163.
4. Larson, *Emergence of African Fiction*, p. 246.
5. Ibid., p. 246.
6. Palmer, *Growth of the African Novel*, p. 259.
7. Jones, *Writing of Wole Soyinka*, p. 156.
8. See Bakhtin, *Problems of Dostoevsky's Poetics*, ch. 4.
9. Neil McEwan, *The Survival of the Novel* (Macmillan, 1981) p. 16.
10. Speaking at the University of Fez in April 1979.
11. Palmer, *Growth of the African Novel*, p. 242.
12. Soyinka, *Myth, Literature and the African World*, p. 127.
13. Ibid., p. 1.
14. Ibid., p. 18.
15. Ibid., p. 16.
16. See Chapter 5 of Anthony Powell, *The Military Philosophers* (Heinemann, 1968).
17. Carroll, *Chinua Achebe*, p. 152.
18. Ibid., p. 134.
19. This remark is made by Ezeulu in Chapter 4 of Chinua Achebe, *Arrow of God* (Heinemann, 1964).
20. Achebe, *Morning Yet on Creation Day*, p. 25.
21. Ibid., pp. 24–5.
22. This is from the opening paragraph of his review of Colin Wilson's *The Outsider*, reprinted in *What Became of Jane Austen? and other Questions* (Cape, 1970).
23. Achebe, *Morning Yet on Creation Day*, p. 26.
24. Ibid., p. 26. Cary wrote of Fada that 'its people would not know the change if time jumped back fifty thousand years'.
25. Ibid., p. 75.
26. E. M. Forster, *Howard's End*, (Abinger edn, Edward Arnold, 1973) p. 43.
27. Robert Fraser, *The Novels of Ayi Kwei Armah* (Heinemann, 1980) p. 25.
28. Achebe, *Morning Yet on Creation Day*, p. 25.
29. Fraser, *Novels of Ayi Kwei Armah*, p. 18.

30. Ibid., p. 25.
31. Achebe, *Morning Yet on Creation Day*, p. 67.

CHAPTER 4

1. Ngugi, *Writers in Politics*, p. 58.
2. See Chapter 6, below; and McDonald (ed.), *Phoenix: the Posthumous Papers of D. H. Lawrence*, p. 528.
3. Palmer, *Growth of the African Novel*, p. 297.
4. Clifford B. Robson, *Ngugi wa Thiong'o* (Macmillan, 1979) pp. 104–10.
5. Terry Eagleton, *Marxism and Literary Criticism* (Methuen, 1976) p. 52.
6. Ngugi, *Writers in Politics*, p. 75.
7. Ibid., p. 3.
8. John Carey, *The Violent Effigy: A Study of Dickens's Imagination* (Faber, 1979) p. 134.
9. Palmer, *The Growth of The African Novel* (Heinemann, 1972) p. 303.
10. Ibid., pp. 303–4. 'They surely reveal themselves as immature adolescents.'
11. See Camara Laye, *The Guardian of the Word*, trans. James Kirkup (Fontana, 1980) p. 19.
12. Adrian Roscoe, *Uhuru's Fire: African Literature East to South* (Cambridge University Press, 1977) p. 234.
13. Alex La Guma, *Time of the Butcherbird* (Heinemann, 1979) p. 106.
14. Ibid., p. 63.
15. Ibid., p. 92.

CHAPTER 5

1. Trollope, *South Africa*, 2 vols (1878) Vol. II, p. 92.
2. Cited in William J. Pomeroy's *Apartheid Axis* (New York, 1971) p. 19.
3. Nadine Gordimer, 'English-Language Literature and Politics in South Africa', in Christopher Heywood (ed.), *Aspects of South African Literature* (Heinemann, 1976) p. 101.
4. Ibid., p. 118.
5. Nadine Gordimer, *July's People* (Cape, 1981) p. 9.
6. Ibid., p. 96.
7. Ibid., p. 8.
8. Rowland Smith, 'The Plot Beneath the Skin: The Novels of C. J. Driver', in Heywood (ed.), *Aspects of South African Literature*, p. 148.
9. Gordimer, *July's People*, pp. 64–5.
10. Dennis Brutus, 'Protest Against Apartheid', in Cosmo Pieterse and Donald Munro (eds), *Protest and Conflict in African Literature* (1969) p. 97.
11. Gordimer, *July's People*, p. 45.
12. Ibid., p. 100.
13. Ibid., p. 72.
14. Ibid., p. 98.
15. Ibid., p. 71.
16. Ngugi, *Writers and Politics*, pp. 14–15. Ngugi writes that English is

'probably the most racist of all human languages'. In the same passage he attacks Trollope for 'racist sickness', on the evidence of Trollope's remarks on signs of laziness among West Indians. Indolence, in any race, could jolt Trollope out of his usual fair-mindedness; most of us would have seemed idle to him. By Victorian standards Trollope was the opposite of a racialist.

17. Nadine Gordimer, *A Guest of Honour* (Harmondsworth: Penguin, 1973) p. 68.
18. Gordimer, *July's People*, p. 89.
19. Ibid., pp. 37–8.
20. Ibid., p. 59.
21. Robert J. Green, 'Politics and Literature in Africa: The Drama of Athol Fugard', in Heywood (ed.), *Aspects of South African Literature*, p. 172.
22. Gordimer, *July's People*, p. 86.
23. Ibid., pp. 62–3.
24. Ibid., p. 29.
25. Ibid., p. 153.
26. Ibid., p. 33.
27. Ibid., p. 120.
28. Ibid., p. 6.
29. Laurens van der Post, *The Heart of the Hunter* (Harmondsworth: Penguin, 1976) p. 103.
30. Ibid., p. 119.
31. Ibid., p. 123.
32. Ibid., p. 12.
33. Achebe, *Morning Yet on Creation Day*, p. 53.
34. Van der Post, *Heart of the Hunter*, p. 167.
35. Ibid., pp. 132–3.
36. Ibid., p. 60.
37. Ibid., pp. 120–1.

CHAPTER 6

1. Quoted in Hans Zell and Helene Silver (eds), *A Reader's Guide to African Literature* (Heinemann, 1972) p. 192.
2. Wole Soyinka, *The Man Died: Prison Notes* (Rex Collings, 1972; Harmondsworth: Penguin, 1975).
3. Ngugi wa Thiong'o, *Detained: A Writer's Prison Diary* (Heinemann, 1981).
4. Christopher Ricks, *Keats and Embarrassment* (Cambridge University Press, 1976) p. 1.
5. Dickens, *Our Mutual Friend*, ch. 11.
6. Ricks, *Keats and Embarrassment*, p. 1.
7. George Novack, *Understanding History: Marxist Essays* (New York: Pathfinder Press, 1972).
8. Ibid., p. 83.

Select Bibliography

The place of publication, unless otherwise stated, is London.

I FICTION

Chinua Achebe

NOVELS
Things Fall Apart (1958); *No Longer At Ease* (1960); *Arrow of God* (1964; second edn 1974); *A Man of the People* (1966).

SHORT STORIES
Girls at War and Other Stories (1972)
Achebe is published by Heinemann.

Elechi Amadi

The Concubine (1966); *The Great Ponds* (1969); *The Slave* (1978)
Amadi is published by Heinemann.

Ayi Kwei Armah

The Beautyful Ones Are Not Yet Born (1968); *Fragments* (1970); *Why Are We So Blest?* (1972); *Two Thousand Seasons* (1973); *The Healers* (1978)
Armah is published by Heinemann.

Nuruddin Farah

From a Crooked Rib (1970); *A Naked Needle* (1976); *Sweet and Sour Milk* (1979)
Farah is published by Heinemann.

Nadine Gordimer

NOVELS
The Lying Days (1958); *Occasion for Loving* (1963); *The Late Bourgeois World* (1966); *A Guest of Honour* (1970); *The Conservationist* (1974); *Burger's Daughter* (1979); *July's People* (1981)

SHORT STORIES
Livingstone's Companions (1972); *Selected Short Stories* (1975)
Nadine Gordimer is published by Cape

Alex La Guma

NOVELS
The Stone Country (1967); *In The Fog, of the Season's End* (1972); *Time of the Butcherbird* (1979)

SHORT STORIES
A Walk in the Night (1967)
Alex La Guma is published by Heinemann.

Camara Laye

The African Child (*L'enfant noir*, 1953); *The Radiance of the King* (*Le regard du roi*, 1954); *A Dream of Africa* (*Dramouss*, 1966); *The Guardian of the Word* (*Le Maître de la Parole*, 1978)
James Kirkup's translations of Camara Laye are published by Fontana. The French texts are published by Librairie Plon, Paris.

Meja Mwangi

Kill Me Quick (1973); *Carcase for Hounds* (1974); *Going Down River Road* (1976)
Mwangi is published by Heinemann.

Ngugi wa Thiong'o

NOVELS
Weep Not Child (1964); *The River Between* (1965); *A Grain of Wheat* (1967); *Petals of Blood* (1977)

SHORT STORIES
Secret Lives (1975)
Ngugi is published by Heinemann.

Ferdinand Oyono

Houseboy (*Une vie de boy*, 1956); *The Old Man and the Medal* (*Le vieux nègre et la médaille*, 1956)
John Reed's translations of Oyono are published by Heinemann. The French texts are published by Editions Julliard, Paris.

Wole Soyinka

The Interpreters (1965); *Season of Anomy* (1973)
The Interpreters is available in paperback from Heinemann and in a Fontana edition. *Season of Anomy* is published by Rex Collings.

Laurens van der Post

Flamingo Feather (1955); *A Story Like the Wind* (1972); *A Far-Off Place* (1974); *The Heart of the Hunter* (1961)
Van der Post is published by the Hogarth Press and in paperback by Penguin Books, Harmondsworth, Middlesex.

II CRITICAL STUDIES

Achebe, Chinua. *Morning Yet on Creation Day*, (Heinemann, 1975)
Bakhtin, Mikhail. *Problems of Dostoevsky's Poetics* (1929, 1963); trans. R. W. Rotsel (Ann Arbor: Ardis, 1973)
Barthes, Roland. *Le plaisir du texte* (Paris: Editions du Seuil, 1973); trans. Richard Miller (Cape, 1976)
Carroll, David. *Chinua Achebe* (Macmillan, 1980)
Eagleton, Terry. *Marxism and Literary Criticism* (Methuen, 1976)
Fraser, Robert. *The Novels of Ayi Kwei Armah* (Heinemann, 1980)
Gontard, Marc. *La violence du texte: la littérature marocaine de langue française* (Paris: Harmattan, 1981)

Heywood, Christopher, (ed.). *Aspects of South African Literature* (Heinemann, 1976)
Jones, Eldred Durosimi. *The Writing of Wole Soyinka* (Heinemann, 1973)
Killam, G. E. D. *The Novels of Chinua Achebe* (Heinemann, 1969)
King, Adele. *The Writings of Camara Laye* (Heinemann, 1980)
Larson, Charles R. *The Emergence of African Fiction* (Bloomington and London: Indiana University Press, 1971)
Mahood, M. M. *The Colonial Encounter: A Reading of Six Novels* (Rex Collings, 1977)
Moore, Gerald. *The Chosen Tongue* (Longman, 1971)
Ngugi wa Thiong'o. *Homecoming: Essays on African and Caribbean Literature, Culture and Politics* (Heinemann, 1972)
Ngugi wa Thiong'o. *Writers in Politics: Essays* (Heinemann, 1981)
Palmer, Eustace. *An Introduction to the African Novel* (Heinemann, 1972)
Palmer, Eustace. *The Growth of the African Novel* (Heinemann, 1979)
Ravenscroft, Arthur. *Chinua Achebe* (Longman, 1969)
Robson, Clifford B. *Ngugi wa Thiong'o* (Macmillan, 1979)
Roscoe, Adrian A. *Mother is Gold* (Cambridge University Press, 1971)
Roscoe, Adrian A. *Uhuru's Fire: African Literature East to South* (Cambridge University Press, 1977)
Soyinka, Wole. *Myth, Literature and the African World* (Cambridge University Press, 1976)
Watson, George. *The Story of the Novel* (Macmillan, 1979)
Watt, Ian. *Conrad: In the Nineteenth Century* (Berkeley, Los Angeles: University of California Press, 1979)

III SUGGESTIONS FOR FURTHER READING

The novels of the exiled South African Bessie Head are the most glaring omission from the present study. She has attracted very able criticism, including Arthur Ravenscroft's essay in Heywood (ed.), *Aspects of South African Literature*. *When Rain Clouds Gather* (Gollancz, 1969), *Maru* (Heinemann, 1972) and *A Question of Power* (Heinemann, 1974) should be read in that order. Amos Tutuola's *The Palm-Wine Drinkard* (Faber, 1952) is a modern classic, and some would say the same of *The Voice* (1964) by the poet Gabriel Okara (available in Fontana). The opening chapters of Mongo Beti's *The Poor Christ of Bomba* (Heinemann) are a *tour de force*, better read in the French: *Le pauvre Christ de Bomba* (Paris: Robert Laffont, 1956). Of francophone fiction from the Maghreb, Driss Chraibi's *Heirs to the Past*, in Len Ortzen's translation, is one of the few North African novels to have been accepted by Heinemann's African Writers Series. The French title is *Succession Ouverte* (Paris: Denoël, 1962). The Egyptian Naguib Mahfouz, the greatest novelist of the Arab world, is best known for *Miramar* (1967), translated by Fatma Moussa-Mahmoud (Heinemann, 1978). The Nigerian Nkem Nkwankwo's *Dauda* (Deutsch, 1964), available in Fontana, is entertaining light reading. Buchi Emecheta's *The Slave Girl* (Allison and Busby 1977), also in Fontana, is a story of 'the women's cause' in Nigeria. Dambudzo Marechera, from Zimbabwe, is a promising younger writer. Heinemann, his publisher, warn (or promise) that 'he uses language without inhibitions' in *Black Sunlight* (1980). John Updike's *The Coup* (1978) is in Penguin.

Index

Achebe, Chinua, 1–8 *passim*, 18, 53, 54, 70, 101, 110
   Arrow of God, 7, 15, 16, 36–9, 111
   A Man of the People, 75–95, 163
   Morning Yet On Creation Day, 2, 3–4, 8, 16, 97–8, 101, 151–2
   No Longer at Ease, 21, 31, 32
   Things Fall Apart, 4, 7, 15, 20–36, 96
Amadi, Elechi, 5, 161
   The Concubine, 16
   The Great Ponds, 16, 19
   The Slave, 16
   Sunset in Biafra, 19, 161
Amis, Kingsley, 57, 71, 88, 90, 95, 96
   One Fat Englishman, 61
Apuleius, 66
Armah, Ayi Kwei, 18, 103
   The Beautyful Ones Are Not Yet Born, 85–101, 102
   Two Thousand Seasons, 162
Austen, Jane, 167 n. 7
   Pride and Prejudice, 4–5

Bakhtin, Mikhail, 6
   Problems of Dostoevsky's Poetics, 6, 66–7, 69
Balzac, Honore de, 103, 104
Barth, John, 2
Barthes, Roland, ix, 2–3, 86, 167 n. 2
Beckett, Samuel, 57
Beerbohm, Max, 37
Bernanos, Georges, 47
Beti, Mongo, *The Poor Christ of Bomba*, 17, 40, 60
Blake, William, 111, 129, 146, 154
Brutus, Dennis, 132
Buchan, John, 142, 151
Burgess, Anthony, 24, 61
   Inside Mr Enderby, 61

Butor, Michel, 17

Camus, Albert, 2
Carey, John, 114
Carroll, David, *Chinua Achebe*, 7, 15, 22, 27, 36, 93
Carroll, Lewis, 51, 72
Cary, Joyce, 7
   Mister Johnson, 13–14, 96, 169 n. 24
Chaucer, Geoffrey, 2
Clemenceau, Georges, 121
Coleridge, S. T., 127
Conrad, Joseph, ix, 6, 7, 31
   Heart of Darkness, 10–14, 16
Crabbe, George, 129

Defoe, Daniel, 1, 6
Dickens, Charles, 1, 2, 6, 55, 84, 87, 97, 105, 112, 114, 163
Dostoevsky, Fyodor, 66

Eagleton, Terry, 106
Ekwensi, Cyprian, 1, 151
Eliot, George, 105, 106

Fanon, Franz, *The Wretched of the Earth*, 14–15, 102, 166
Farah, Nuruddin, 113, 127
   From a Crooked Rib, 119
   A Naked Needle, 65
   Sweet and Sour Milk, 18, 117–21
Fielding, Henry, 2
   Joseph Andrews, 41
Forster, E. M., *Howard's End*, 97
Fraser, Robert, 99–100
Frayn, Michael,
   The Tin Men, 6

Ghanem, Fathy
  The Man Who Lost his Shadow, 41
Golding, William, 57
  The Scorpion God, 33
Gontard, Marc
  La violence du texte, 3
Gordimer, Nadine, 124, 128, 129
  The Conservationist, 137
  A Guest of Honour, 135
  July's People, 130–41
  The Late Bourgeois World, 131
Graves, Richard, 112
Green, Robert J., 137
Greene, Graham, 51, 57, 75

Haggard, Rider, 81, 151
Hardy, Thomas
  Jude the Obscure, 87, 106
Hartley, L. P., 107
  The Go-Between, 36
Homer, 19, 152

James, Henry, 47, 94
Jones, Eldred, 5
  The Writing of Wole Soyinka, 62, 65
Joyce, James, 2, 6, 121
Jung, C. G., 10, 142, 151, 153

Kafka, Franz, 2, 47, 49
Kellogg, Robert, *The Nature of Narrative*, 128
King, Adele, *The Writings of Camara Laye*, 55, 59, 60
Kipling, Rudyard, 51
Kirkup, James, 47, 48, 59

La Guma, Alex, 161
  Time of the Butcherbird, 124–7, 162
  A Walk in the Night, 124
Lamb, Charles, 84
Larson, Charles R., *The Emergence of African Fiction*, 21, 27, 49, 54, 61–2, 64, 65
Lautréamont, comte de, 47
Lawrence, D. H., 2, 6, 7, 113

Laye, Camara, 17, 161
  The African Child, 47, 54
  Dramouss, 56
  The Guardian of the Word, 48, 57
  The Radiance of the King, 17, 47–60
Leonardo da Vinci, 47
Lucian, 66, 69
Lugard, F. D., 1st. baron, 38
Lukács, Georg, 106

McEwan, Neil, *The Survival of the Novel*, 66
Mahood, M. M., 35, 36
Mao Tse-Tung, 114
Marx, Karl, and Marxism, 4, 8, 14, 30, 75, 76, 103, 107, 113, 118, 164–6
Maupassant, Guy de, 2, 97
Milton, John, 129
Moravia, Alberto, 9–10, 163
Murdoch, Iris, 41, 57, 88, 164
Mwangi, Meja, 127, 162
  Carcase for Hounds, 122
  Going Down River Road, 122–4
  Kill Me Quick, 122

Nabokov, Vladimir, 2
Naipaul, V. S., 8
Ngugi wa Thiong'o, 1, 18, 19, 34, 127, 161
  Detained, 161
  Devil on the Cross, 103
  A Grain of Wheat, 116
  Homecoming, 3, 17, 75
  Petals of Blood, 18, 23, 102–17, 118, 162, 163
  The River Between, 116
  Weep Not, Child, 116
  Writers in Politics, 9, 13, 14, 22, 30, 102, 106, 113, 114, 134, 170 n. 16
Nkwankwo, Nkem 73
Novack, George, *Understanding History*, 164–5

Ousmane, Sembene, *God's Bits of Wood*, 102

Oyono, Ferdinand, *Houseboy*, 17, 40–7
Oyono-Mbia, Guillaume, 7, 89, 108
Chronicles of Mvoutessi, 7

Palmer, Eustace, *The Growth of the African Novel*, 45–6, 65, 74, 79, 105, 114–15
Powell, Anthony, *A Dance to the Music of Time*, 82
Powys, J. C., 155
Pringle, Thomas, 128–9

Rabelais, 66
Ravenscroft, Arthur, *Chinua Achebe*, 31
Richardson, Samuel, 6
Pamela, 41
Ricks, Christopher, *Keats and Embarrassment*, 163
Robbe-Grillet, Alain, 17, 64, 69
Robson, C. B., *Ngugi wa Thiong'o*, 105
Roscoe, Adrian, *Uhuru's Fire*, 124
Roth, Philip, 3

Said, Edward, *Orientalism*, 164
Sartre, Jean-Paul, 96
Scholes, Robert, *The Nature of Narrative*, 28
Schreiner, Olive, 155
The Story of An African Farm, 10–11
Sefroui, Ahmed, 56
Senghor, Leopold Sedar, 8, 60
Shakespeare, 68, 84, 115–16, 129, 136
Sidney, Sir Philip, 55
Smith, Rowland, 131
Soyinka, Wole, 1, 33, 101, 161
The Interpreters, 18, 61–79, 163
The Man Died, 161

Myth, Literature and the African World, 3, 18–19, 49, 51, 75–6, 78
Season of Anomy, 161–2
Steiner, George, 165
Swift, Jonathan, 66

Taylor, John, *The Primal Vision*, 60
Tempels, Father Placide, 17
Thomas, Dylan, 6, 167 n. 9
Tönnies, Ferdinand, 31
Trollope, Anthony, 87, 112
South Africa, 128
Tutuola, Amos, 1
The Palm-Wine Drinkard, 5–6

Updike, John, 3
The Coup, 165–6

van der Post, Sir Laurens, 34, 128, 129, 161
A Far Off Place, 142, 145, 149, 150, 157
The Heart of the Hunter, 146, 151, 157, 159
Jung and the Story of Our Time, 151
A Story Like the Wind, 141–60, 162
Virgil, 9, 19, 159

Watson, George, *The Story of the Novel*, 4, 28
Watt, Ian, 31
Waugh, Evelyn, 37, 84
Wilson, Sir Angus, 37
Wordsworth, William, 154

Yeats, W. B., 15–16, 21, 106, 154

Zola, Emile, 2

DATE DUE

#47-0108 Peel Off Pressure Sensitive